Indonesia's Overseas Labour Migration Programme, 1969–2010

Verhandelingen van het Koninklijk Instituut voor Taal-, Land- en Volkenkunde

VOLUME 307

The titles published in this series are listed at *brill.com/vki*

Indonesia's Overseas Labour Migration Programme, 1969–2010

By

Wayne Palmer

BRILL

©2016

LEIDEN | BOSTON

Cover illustration: Map of South East Asia. iStock.com/VM_Studio

The Library of Congress Cataloging-in-Publication Data is available online at http://catalog.loc.gov
LC record available at http://lccn.loc.gov/2016028917

Typeface for the Latin, Greek, and Cyrillic scripts: "Brill". See and download: brill.com/brill-typeface.

ISSN 1572-1892
ISBN 978-90-04-32544-9 (hardback)
ISBN 978-90-04-32548-7 (e-book)

This book is printed on acid-free paper and produced in a sustainable manner.

Printed by Printforce, the Netherlands

Contents

Preface

This book is the product of more than eight years observation of Indonesia's often controversial overseas labour migration programme and the systematic exploitation of those who use it to find jobs abroad. My experience volunteering for a non-governmental organization that provides paralegal assistance to Indonesian labour migrants in Hong Kong during 2007 alerted me to some of the most baffling realities associated with the programme. Very quickly I learned that Indonesian labour migrants made a distinction between the date of birth in their passport and their true one, a fact that could land them in prison with a hefty fine. They knew very little about how their recruitment debt was financed, but followed agents' instructions to hand over most of their pay for up to seven months. Strangely too the Indonesian consulate seemed to exercise extraordinary power over Hong Kong-licensed agents, which at times made the local law enforcement agencies look like toothless tigers. While the Indonesian consulate promptly retrieved passports from agents behind closed doors, the Hong Kong police accompanied the migrant to her agent's office to do so but would then accept excuses, including that her Indonesian recruitment debt was still not fully settled, to hold on to the document. The crucial role that host states should play in law enforcement is indisputable but practices that partly have their origin in another country can certainly complicate efforts to do so.

My purpose here is to further examine Indonesia's overseas labour migration programme, which sets standards for legal movement of Indonesian citizens into jobs outside the country, and chart the state's technical and political involvement in migrant labour export to destinations like Hong Kong. Early on I was tempted to include accounts of how labour migrants experience the system. Fortunately, we have a raft of work that documents this perspective and demonstrates that the system has developed an exploitative tendency, which enables state and non-state intermediaries to reap profits at the expense of labour migrants, their employers and even the state itself. With time I came to see that we needed more knowledge about relationships between different parts of the bureaucracy and of individual bureaucrats' motivations for action in Indonesia to better understand the state's role in the programme. The purpose of the book lies here. It provides for the first time a detailed critical analysis of the programme's administration and how this fits with other developments within the Indonesian government. More material like this will help us produce more evidence-based recommendations that aim to develop and implement a fairer system for Indonesia's labour migrants.

A few qualifiers about the book's limitations are in order. First, I do no not examine every major administrative site of the overseas labour migration programme within Indonesia. There were 18 such cities dotted across Indonesia in 2010 when I concluded my main round of fieldwork. I examined half that number, including four sites in Java (Jakarta, Semarang, Surabaya and Yogyakarta), three in mainland Sumatra (Banda Aceh, Medan and Pekanbaru), and two that share an international border with Malaysia and/or Singapore (Nunukan and Tanjung Pinang) to get a strong sense of variations in the system. Of these I selected six cities – Jakarta, Medan, Nunukan, Semarang, Surabaya, Tanjung Pinang, which accounted for one third of the system – to present a snapshot of implementation and an insight into its remarkable heterogeneity. The programme differs from decentralized interventions in that national law requires implementation to be much more homogeneous. This selective approach teased out themes that help explain the diversity of practice. It produced a set of indicators that may be used as a point of reference for examination of the remaining sites or other such national programmes.

This book deals exclusively with the western part of Indonesia, excluding some of the country's poorest regions. Eastern Indonesia is much less densely populated than the west and the islands lie much further away from the international borders that Indonesian citizens frequently cross in search of work. As a result, three quarters of the programme's offices were located in Western Indonesia, where 91 per cent of labour migrants were processed. However, this is not to say that Eastern Indonesians do not cross international borders in search of work. They do; however, the majority do not do so through the government's overseas labour migration programme, which they circumvent through the use of alternative networks that secure jobs overseas. Despite this their labour migration involves a degree of bureaucratic compliance, as Eastern Indonesians may use passports and declare their intention to work abroad at border crossings. My observations in Nunukan, where Eastern Indonesians transit on the way to work on plantations in the East Malaysian State Sabah, further confirmed this view. They hinted at the necessity for more studies that examine (1) why the programme's infrastructure is still so densely located in the west and (2) how politics play out around administering labour migration to East Malaysia, East Timor and Papua New Guinea.

I also focus squarely on the programme's operation in urban areas at the final stages of the pre-departure process. The 18 sites determine the ability of labour migrants to legally leave the country for work overseas through their provision of an overseas identity card, which immigration officials wanted to sight in addition to a valid passport at the border. In short, the cities operated as a departure point for migrants to a range of destination countries. This book does not examine in detail the relationship between government agencies and the motivations of individuals at the stages where labour migrants are recruited and registered, which mostly takes place in rural areas and always involves a combination of direct and indirect interaction with local government. I collected interview data in a range of rural areas in East Java, but omitted them from the book. On the basis of this small sample, it was not possible to draw rigorous, evidence-based conclusions about the recruitment-administration nexus in rural areas.

Finally, it is worth noting that the chapter on administration of the programme from within Indonesian consular offices draws exclusively on data collected in the Asia-Pacific region. At this time, this area was the second most popular destination for Indonesian labour migrants after the Gulf region, where Saudi Arabia had provided informal sector employment to Indonesia for almost 40 years. Attention to the politics around implementation of the programme in these states would have yielded complementary data about the factors that drove the intra-state conflict that is the focus of Chapter 3. But although each country regardless of region presents a unique extraterritorial context in which to implement the programme, the associated opportunities and constraints are not always place-specific. Examination of the role and work of Indonesian labour attachés in Hong Kong, Kuala Lumpur and Singapore brings this experience into relief, which provides a starting point for a wider, comparative analysis of implementation in other Asia-Pacific countries, including Brunei Darussalam, Taiwan and South Korea. Anecdotal evidence suggests that these inferences may also help make sense of Indonesia's administration of the programme in the Gulf region, certain parts of Africa, the Americas, Europe and Oceania within a more global setting.

Acknowledgements

This book would not have been possible without the help and generosity of so many people. Professor Michele Ford deserves a special mention here for the excellent supervision she gave me while writing the PhD thesis on which this book is based. I cannot thank Michele enough for her honesty and advice. This project also benefited from input from my associate supervisor, Professor Simon Butt, who commented on drafts and shared his knowledge about law in Indonesia, and conversations with Dr Anne McNevin about states and migrants. Professors Howard Dick and Graeme Hugo also provided useful guidance. I would also like to thank Dr Keith Foulcher, who introduced Indonesia to me as an undergrad 14 years ago and has encouraged my commitment to learning more about the country ever since.

In Indonesia, I am grateful to Dr Endang Sulistyaningsih. Her willingness to act as my in-country supervisor during my Postgraduate Prime Minister's Australia-Asia Endeavour Award was vital to the success of my project. I also greatly appreciate the fact that she made time to meet with me when I passed through Jakarta to one of my field sites. I am grateful to Dr Aswatini Raharto at the Indonesian Institute of Social Sciences (Lembaga Ilmu Pengetahuan Indonesia, LIPI) for taking an interest in my project and the invitation to participate in their policy forum. I would also like to express my deepest appreciation to the 121 informants who met with me to discuss my project. Their experience and perspectives added a richness to this project that would have been very difficult (if not impossible!) to find elsewhere. Keeping my word, I have done my best to maintain their anonymity. With time, the information they shared will become less politically sensitive: I look forward to this as an opportunity to put names to claims.

Parts of Chapter 5 draw on material previously published in: Palmer, Wayne. "Discretion and the Trafficking-like Practices of the Indonesian State." In Labour Migration and Human Trafficking in Southeast Asia: Critical Perspectives, edited by Michele Ford, Lenore Lyons, and Willem van Schendel, pp. 149–66. London: Routledge, 2012. This chapter also draws on material previously published in: Palmer, Wayne. "Public-Private Partnerships in the Administration and Control of Indonesian Migrant Labour in Hong Kong." Political Geography 34 (2013): pp. 1–9.

List of Organigrams

Abbreviations

APJATI	Asosiasi Perusahaan Jasa Tenaga Kerja Indonesia, Association of Indonesian Labour Service Companies
ASPAL	asli tapi palsu, real but fake
BAC	Business Accreditation Certificate
BNP2TKI	Badan Nasional Penempatan Tenaga Kerja Indonesia, National Agency for the Placement and Protection of Overseas Indonesian Workers
BPK	Badan Pemeriksa Keuangan, National Audit Agency
DKI Jakarta	Daerah Khusus Ibukota Jakarta, Special Capital Region of Jakarta
DPD	Dewan Perwakilan Daerah, Regional Representative Council
DPR	Dewan Perwakilan Rakyat, People's Representative Council
FPI	Front Pembela Islam, Islamic Defender's Front
GASPERMINDO	Gabungan Serikat Pekerja Merdeka Indonesia, Amalgamated Free Trade Unions of Indonesia
GATT	General Agreement on Tariffs and Trade
GSP	General System of Preferences
GOLKAR	Golongan Karya, Functional Groups
G30S	Gerakan 30 September, 30 September Movement
Gerindra	Partai Gerakan Indonesia Raya, Great Indonesia Movement Party
ILO	International Labour Organization
IMSA	Indonesian Manpower Supply Association
INP	Kepolisian Republik Indonesia, Indonesian National Police
IOM	International Organization for Migration
JMA	Jakarta Metropolitan Area
KOPBUMI	Konsorsium Pembela Buruh Migran Indonesia, Consortium for the Defence of Indonesian Migrant Workers
Kopkamtib	Komando Operasi Pemulihan Keamanan dan Ketertiban, Operational Command for the Restoration of Security and Order
KPK	Komisi Pemberantasan Korupsi, Corruption Eradication Commission
KSPSI	Konfederasi Serikat Pekerja Seluruh Indonesia, Confederation of All Indonesia Workers Unions
LIPI	Lembaga Ilmu Pengetahuan Indonesia, Indonesian Institute of Social Science
Malari	Malapetaka Limabelas Januari, 15 January Incident
MPR	Majelis Permusyawaratan Rakyat, People's Consultative Assembly
MUI	Majelis Ulama Indonesia, Indonesian Council of Islamic Scholars

NGO	Non-governmental organization
OPEC	Organization of the Petroleum Exporting Countries
PAPA	Persatuan Agensi Pembantu Rumah Asing, Association of Foreign Maid Agencies
PAN	Partai Amanat Nasional, National Mandate Party
PD	Partai Demokrat, Democratic Party
PDI	Partai Demokrat Indonesia, Indonesian Democratic Party
PDIP	Partai Demokrat Indonesia Perjuangan, Indonesian Democratic Party of Struggle
PKB	Partai Kebangkitan Bangsa, National Awakening Party
PKI	Partai Komunis Indonesia, Indonesian Communist Party
PKS	Partai Keadilan Sejahtera, Prosperous Justice Party
PPP	Partai Persatuan Pembangunan, United Development Party
PTUN	Pengadilan Tata Usaha Negara, Administrative Court
Pusat AKAN	Pusat Antar Kerja Antar Negara, Overseas Employment Centre
SMS	Short Message Service (text message)
UNDP	United Nations Development Programme

Map of Sites in Southeast Asia

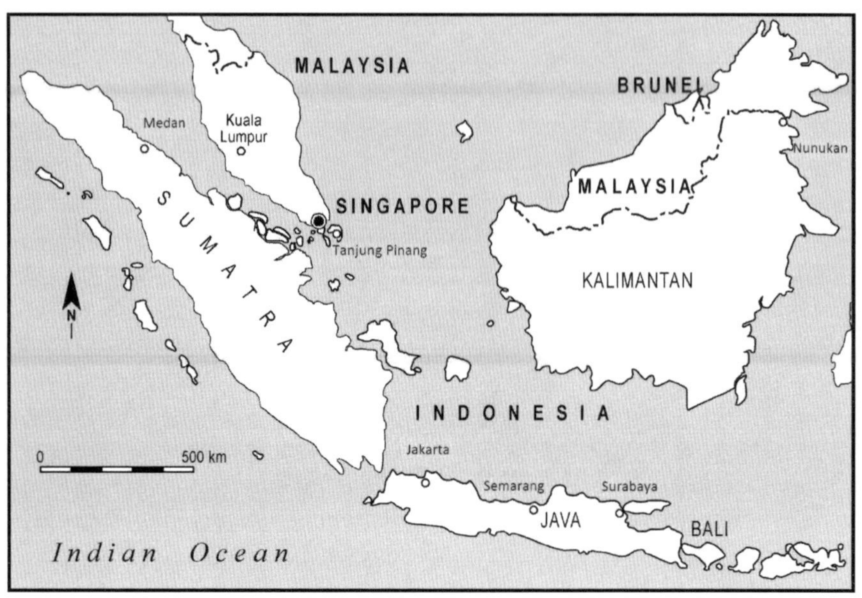

CHAPTER 1

Law and Discretion

One day during a courtesy call to the Indonesian Ministry of Manpower, a junior official confided that her boss had made her break the law. Later a middle ranking official with the National Agency for the Placement and Protection of Overseas Indonesian Workers went on to talk about how the lawbreaking official's ministry had started duplicating her agency's services. She shook her head while saying that senior management in both institutions had had a falling out, were now competing with each other and making life hard for those bureaucrats who just wanted to do their job. These confessions were confronting because they positioned officials as victims of Indonesia's overseas labour migration progamme. Surely the real victims were the migrant workers imprisoned in training centres by thuggish recruiters, given forged passports by corrupt officials and denied wages by unscrupulous employers. Of course they are. But the programme benefits and disadvantages a wide range of people, and officials are often concerned with how they are – and are not supported – to achieve their goals.

Indonesian bureaucrats generally have a reputation for subverting procedure when they do their jobs, for example, by granting exemptions in return for bribes or turning a blind eye to inconvenient facts. In administration of the overseas labour migration programme, they are often corrupt and negligent in their interactions with migrant workers and their recruiters. The officials have also shown little interest in intervening against recruiters who routinely break laws designed to protect the well-being of migrant workers.[1] Corruption and negligence are indeed rife within all aspects of the programme, including authorization of recruitment, verification of labour migrants' documents and certification of vocational competencies.[2] Regular failure to comply with the system's own standards has contributed to the popular perception that those requirements can simply be waived for the right price.[3]

1 Lindquist, "Labour Recruitment, Circuits of Capital and Gendered Mobility: Reconceptualizing the Indonesian Migration Industry"; Lindquist, "The Elementary School Teacher, the Thug and His Grandmother: Informal Brokers and Transnational Migration from Indonesia"; Killias, "'Illegal' Migration as Resistance: Legality, Morality and Coercion in Indonesian Domestic Worker Migration to Malaysia"; Killias, "The Politics of Bondage in the Recruitment, Training and Placement of Indonesian Migrant Domestic Workers."

2 International Organization for Migration, "Labour Migration from Indonesia: An Overview of Indonesian Migration in Selected Destinations in Asia and the Middle East," 27–31.

3 Human Rights Watch, "Help Wanted: Abuses against Female Domestic Workers in Indonesia and Malaysia," 23.

 | DOI 10.1163/9789004325487_002

Major strategies to reduce corruption aim to limit government officials' discretion in the use of resources and ability to extract fees in exchange for services.[4] Eliminating the capacity for discretionary decision-making ought to impede, or at least reduce, various forms of corruption.[5] The underlying assumption is that opportunities to profit personally from government business are limited when government officials are deprived of the ability to use discretion, for example, in awarding procurement contracts or outsourcing government services to private companies. However, while eliminating the discretionary capacity of bureaucrats may take some element of choice away from how they perform their roles, there are cases where it is practically impossible to follow pre-determined rules.[6] In such situations, the rule-versus-discretion model for controlling the level of corruption is not fit for the task, drawing attention to the fact that it uses a narrow understanding of discretion that ignores its role in creating capacity to implement policy.[7]

This book presents one such case in which discretion generates opportunities for corruption, but then also serves to maintain the viability of state agencies in the face of legal and institutional uncertainty. Many studies analysing the state's involvement in migration processes have captured the prevalence of corruption within the bureaucracy in Indonesia.[8] However, there is no comprehensive study of interactions between the various government agencies, units and individuals that make up the country's 'migration bureaucracy'.[9] Where existing studies engage with intra-state dynamics, they generally do so as part of a broader analysis of the labour migration experience rather than focusing specifically on the state's internal politics.[10] To the foray, this study adds a detailed examination of the internal politics at play when bureaucrats

4 Hamilton-Hart, "Anti-Corruption Strategies in Indonesia," 67.

5 Rose-Ackerman, *Corruption and Government: Causes, Consequences, and Reform*, 39–42.

6 Taylor, "Discretion versus Policy Rules in Practice," 195.

7 Brietzke, "Administrative Reform in Indonesia," 110.

8 For example, see Silvey, "Unequal Borders: Indonesian Transnational Migrants at Immigration Control"; Ford and Lyons, "Travelling the Aspal Route: 'Grey' Labour Migration through an Indonesian Border Town"; Killias, "'Illegal' Migration as Resistance: Legality, Morality and Coercion in Indonesian Domestic Worker Migration to Malaysia."

9 For a detailed discussion of how 'migration bureaucracy' is used to describe the overseas migration programme in The Philippines, see Rodriguez, *Migrants for Export: How the Philippine State Brokers Workers to the World.*

10 For exceptions, see Jones, *Making Money off Migrants*; Tirtosudarmo, *Mencari Indonesia: Demografi-Politik Pasca-Soeharto*; Ford, "After Nunukan: The Regulation of Indonesian Migration to Malaysia"; Ford and Lyons, "Travelling the Aspal Route: 'Grey' Labour Migration through an Indonesian Border Town."

perform illegal acts. It shifts the focus from the *modus operandi* of corruption to the individual and institutional factors that enable and limit corrupt and negligent behaviour on the part of those tasked with administering and managing the programme.

The inter-agency conflict between the Ministry of Manpower and the National Agency for the Placement and Protection of Overseas Indonesian Workers and the confusion it caused among officials, recruiters and migrants are a core focus of this book. Before March 2007, migrants and recruiters engaged primarily with the Ministry of Manpower. But with the establishment of the National Agency for the Placement and Protection of Overseas Indonesian Workers (Badan Nasional Penempatan dan Perlindungan Tenaga Kerja Indonesia, BNP2TKI), responsibility for much of the overseas labour migration programme was transferred to this new institution. Conflict ensued as the Ministry fought to maintain influence over the programme. At the lowest point, the Minister for Manpower and head of the BNP2TKI authorized personnel to duplicate services provided to migrants and recruiters. In Jakarta, the Ministry set up a rival service to issue recruitment certificates, provide pre-departure training and finalize migrants' permission to travel. Elsewhere, it authorized provincial governments to do the same. In response, the BNP2TKI instructed its offices in Jakarta and 17 other locations to ignore the ministry's regulations and continue business as usual.

Taking this as a starting point, the book then goes on to identify factors that generate such conflict, including discipline and hierarchy, which can and do influence the decision-making of individual officials. Rather than assessing how inter-agency conflict affects the state's capacity to achieve particular objectives, it focusses on the ways in which individuals and groups of officials do so amid contradictory claims for authority to administer the programme. At an organizational level, the examination shows how different government bodies work to strengthen their respective positions in struggles for power and influence. In terms of personnel, it also reveals the central role of discretion in the production, maintenance and resolution of at least some intra-state conflict around interpretation of legal and policy frameworks in pursuit of institutional objectives. The following sections summarize theories that help make sense of what happened in Indonesia.

Setting Institutional Objectives

Policy-making in Indonesia is no simple task. The national government can not always count on sub-national levels of the state to share the same objectives, regardless of their level and geographic location.[11] This is partly due to the fact that the state is large with sprawling territories and uneven population distributions. As this suggests, place-specific considerations are important when deciding how – or if – to implement national policy. In locations where multiple levels of government are present such as provincial capital cities, national and sub-national institutions can come to share place-specific objectives that sometimes subvert national policy. Inter-scalar relationships in a certain location are indeed a product of contextual factors, including history and place, but they are also affected by the larger system of government of which they are a part.

The 'decentralized unitary state' has emerged as a compromise between the unitary system, which puts a premium on unity, uniformity and hierarchy, and the federal system that is structured to better accommodate plurality, diversity and autonomy.[12] As a result, sub-national political contexts, which are arranged according to place, are formalized within a single frame of the state. Within such contexts, decentralization programmes affect the pattern of relations between national and sub-national government institutions. In 2001, Indonesia legislated a package of decentralization measures that shifted the bulk of policy-making authority and allocated a much larger share of the national budget to the state's lowest sub-national tier.[13] Direct elections for governors, district heads and mayors were also introduced. But problems with the implementation of decentralization have raised questions about whether it serves as a proxy for democratization.[14] Free from the level of scrutiny found higher up in the hierarchy,[15] it has widened opportunities for corruption and other illegal practices.[16] Decentralization has also promoted the development of a local oligarchy, which typically has a strong 'desire to influence and

11 Aspinall and van Klinken, *The State and Illegality in Indonesia*; Barker and van Klinken, *State of Authority: State in Society in Indonesia.*

12 Toonen, "The Unitary State as a System of Co-Governance: The Case of The Netherlands," 282.

13 Aspinall and Fealy, *Local Power and Politics in Indonesia: Decentralisation and Democratisation.*

14 See Chapter 2 for an account of how the decentralization package impacted the overseas labour migration programme.

15 Koppelman, "How 'Decentralization' Rationalizes Oligarchy: John McGinnis and the Rehnquist Court."

16 These consequences are often relegated in favour of claims that decentralization will ultimately help deepen democracy. See Heller, Harilal, and Chaudhri, "Building Local Democracy: Evaluating the Impact of Decentralization in Kerala, India," 627–628.

participate in public choices',[17] around which new patron-client relationships have developed.[18]

But this says little about how those institutions then relate to national government units that continue to operate in those places. The decentralization laws and implementing regulations set out the format for the formal dimension of institutional relations. However, exclusive focus on this dimension runs the risk of only seeing an 'illusory account of practice'.[19] For bureaucrats, such accounts of practice are useful to convey the impression that the diverse array of institutions that comprise the state share the same purpose. Such accounts also make it possible for those bureaucrats to represent their activity as legal-rational and therefore more or less disinterested, even though this is rarely the case.[20] As a result, these efforts produce something akin to a 'state effect', whereby the 'complexities of the various networks, factions, and institutions' that constitute the state are kept from public view.[21] Rumours of politics within and between these institutions are bountiful. But sometimes bureaucrats go public by taking complexities to the mass media as part of an attempt to get the upper hand on rivals who claim superiority in the same field of activity. This book presents one such case.

Focus on interaction between institutions suggests that the state might also be usefully viewed as a collection of relationships and strategies. This shifts attention away from the conditions that produce unity or conflict to the actors and the logic they use when deciding how best to achieve institutional objectives, such as policy implementation. It recasts the state as 'an elaborate web of distributed agency'.[22] Using the network model, the state can be reduced to a system of nodes (actors) and ties (relationships), which may vary in strength between the same sets of actors in different settings. To illustrate, the head of an Immigration Office in one regional city may have a much stronger

17 Bourguignon and Verdier, "Oligarchy, Democracy, Inequality and Growth."

18 For examples of the Indonesian literature on oligarchy, see Ford and Pepinsky, "Beyond Oligarchy? Critical Exchanges on Political Power and Material Inequality in Indonesia"; Winters, "Oligarchy and Democracy in Indonesia"; Hadiz and Robison, "The Political Economy of Oligarcy and the Reorganization of Power in Indonesia." For a discussion of these relationships in relation to the overseas labour migration programme at the state's centre, see Chapter 3. Chapter 4 refers to them in six decentralized contexts.

19 Abrams, "Notes on the Difficulty of Studying the State (1977)," 58.

20 Matheson, "Rationality and Decision-Making in Australian Federal Government."

21 Pierce, "Looking like a State: Colonialism and the Discourse of Corruption in Northern Nigeria," 898.

22 Passoth and Rowland, "Actor-Network State: Integrating Actor-Network Theory and State Theory," 822–823, 827.

relationship with local government than the head of the same office in another city because of factors such as kinship ties. As a result, the former office may have more success in soliciting the cooperation of local government to limit the production of real but fake (*asli tapi palsu, aspal*) identity documents for citizens who want passports. An Indonesian Immigration Office's attempt to achieve this outcome in West Kalimantan upset the local government and resulted in threats of violence so the head of that office made a peace offering in line with local customs to normalize the institutional relationship in that particular place.[23]

Role of Legal Authority

The state's institutions and laws that govern them are mutually constitutive. An institution is a 'network of formal, norm-created and norm-creating' entities operated by individuals who have authority to command others.[24] In practical terms, this means that law authorizes the establishment of state institutions and then delegates to them legal authority to apply the law. One way to visualize the relationship between institutions and the law is to see them as two congruent pyramids: a normative structure of positive law and an institutional one that organizes individuals and organizations into hierarchies and sectors with authority to implement policy within an area over which they hold legal authority.[25] This structural approach provides those who study the state with a schema to examine the relationship between laws, regulations and policies on the one hand, and government agencies, units and individual officials on the other.

23 See Dewan Perwakilan Rakyat, *Risalah Rapat Panitia Khusus Rancangan Undang-Undang Tentang Pemberantasan Tindak Pidana Perdagangan Orang: Rapat Dengar Pendapat Umum*, 2006; Dewan Perwakilan Rakyat, *Risalah Rapat Panitia Khusus Rancangan Undang-Undang Tentang Pemberantasan Tindak Pidana Perdagangan Orang: Rapat Dengar Pendapat Umum*, 2006; Dewan Perwakilan Rakyat, *Risalah Rapat Panitia Khusus Rancangan Undang-Undang Tentang Pemberantasan Tindak Pidana Perdagangan Orang: Rapat Dengar Pendapat Umum*, 2006.

24 Akzin, "Analysis of State and Law Structure," 3–4. Benyamin Akzin is a student of Hans Kelsen to whom this definition of the state's institutional and legal frameworks belong. Akzin adds value to Kelsen's definition by fleshing out the institutional and legal structures as well as the relationships between them. These Akzin-Kelsen structures and relationships continue to inform the way in which government officials in some states are trained to understand the legal-administrative context in which they work. For example, see the strong emphasis that the Indonesian Director-General for Regulations and Laws in the Indonesian Ministry of Law and Human Rights places Kelsen's hierarchy of norms in Masitah, "Urgensi Naskah Akademik Dalam Pembentukan Peraturan Daerah," 111–112.

25 Akzin, "Analysis of State and Law Structure," 3.

This approach is used in a social-legal study on Indonesia's administrative courts to examine spaces of tension and harmony that exist between these institutions and law.[26] In general, the 'living reality' in most situations is that bureaucrats treat law as their primary referent when assessing the validity of other laws.[27] In response to criticisms of their own acts, bureaucrats also often make the claim, 'I do not make law, I follow it'.[28] They are encouraged to adhere strictly to rules in the name of consistency, which can in turn help prevent caprice and whimsical exercise of their authority.[29] Viewed more critically, strict adherence to procedure provides bureaucrats with a 'way to avoid emphatic understanding and a way to *deny* moral choice in legal decision-making'.[30] But by paying attention to 'the games bureaucrats play', it also becomes apparent that while they might follow the law, they might also do so in pursuit of an entirely different objective from that envisaged by legislators.[31] This case study about intra-state conflict around administration of Indonesia's overseas labour migration programme offers just such a narrative.

Legal authority is as a key concept to make sense of the relationships between the programme's institutions and laws. In particular, it is useful to test the limits of how law is used to implement the programme.[32] Hans Kelsen interprets the relationships through the lens of an identity thesis,[33] which treats the law and institutions as 'two words for the same thing'.[34] The first reading of this thesis – that the law is the state – has repercussions for the legal authority of institutions in the sense that they lack the capacity to contravene the law.[35] In other words, only legal acts may be attributed to the state. To explain the

---

26 Also, see Chapter 3 for an account of this tension in the context of the overseas labour migration programme.

27 Hart, *The Concept of Law*, 293.

28 Henderson, "Legality and Empathy," 1590.

29 Massaro, "Empathy, Legal Storytelling, and the Rule of Law: New Worlds, Old Wounds?" 2103.

30 Henderson, "Legality and Empathy," 1587 emphasis in original.

31 For detailed discussions about instances where bureaucrats in the United States narrowly interpreted law to protect their collective interests, see Katz, "The Games Bureaucrats Play: Hide and Seek under the Freedom of Information Act." This behaviour accurately reflects some of the behaviour described in Chapter 3.

32 Here legal authority is used to describe the ability to apply the law. Alternatively, this concept has been used to describe the 'weight of a text in a legal argument'. See Jansen, *The Making of Legal Authority: Non-Legislative Codifications in Historical and Comparative Perspective*, 138.

33 Kelsen, *Pure Theory of Law*.

34 Troper, "Lars Vinx, Hans Kelsen's Pure Theory of Law: Legality and Legitimacy," 523.

35 Vinx, *Hans Kelsen's Pure Theory of Law: Legality and Legitimacy*.

fact that institutions engage in illegal practices, blame is shifted to individual officials who come to use their legal authority inappropriately because of 'laziness, viciousness, rebelliousness' or human error.[36] Referred to as *oknum* in Indonesia, these officials are often the target of internal and external efforts to align how government implements programmes and manages its resources with the law.[37]

An inverse reading of the identity thesis – that the state is the law – reveals another debate about the boundaries of legal authority: that all acts done in the state's name are legal. Because the state is the law, everything done in its name is legal. Many are uncomfortable with this reading because it legitimizes practically any use of institutions, 'including [for] the most barbaric' purposes.[38] A hallmark of Indonesia's New Order regime (1967–1998), for example, is that it prioritized the achievement of institutional objectives over the legality of acts that made it possible.[39] Most institutions have internal mechanisms to review instances where those with legal authority authorize activity that somehow conflicts with the law. Accessing these mechanisms is not always easy. In fact, it can sometimes be impossible. But where it is possible, the purpose is to reverse uses of legal authority that do not conform to some aspect of the law.[40] This does not mean, however, 'that the state cannot conceivably depart from the law'.[41] The very existence of these mechanisms demonstrates quite the opposite but shows that it is not generally desirable.

By recognizing the capacity of institutions to act beyond the strictures of the laws that govern their work, it becomes possible to focus on how political relationships between state agencies can over-ride their technical relationship. Unpacking the identity thesis, for example, enables a discussion of the technical and political aspects of legal authority, which is key to understanding how institutions come to engage in illegal practices. This depiction of the state is necessarily partial, both because institutions and law are not identical, and because the state is a much more complex structure than its mutually constitutive parts. Nevertheless, these tools provide an evidence-based technique to examine situations in which Indonesian officials use legal authority to

36 Christie, "Lawful Departures from Legal Rules: 'Jury Nullification' and Legitimated Disobedience," 1289.

37 Aspinall and van Klinken, *The State and Illegality in Indonesia.*

38 Akzin, "Analysis of State and Law Structure," 2.

39 See Chapter 2 for an account of specific ways in which the New Order regime did so.

40 Troper, "Lars Vinx, Hans Kelsen's Pure Theory of Law: Legality and Legitimacy," 523; Jeffries Jr., "Legality, Vagueness, and the Construction of Penal Statutes," 212.

41 Tanguay-Renaud, "The Intelligibility of Extralegal State Action: A General Lesson for Debates on Public Emergencies and Legality," 163.

authorize illegal acts. The approach opens up new topics for discussions about the state's relationship to legality by moving beyond the focus of legal authority on the illegal acts of individual officials to the network that constitutes the state. Next it is worth considering how bureaucrats make decisions.

Legal Relations, Justification and Authorization

There are many layers of law, which can make it difficult to see which one should apply in a particular situation. It is useful to picture law as a hierarchical structure of norms with fewer and often more general laws at the top and a greater number of more particular ones closer to its base. In Indonesia, the constitution is the highest law in the land, followed by statutes, government regulations, presidential regulations and regional regulations to provide general and abstract norms.[42] Individual and concrete laws take the form of decrees and instructions and are generally used by heads of institutions to set some kind of specific policy or procedure. This formulation of law as structure gives the impression that law has a form. But it is also possible to view law in a different light, for example, by moving away from this concern with where rules fit into the hierarchy of laws to focus on how and why they are produced. This idea of 'law as process' takes into consideration why a particular law came to stipulate a particular view at a certain point in time, what the law adds or takes away in that context, and how that law is interpreted with the passage of time.[43]

Identifying the most appropriate law can also be a technically difficult task. Legal relations offer one way to narrow down the possibilities. The legal concept describes ties between the person who is affected by the law, which stipulates that 'certain facts will normally be followed by … consequences in the form of action or non-action', and that one or more government officials are authorized to impose those consequences.[44] Terms of the law, such as marriage and property, never represent a single relationship, so it is necessary to ask what the person who is affected by the law may do without penalty, must do under the threat of penalty or can do to change legal relations. Doing so teases out a variety of legal relations and establishes the rights, privileges, powers and immunities of all those involved.

But bureaucrats are primarily concerned with two legal concepts: authorization and justification. They deem it necessary that their actions are authorized

42 See Chapter 3 for a detailed explanation of this hierarchy of laws in relation to the overseas labour migration programme.

43 Falk, *Law as Process: An Anthropological Approach*, xi, xvi–xxii.

44 Corbin, "Legal Analysis and Terminology," 164–165.

by the law, begging the question: what aspect of the law authorizes them to choose a particular law over another to justify their decisions? The distinction between formal and material authorization provides a starting point to answer this question. Unlike material authorization, which enables bureaucrats to use the law in line with higher order norms, formal authorization is related to the power that a particular individual has to do so.[45] Formal authorization enables officials to create and apply norms that conflict with higher order ones, such as statutes. In other words, provided that officials act '*within the limits* of their authorization', their decisions have normative force regardless of their legality.[46] Formal authorization, then, constitutes a resource that allows a government institution to act illegally when those who are authorized to do so deem it necessary.

To access this resource, bureaucrats need only justify their use of the law through reference to some higher level legal or political principle.[47] In Indonesia, for example, the substantive provisions of an implementing regulation is preceded by two sections that justify it. The 'considering that' (*menimbang*) part makes arguments for the necessity of the decisions that follow, usually citing the enactment of a new statute, a meeting or some development that requires an amendment. This is then followed by a 'remembering that' (*mengingat*) section, which lists the higher level laws that authorize an individual to issue the decision. There is broad agreement that bureaucrats should not have a 'recourse role' that enables them to justify their refusal to follow the law.[48] However, it is possible for them to do just that by using 'some other basic end of the legal and political order'.[49] An agency might choose, for example, to list the statutes that support their decisions while making an argument about how other conflicting laws are out of step with the broader political programme of the government in power. In 2008 Indonesia's Minister for Manpower did just that in its turf war with the BNP2TKI, providing the empirical basis for the discussion in this book.

---

45 Paulson, "Material and Formal Authorisation in Kelsen's Pure Theory," 172.

46 Vinx, *Hans Kelsen's Pure Theory of Law: Legality and Legitimacy*, 83.

47 Kadish and Kadish, *Discretion to Disobey: A Study of Lawful Departures from Legal Rules*, 11.

48 '[R]ecourse roles…enable their agents to take acion in situations where the role's prescribed ends conflict with its prescribed means, including grants of discretion broad or narrow'. For a detailed discussion of these roles, see Christie, "Lawful Departures from Legal Rules: 'Jury Nullification' and Legitimated Disobedience," 1289–1291.

49 Ibid., 1290.

Achieving Institutional Objectives

Both formal structures and informal institutions help the state to achieve its objectives. Formal structures provide a 'blueprint for activities', setting out goals and policies that constitute a kind of rational theory about how institutional objectives ought to be achieved.[50] They are 'facts which must simply be taken into account'.[51] But there is a sharp distinction between this blueprint and how institutional objectives are actually achieved. The distinction is most visible in situations where formal structures fail to take account of local context.[52] For example, the corrupt practices of government officials in these places may be be a 'local community-sanctioned response to managing the impact and limitations of a central government policy' that fails to do so.[53] But before considering excuses for informal institutions such as these, it is important to discuss bureaucrats' other motives to undermine the law.

Officials may ignore the law because doing so enables them to pursue private interests, such as accumulation of wealth through the collection of bribes.[54] However, examination of the principal-agent problem inherent in their role as an agent of the state opens up another dimension to this activity.[55] When the head of an institution is identified as the principal, for example, officials can become internally accountable. Heads of institutions have the necessary tools to level administrative sanctions against subordinates who do not toe the line, and it is partly for this reason that officials come to practise a high level of fealty to public office.[56] This fealty, in turn, can be harnessed as part of an attempt to direct officials towards the achievement of institutional objectives irrespective of what is permitted by the law and so may have little to do with private ambitions.

---

50 Meyer and Rowan, "Institutionalized Organizations: Formal Structure as Myth and Ceremony," 342.

51 Ibid., 341.

52 Ibid., 346.

53 Ford and Lyons, "Travelling the Aspal Route: 'Grey' Labour Migration through an Indonesian Border Town," 122.

54 Butt, *Corruption and Law in Indonesia*.

55 Principal-agent theory describes a "relationship that arises when one person ('a principal') manifests assent to another person ('an agent') that the agent shall act on the principal's behalf and subject to the principal's control". Metzger, "Privatization as Delegation," 1463.

56 Weber, "Bureaucracy," 959.

Officials may also look for opportunities to augment their power *vis-à-vis* one another. This may entail augmenting the power of their institution in relation to another state agency or in their relationships with society.[57] Budget maximization theory, which predicts that officials seek ever larger budget allocations offers one way in which to study these phenomena.[58] Organizationally, this might be justified by the addition of new services to the portfolio of programmes. On an individual level, the theory of utility maximization indicates that bureaucrats may also do so because of the increase in 'income, prestige, power, emolument and other amenities' that come with greater budget allocations.[59] However, empirical studies show that government agencies do not always seek to maximize their budget, nor do officials always seek to maximize the private utility of resources under their control. This case study about individuals and groups of officials in Indonesia shows that they may also do so to maintain the *status quo* and secure promotions.[60]

The power to pursue individual and institutional objectives can manifest itself in forms such as competition that pits individuals, units, agencies, branches and even tiers of government against one another. Competition is also structured into the state's design, as some government agencies are intended to monitor and even challenge fellow institutions. States frequently create such agencies to enhance the credibility of their policies by incorporating oversight into the institutional system.[61] The importance of transparency for institutional legitimacy is also highlighted by the creation of independent agencies, which states set-up regardless of the 'severe problems of coordination, legitimacy and control' they may create.[62] Independent anti-corruption agencies are a popular choice in countries where the government is seeking political legitimacy ahead of a general election or fulfilling conditions for access to funds from international donors.[63] The BNP2TKI is one such agency, as

57 Fyre, "Capture or Exchange? Business Lobbying in Russia," 1020.

58 Niskanen, "Nonmarket Decision Making: The Peculiar Economics of Bureaucracy."

59 Breton and Wintrobe, "The Equilibrium of a Budget-Maximizing Bureau: A Note on Niskanen's Theory of Bureaucracy," 195–196.

60 See Chapter 3.

61 Gilardi, "Policy Credibility and Delegation to Independent Regulatory Agencies: A Comparative Empirical Analysis," 873.

62 Shapiro, "The Problems of Independent Agencies in the United States and the European Union," 276.

63 International aid donors that attach the condition of sustainable anti-corruption strategies to financial support are also partly responsible for the proliferation of nominally independent anti-corruption agencies. See Doig, "Good Government and Sustainable Anti-Corruption Strategies: A Role for Independent Anti-Corruption Agencies," 151.

demonstrated in the following chapter, which examines the motivation for its establishment and evolution of institutions and laws that preceded it. A core objective of the BNP2TKI was to cooperate with the Ministry for Manpower, but in reality this and other independent agencies are often pitted against the very institutions they should be working with.

These agencies, for the most part, do not share a single view on how things should be done – indeed, they may also have opposing purposes. Even where there is general agreement in a particular policy area, individual agencies can hold different interpretations about what factors are more relevant.[64] Extreme forms of institutional fragmentation such as this are evident in parts of the developing world, where at times the state is unable to project an appearance of unity due to deep internal divisions.[65] In less extreme cases, a plurality of understandings may reflect the fact that state institutions use legal terminology that relates to their particular function and so tend to re-interpret situations and practices in those terms. Such fragmentation can weaken the state's capacity to 'coordinate and plan', leading to 'functional and jurisdictional overlap', which can reduce efficiency through 'duplication and waste'.[66] Formal structures such as the law may well seek to prevent these situations, but those with legal authority can and do create informal institutions that make them a reality.

Cultures of Administration

Administrative culture offers a way to identify a wider range of practices used to achieve institutional objectives. Bureaucrats operate within an administrative culture that instructs them on why and how to use the state's formal structures.[67] Within organizational studies, administrative culture describes the distinctive values and patterns of behaviour found within communities of individuals working in formal institutions. One model divides administrative culture into four broad analytical categories using a two-by-two grid with 'preferences regarding structure' (control or flexibility) on the vertical axis and 'organizational focus' (internal and external) on the horizontal plane.[68] As tiered

64 Palmer, "Discretion and the Trafficking-like Practices of the Indonesian State," 153–156.

65 Rubin, *The Fragmentation of Afghanistan: State Formation and Collapse in the International System*, x.

66 Rhodes, "The Hollowing of the State: The Changing Nature of the Public Service in Britain," 149.

67 Hofstede, Hofstede, and Minkov, *Cultures and Organizations: Software of the Mind.*

68 Quinn et al., "A Competing Value Framework for Analyzing Presentational Communication in Management Contexts," 217.

organizations, states fall into the bottom two quadrants. Those with a strong external focus tend to have correspondingly strong legal-rational cultures, which include productivity and efficiency as objectives in the performance of public functions. Those with an inwardly focussed orientation generally have more hierarchical cultures that have as their primary objective 'management of internal communication … stability and control'.[69]

Scrutinizing patterns 'of and for' administrative behaviour makes it possible to identify the value that bureaucrats attribute to a particular course of action.[70] These values are sometimes articulated in formal documents, which may claim to promote impartiality, commitment to service, accountability, respectfulness and ethics among those in its employ. Indonesian law also requires officials to prioritize legal certainty and special treatment of vulnerable groups of people in relation to public services.[71] Informally, administrative culture might also encourage other values, such as fairness, consensus, trust, secrecy, pragmatism, accommodation and territorialism.[72] Evidence of these values in the Indonesian bureaucracy can be found in studies of diverse topics, ranging from law enforcement, elections, environmental resource management, construction to international migration.[73]

Infrastructure in a given institution's environment moulds the contours of administrative culture.[74] For example, they can make some forms of interaction easier than others. In office spaces that have photocopiers and water coolers, for example, staff are likely to have informal conversations with one another in those areas, and in so doing develop informal social networks.[75] Informal interactions such as these tend not only to be brief and unplanned but also frequent, serving to support 'execution of work-related tasks; co-ordination of group activity; transmission of office culture; and social functions such as team building'.[76] However, there are also disadvantages to this informality from the organization's point of view, as it can, for example, replace formal modes of communication, which are important for documenting conversations and

69 Hajnal, "The Spirit of Management Reforms," 502.

70 Dwivedi and Gow, *From Bureaucracy to Public Management: The Administrative Culture of the Government of Canada*, 19.

71 *Law No. 25 on Public Service*, article 4.

72 Rhodes, "Intergovernmental Relations in the United Kingdom," 52.

73 Barker and van Klinken, *State of Authority: State in Society in Indonesia.*

74 Schein, *Organizational Psychology*.

75 Fayard and Weeks, "Photocopier and Water-Coolers: The Affordances of Informal Interaction," 605.

76 Wittaker, Frohlich, and Daly-Jones, "Informal Workplace Communication: What Is It like and How Might We Support It?" 131.

decisions. This analysis of physical environments within a single office setting is useful to examine the administrative landscapes of cities and towns involved in management of the Indonesia's overseas labour migration programme. The physical proximity of government offices in a particular location can assist officials, regardless of their institutional affiliation, to develop the kinds of informal institutions for communication recognized to support, undermine or even displace formal structures as discussed in Chapter 4.[77]

As a manifestation of administrative culture, then, informal institutions may develop in response to formal structures, such as the political organization of government agencies and the law. Some informal activity also has its origins in 'malfunctionings of bureaucracy'.[78] Take institutionalized corruption, for example. The practice is often evidence of institutional break down,[79] during which it can provide a means to bolster administrative hierarchies. Fear of investigation, prosecution and punishment provides presidents with a mechanism of control that allow their inner circle to exercise greater coercive power over the bureaucracy than would have otherwise been the case.[80] These kinds of networks can prove difficult to unravel, as demonstrated by the experience in Indonesia following the regime change that replaced the New Order government in 1998.[81] While in place, however, they can nevertheless serve as a cohesive device in what might otherwise be a chaotic system, effectively instituting an alternative but 'potent ... state command structure'.[82] Ultimately, it is officials at the management level of institutions, such as unit heads, directors and so on, who determine whether such practices are permissible.[83]

Law and Discretion as a Resource

In Indonesia and elsewhere, law is only one of many sets of institutionalized norms that inform bureaucrats' decision-making processes. The norms claim autonomy from the social system in which they are embedded,[84] but must in

77 Grzymala-Busse, "The Best Laid Plans: The Impact of Informal Rules on Formal Institutions in Transitional Regimes," 311–326.

78 Lomnitz, "Informal Exchange Networks in Formal Systems: A Theoretical Model."

79 Darden, "The Integrity of Corrupt States: Graft as an Informal State Institution," 35.

80 Darden, "Blackmail as a Tool of State Domination: Ukraine under Kuchma," 2001, 71.

81 See Chapters 2 and 3 for an account of how senior management in the overseas labour migration programme accommodated the networks put in place by former managers.

82 Darden, "Blackmail as a Tool of State Domination: Ukraine under Kuchma," 2001, 71.

83 Schillemans, "Accountability in the Shadow of Hierarchy: The Horizontal Accountability of Agencies," 189–192.

84 Henderson, "Legality and Empathy," 1588.

reality compete against other norms that seek to regulate everyday life.[85] Part of the reason why the law is not always prioritized is that officials with the authority to apply it might not agree with, for example, the way in which it orders the economic, political and social interests of different groups.[86] In effect, law is framed in terms of 'good rules' and 'bad rules' by the bureaucrats charged with its implementation.[87] A designation of 'bad' may then be used to legitimate practices that subvert the law, such as accepting bribes.[88]

Those advocating better institutional enforcement of law recommend practical solutions, such as increasing officials' salaries. But just as the agencies' relationship to the law is complex, so too is the concept of enforcement. Enforcement is generally judged in terms of its 'success' or 'failure',[89] where failure is characterized by a low probability of enforcement and light sanctions.[90] But it is also possible to frame law enforcement in terms of degrees and levels to reflect the fact that it is determined in large part by factors such as effort and resources.[91] The extent to which agencies enforce law is thus a function of institutional capacity, as institutions must be able to exercise legitimate authority, make strategic choices and deliver incentives and sanctions.[92]

Law enforcement is seldom the only – or even primary – purpose of government institutions. Institutional objectives are rather a commitment to bring about 'some desired set of … consequences' such as a change in social behaviour or the raising of more revenue.[93] Within that context, law may prove a useful tool, for example, to help garner support for political projects and justify interventions that might otherwise be deemed illegitimate. By making alternatives illegal, it becomes possible to generate legitimacy for otherwise

---

85 McCarthy, "The Limits of Legality: State, Governance and Resource Control in Indonesia," 97.

86 Massaro, "Empathy, Legal Storytelling, and the Rule of Law: New Worlds, Old Wounds?" 2116.

87 Ibid., 2120.

88 Gootenberg, "Talking like a State: Drugs, and the Language of Control," 114.

89 Becker and Stigler, "Law Enforcement, Malfeasance, and Compensation of Enforcers," 3.

90 Although not always the case, this mix of conditions is understood to have a positive correlation with the probability of illegal activity. See Garoupa, "The Theory of Optimal Law Enforcement," 267.

91 Becker and Stigler, "Law Enforcement, Malfeasance, and Compensation of Enforcers," 3.

92 Olowo, "Pride and Performance in African Public Services: Analysis of Institutional Breakdown and Rebuilding Efforts in Nigeria and Uganda," 130.

93 McCarthy, "The Limits of Legality: State, Governance and Resource Control in Indonesia," 90–91.

'insupportable and intolerable' activity.[94] A legal mandate may also – though not always – have the effect of foreclosing further discussion about the inherent complexity of the issue at hand.[95] This effect flows partly from the assumption that the law not only provides 'clean-cut answers' to problems,[96] but that it is also in some sense right. This idea of illegality as a narrative rather than a technical category, as it is most commonly understood, opens up space to examine how and why law is used for purposes that sometimes have little or nothing to do with enforcement.

Discretion is a key resource in bureaucrats' application of law, which is not always consistent. Defined as 'the power or the right to decide according to one's own judgement',[97] bureaucratic discretion is vital in the modern state. Executive agencies have a great deal of discretion in the design and implementation of government policy as a consequence of the fact that the legislature delegates so much rule-making authority to them.[98] Indeed, the exercise of discretion can result in the creation and implementation of informal, discriminatory and personalized regimes for performing public functions.[99] But this is not always a certain outcome.

The concept of legitimacy offers a way to move the debate around the effects of discretion forward. It is not always possible to infer legitimacy based solely on whether an act is technically legal.[100] Rather, the rubric for determining legitimacy derives standards from an external source, such as 'tradition, following established procedures, reflecting shared values, and so on'.[101] An act can never be 'legitimate in and of itself'.[102] Legitimacy is expressed in reactions, which may be pragmatic (whether the act had benefits), moral (whether it was the right thing to do), or cognitive (whether it was inevitable.)'[103] This

94 Abrams, "Notes on the Difficulty of Studying the State (1977)," 76.

95 McCarthy, "The Limits of Legality: State, Governance and Resource Control in Indonesia," 93.

96 Massaro, "Empathy, Legal Storytelling, and the Rule of Law: New Worlds, Old Wounds?" 2110.

97 Langbein, *Bureaucratic Discretion*, 2:53–58.

98 Epstein and O'Halloran, *A Transaction Cost Politics Approach to Policy Making under Separate Powers*, 27.

99 Rosenbloom, "Israel's Administrative Culture, Israeli Arabs, and Arab Subjects."

100 Dowling and Pfeffer, "Organizational Legitimacy: Social Values and Organizational Behaviour," 124.

101 Vinzant and Crothers, *Street-Level Leadership: Discretion and Legitimacy in Front-Line Public Service*, 49.

102 Ibid.

103 Suchman, "Managing Legitimacy: Strategic and Institutional Approaches," 578–584.

more complex definition of legitimacy is useful when discussing the decisions of government officials, who are 'asked to make choices that are in accord or compliance with multiple and sometimes conflicting norms, laws, values, and rules'.[104] Discussing these acts in terms of legitimacy rather than legality offers a way in which to understand why bureaucrats sometimes choose to act illegally in the pursuit of institutional objectives. It is this approach that drives this book's main argument.

Structure of the Book

This chapter presented a theoretical framework, which distinguishes between institutions and the law as two major components of the state. It provided a means of focusing specifically on alignments and tensions between the state's constituent parts and a lens through which to interpret the relationships between them. The chapter advanced the argument that discretion can and does play a vital role in lubricating the modern state's machinery, especially when the state's formal structures are somehow deficient. For example, bureaucrats may use it to achieve institutional objectives when institutions breakdown. Their tactics may include strategic use of the law, which are not always legal, and which which may be primarily aimed at personal gain or the furthering of sectional interests.

Chapter 2 provides a history of the institutional and legal evolution of Indonesia's overseas labour migration programme in its changing economic and political context. The first section shows that state infrastructure grew around international labour migration in the context of attempts to address problems in the Indonesian economy. This development later encouraged the rise of a purpose-specific recruitment industry, which in turn fuelled an increasingly authoritarian approach within the programme as officials accommodated private sector interests in return for access to its economic resources. Second, the chapter shows how the context shifted in the late 1980s, prompting further adjustments to bring the programme more in line with the trend towards greater economic and political liberalization of the times. This section also explains how the consequences of the 1997 Asian Financial Crisis made meaningful reform difficult in the period immediately following the resignation of President Suharto in 1998. Finally, the chapter documents changes over the nine

104 Vinzant and Crothers, *Street-Level Leadership: Discretion and Legitimacy in Front-Line Public Service*, 49.

years before the BNP2TKI took control of the programme from the Ministry of Manpower.

Chapter 3 presents a worm's eye view of the relationship dynamics between government agencies in the following four years. It starts with an analysis of the factors that initially drove the two government agencies into conflict. This section reveals that the ensuing conflict was fuelled by disagreement concerning their respective roles as operator or regulator, access to labour recruitment companies as an economic resource, and the career advancement ambitions of individual bureaucrats. The chapter then examines the phase in which the agencies duplicated services, with a focus on the consequences of duplication for administration of the programme in Jakarta. It describes judicial and legislative interventions in the dispute as well as the way in which the agencies engaged with the public in their battles for popular support. The final section identifies the event at which the agencies agreed to seek a compromise, discusses the President's role in it and the implications that past staffing decisions had for the negotiations. It ends with an analysis of the events that precipitated a speedy closure of the most obvious gaps between the law and and institutional practice in this policy area.

Chapter 4 uses one of the many dilemmas that this conflict created for bureaucrats as a starting point for six case studies on how it played out in different places. The BNP2TKI issued notice that in January 2010 labour recruitment companies must organize overseas identity cards for migrant workers. These identity cards could be obtained at its units in 18 locations across the country. A contradictory notice was issued by the Ministry of Manpower, which instructed companies to apply for the documents at its unit in Jakarta or at a provincial government office in the regions. The case studies show how and why the consequences of these conflicting policies differed from place to place. The Jakarta and Tanjung Pinang experiences reveal that bureaucrats prioritized horizontal relationships with officials from other agencies in their location over their relationships with the national government. However, Medan and Semarang show that tier of government trumped place-specific factors, such as collegiality. Nunukan and Surabaya show what can happen when a tier of government is missing.

Chapter 5 analyses the role that Indonesian consular officers played in setting up systems to deal with labour migration in Hong Kong, Kuala Lumpur and Singapore during the period examined in Chapters 3 and 4. The chapter is divided into two sections, the first of which details how systems were established, including the role played by individual officials in their extraterritorial setting. In Hong Kong, the system was designed to outsource migrant labour matters to local labour recruitment companies. The system in Kuala Lumpur, by contrast, harnessed the economic resources of their counterparts in Indonesia to help cover the costs of labour migrants who fall foul of Malaysian immigration law. In Singapore, adjustments to the system synchronized the embassy's standards with those of the Ministry of Manpower in Indonesia in response to lobbying on the part of the recruitment industry for greater legal certainty. The second section examines how labour attachés handled cases of passport confiscation by labour recruitment companies, lack of capacity in the emergency shelter for women, and the uncovering of fake data in official documents. This reveals the extent to which the attachés personal decision-making, rather than the systems' legal framework or a set of institutional procedures, determines the day-to-day operation of the programme.

Chapter 6 offers a brief conclusion that sums up how individuals and agencies in contemporary Indonesia operationalize discretion as a key resource to deal with disjuncture between the legal framework governing the overseas labour migration programme and institutional practice, as embodied in the activities of individuals as they decide how to carry out their tasks within particular local contexts. The case studies offer a snapshot of interaction between formal and informal institutions, demonstrating how discretion can provide an 'institutional fix'[105] to problems caused by the misalignment of the state's formal structures. It confirms that while discretion poses a threat to legal certainty, it can also make it possible for formal institutions to continue operating in the absence of workable processes and procedures. These issues are considered the in following chapters.

105 For discussions that also use 'institutional fixes' to describe arrangements in which states attempt to close gaps between laws and institutional objectives in other attempts to manage migration matters, see Rodriguez, *Migrants for Export: How the Philippine State Brokers Workers to the World*, xxii; Palmer, "Public-Private Partnerships in the Administration and Control of Indonesian Migrant Labour in Hong Kong," 1.

CHAPTER 2

Indonesia's Overseas Labour Migration Programme

Indonesia's overseas labour migration programme has undergone considerable legal and institutional change in its more than 40 years of existence, during which time it both influenced and responded to migration flows.[1] The system developed as part of the New Order government's larger economic development strategy, which began in the late 1960s. It aimed to find overseas employment for Indonesian workers as part of a stop gap solution for the lack of adequate gainful employment in densely populated areas of the country, such as rural Java.[2] In subsequent years, the initiative was harnessed to serve other objectives, such as helping the country tap an alternative source of foreign exchange revenue. However, not all adjustments were made with an eye to economic, political and social benefits at home. In 2004 the legislature passed Indonesia's first overseas migration law, which expanded the monitoring role of government agencies over recruitment industry practices that had negative consequences for labour migrants, such as the provision of sub-standard board and lodgings during training. In response to predictions that the Ministry of Manpower would struggle in applying these standards, the BNP2TKI was established in 2007.

Broad policy shifts and the experiences of migrants themselves are a major focus of academic literature on labour migration from Indonesia.[3] Missing from this narrative is a close consideration of the evolution of specific government programmes. Tracing the overseas labour migration programme's policy direction over time enables the identification of ruptures and continuities that do not necessarily correspond with changes in the national political context.

1 See, for example, Hugo, "Indonesian Labour Migration to Malaysia: Trends and Policy Implications"; Robinson, "Gender, Islam, and Nationality: Indonesian Domestic Servants in the Middle East"; Spaan, "Taikongs and Calos: The Role of Middlemen and Brokers in Javanese International Migration"; Cremer, "Deployment of Indonesian Migrants in the Middle East: Present Situation and Prospects"; Lindquist, "The Elementary School Teacher, the Thug and His Grandmother: Informal Brokers and Transnational Migration from Indonesia"; Silvey, "Unequal Borders: Indonesian Transnational Migrants at Immigration Control."

2 *Law No. 14 on Important Points about Labour.*

3 See, for example, Silvey, "Unequal Borders: Indonesian Transnational Migrants at Immigration Control"; Silvey, "Transnational Domestication: State Power and Indonesian Migrant Women in Saudi Arabia"; Jones, *Making Money off Migrants.*

 | DOI 10.1163/9789004325487_003

Close attention to the history of amendments to the overseas labour migration programme's institutions and the laws that govern them reveals when and why various networks of executive and legislative officials authorized the changes they did. In addition to building a history of service provision by the Indonesian state, a nuanced study of policy direction in this particular context fleshes out existing accounts of Indonesian political history and uncovers incidents that challenge the assumption that government institutions respond to political change in broadly the same way.

The chapter begins with an analysis of the economic drivers of policies governing the overseas labour migration programme from the 1970s until the mid-late 1980s before shifting its attention to the period between the mid-1980s and the immediate aftermath of the resignation of President Suharto in 1998. In this period, one of the primary drivers of migration policy was a desire to protect the business interests of individuals, ranging from licensed labour recruitment companies to their bureaucratic patrons. The final section focuses on the implications of the introduction of decentralization for the management of the programme. It was in this period that authority over the administrative and operational aspects of the programme was transferred to the BNP2TKI from the ministry, whose mandate was largely reduced to policy-making and regulatory functions regarding the licensing of labour recruitment companies. The programme's 40 year legacy provides instructive insights into why these two central government agencies quickly became embroiled in the contest for control described in Chapter 3.

Economic Development

Indonesia's contemporary overseas labour migration programme was first conceptualized in the late 1960s by the New Order regime. It was part of an attempt to claim political legitimacy based on an agenda that prioritized economic development and political stability following the turbulent decades of the Sukarno era (1945–1967).[4] President Suharto had pledged to immediately stabilize Indonesia's international relationships, normalizing bilateral

4 Hein, "Indonesia in 1981: Countdown to the General Elections," 200. By contrast, the colonial regime delivered largely Javanese workers to other Dutch territories, including Sumatra and Suriname, as part of a programme that ensured capital had greater access to labour for the production of agricultural exports. See, for example, Houben and Lindblad, *Coolie Labour in Colonial Indonesia: A Study of Labour Relations in the Outer Islands, C. 1900–1940*; Feuer, "End of Coolie Labor in New Caledonia."

relations with Malaysia and the United States and re-joining the United Nations. The New Order regime also promised state-led, technocratic management of the country that would harness human and natural resources for the purpose of furthering economic development with the view to make the Indonesian population wealthier.[5] The New Order regime quickly adopted the development strategy proposed by United States-educated economists as part of an attempt to overcome problems created by high levels of inflation.[6] It was in this economic and political context that the overseas labour migration programme was also introduced.

The programme took its form from an existing attempt to address imbalances in the internal labour market. In the early 1950s, the Sukarno government reactivated an internal colonial era labour supply network to address the problem,[7] with the Minister for Labour requiring that state agencies not only act as an intermediary but also underwrite loans for workers' travel expenses to other regions.[8] However, the problem persisted, threatening political stability not only in oversupplied sub-national labour markets such as East Java, where social grievances could quickly turn into anti-government sentiment, but in undersupplied areas like East Sumatra, where a lack of labour had the potential to disrupt plantation exports. With a labour force of around 75 million workers, conservative estimates in the late 1960s set unemployment at between 12 and 15 million in the countryside. The entrance each year of between 1 and 1.5 million young Indonesians to the labour market compounded the problem.[9]

Suharto's First Development Cabinet (1968–1973) saw the transmigration programme's potential to ameliorate problems that have their roots

---

5 Hill, *The Indonesian Economy.*

6 Anderson, "Old State, New Society: Indonesia's New Order in Comparative Historical Perspective," 488.

7 For a detailed account of the colonial system, see Houben and Lindblad, *Coolie Labour in Colonial Indonesia: A Study of Labour Relations in the Outer Islands, C. 1900–1940*. For a general discussion of the colonial state's bureaucratic qualities in relation to society, see Heather Sutherland, *The Making of a Bureaucratic Elite: The Colonial Transformation of the Javanese Priyayi*; Ruth McVey, "The Beamtenstaat in Indonesia."

8 *Ministerial Regulation (Manpower) No. 38/1952 on Panjar Biaya Perjalanan Dan Pemindahan Tenaga Kerja*. During the Sukarno period the ministry had developed a reputation for involvement in worker unrest. It was later renamed the Ministry of Manpower to remove the negative connotations of the word 'labour' following the failed coup of the 30 September Movement (Gerakan 30 September, G30S). See Reeve, *Golkar of Indonesia: An Alternative to the Party System*, 284.

9 Pauker, "The Age of Reason?" 140.

in underemployment, but also that it was not in itself enough.[10] As a consequence, the Indonesian government looked to international labour markets to alleviate the pressure on labour markets at home. The Minister for Manpower at the time, Mursalin Daeng Mamangung, coordinated the passage of a new law concerning labour shortly after his appointment. Mamangung was both outgoing vice chairperson of the national legislature and chairperson of the Functional Groups Party (Golongan Karya, Golkar) Secretariat, which helped expedite the passage of the law. It also certainly helped his cause that the New Order government already had overwhelming support from lawmakers loyal to Suharto leadership,[11] which had parachuted many retired defence personnel into the legislature to replace parliamentarians from the Indonesian Communist Party (Partai Komunis Indonesia, PKI) following the anti-communist purges of 1965–1966. Within a year the legislature had rubber-stamped the executive-authored Law No. 14/1969 on the Important Points about Labour, which in turn enabled Mamangung's ministry to intervene in domains of activity that influence the quantity and quality of labour supply,[12] including for the overseas labour market.

The law also called on the executive to steer activity towards ways of distributing labour that were more 'efficient and effective'.[13] Mamangung followed up by passing a decree that articulated a clear administrative role for the ministry in the recruitment of Indonesian labour in surplus areas for employment in and outside the country.[14] One of the ministry's first initiatives was to harness international labour migration that was already taking place. Statistics show that the main destinations were European countries, such as the Netherlands and West Germany,[15] and New Caledonia,[16] which was one of the countries where indentured labour had been sent to work in plantations during

10 The transmigration programme moves landless people from densely populated areas to less populated ones.

11 Emmerson, "Understanding the New Order: Bureaucratic Pluralism in Indonesia"; Jenkins, *Suharto and His Generals: Indonesian Military Politics, 1975–1983*. Mamangung himself had reached the rank of Vice Admiral in the navy and would not retire until 1977. During his time in the legislature, he chaired internal committees that made decisions about the institution's budget and house rules. See "Detail Biodata: Pejabat Menteri."

12 *Law No. 14 on Important Points about Labour*, article 5(1).

13 Ibid., article 5(2).

14 *Ministerial Regulation (Manpower) No. 4/1970 on Pengerahan Tenaga Kerja*, article 1.

15 RDCMD-YTKI, *Prospek Pasar Kerja Di Arab Saudi Bagi Tenaga Kerja Indonesia*, 128.

16 Departemen Tenaga Kerja Transmigrasi dan Koperasi, "Bulletin Tahunan: Statistik Tenaga Kerja Indonesia," 1972, 56–57.

the colonial period.[17] Much of this labour migration was recruited through networks developed in the years since Indonesian independence in 1945. But in the case of some destinations, such as New Caledonia, the movement also included some individuals who had returned to Indonesia with the hope of finding gainful employment after independence, but then sought ways to re-migrate.[18] The ministry encouraged them to do so by offering to use its clout with other state agencies to expedite the issuance of state documents, such as birth certificates and passports.

Only a relatively small number of international labour migrants were registered by ministry officials in the first decade. Around 90,000 Indonesian workers were recorded as having left the country between 1969 and 1979.[19] But these statistics did not record the real scale of international migration from Indonesia, as many more people moved through tried and true migration channels in which state organizations sometimes played little or no role. The majority of labour migrants to East and West Malaysia crossed international borders outside immigration checkpoints.[20] In part, the reason they did so was because there was almost an entire absence of information about official procedures, but also because state agencies that issued travel documents did not have a presence in many source areas for irregular migration, and because authorized international carriers, such as ferry and airplane companies, specialized in conveying passengers with valid passports.[21] Migration flows to Saudi Arabia, which also had strong historical roots, demonstrated by the existence of an

---

17 Feuer, "End of Coolie Labor in New Caledonia"; Maurer, *Les Javanais Du Caillou: Des Affres de L'exil Aux Aléas de L'intégration: Sociologie Historique de La Communauté Indonésienne de Nouvelle-Calédonie.*

18 Maurer, "The Thin Red Line between Indentured and Bonded Labour: Javanese Workers in New Caledonia in the Early 20th Century," 872.

19 Hugo and Bohning, "Providing Information to Outgoing Indonesian Migrant Workers"; Departemen Tenaga Kerja Transmigrasi dan Koperasi, *Bulletin Tahunan: Statistik Tenaga Kerja Indonesia*, 1972; Departemen Tenaga Kerja Transmigrasi dan Koperasi, *Bulletin Tahunan: Statistik Tenaga Kerja Indonesia*, 1975; Departemen Tenaga Kerja Transmigrasi dan Koperasi, *Bulletin Tahunan: Statistik Tenaga Kerja Indonesia*, 1977; Departemen Tenaga Kerja Transmigrasi dan Koperasi, *Bulletin Tahunan: Statistik Tenaga Kerja Indonesia*, 1978; Departemen Tenaga Kerja Transmigrasi dan Koperasi, *Bulletin Tahunan: Statistik Tenaga Kerja Indonesia*, 1983.

20 Spaan, "Taikongs and Calos: The Role of Middlemen and Brokers in Javanese International Migration"; Cremer, "Deployment of Indonesian Migrants in the Middle East: Present Situation and Prospects."

21 Lindquist, "Labour Recruitment, Circuits of Capital and Gendered Mobility: Reconceptualizing the Indonesian Migration Industry."

Indonesian settler community (*mukim*),[22] was also at times illegible to state organizations because many Indonesians travelled to the Middle East as pilgrims rather than with the intention of settling there.[23]

Towards the end of the 1970s, the ministry attempted to scale up the state's involvement in processes that led to the employment of Indonesian citizens in these and other countries by introducing administrative requirements to capture part of that migration. Recognizing the demand for Indonesian migrant labour in the Malaysian state of Sabah in 1978, policymakers within the ministry participated in a coordinating meeting with relevant Sabahan authorities and left with ideas about how to insert the state's administrative apparatus into the existing migration system.[24] The ministry encouraged Sabahan companies to submit requests for Indonesian labour to the Indonesian consulate and asked them to pay for the costs associated with supplying it. In this particular location, the state only recorded a negligible 1,225 departures in the first two years (1979–1981),[25] during which the ministry estimated that each month roughly 3,000 people used the unofficial system. In this and other cases, the state's new programme had to compete with established migration systems in which intermediaries sourced Indonesian labour and where passports were not considered necessary by workers or by those who facilitated international movement or their employers overseas.

An Alternative Source of Foreign Exchange

This policy was developed at a time when oil and gas revenues had started to decline, prompting policymakers to look for alternative sources of foreign exchange income.[26] Windfalls from the oil shocks in the 1970s had provided Indonesia with the resources to bankroll economic activity that created jobs at home. Indonesian crude oil had sold for only USD 1.7 a barrel at the beginning of the decade. Ten years later, it fetched USD 35 on the international market.[27] Revenue from petroleum exports was so significant that it accounted for around 50 per cent of Indonesia's Gross Domestic Product and 70 per cent of the national budget.[28] The New Order used its petrodollars to invest in the

---

22 Diederich, "Indonesians in Saudi Arabia."

23 Vredenbregt, "The Haddj: Some of Its Features and Functions in Indonesia."

24 Departemen Tenaga Kerja, *Perluasan Kesempatan Kerja Melalui Antar Kerja Antar Negara Ke Malaysia Timur*, 8–9.

25 Ibid., 18.

26 For an edited volume that examines government policy during this period, see Booth, *The Oil Boom and after: Indonesian Economic Policy and Performance in the Soeharto Era.*

27 Pauker, "Indonesia in 1980: Regime Fatigue?" 232.

28 Hein, "Indonesia in 1981: Countdown to the General Elections," 206.

construction and rehabilitation of crucial infrastructure, partly compensating for the neglect during the Sukarno years.[29] Petrodollars also meant, however, that the government was able to forestall restructuring work on the Indonesian economy.[30] Instead, protection from competition was made available to investors who produced goods in Indonesia for domestic consumption and export, creating employment with the view to reducing expenditure on imports.

Towards the end of the 1970s, the regime's leading economic managers became increasingly uneasy about the country's reliance on petroleum exports.[31] Exports of coffee, tea and timber had decreased partly in response to the global recession. Further complicating matters, the United States denied Indonesia preferential trade status for maintaining its membership in the exclusive OPEC (Organization of the Petroleum Exporting Countries).[32] Rising internal consumption of petroleum products also increased fiscal expenditure because refined fuel was imported and heavily subsidized.[33] These developments prompted concern about the poor diversification of Indonesia's export portfolio when Indonesia's foreign exchange reserves had started to decline. This motivated President Suharto to intervene, establishing a taskforce for the purpose of coordinating Indonesia-based activity to exploit commercial opportunities in the Middle East,[34] where the economy continued to boom as a result of rising revenues from petroleum exports. The president appointed the former anti-regime Muslim activist turned regime supporter Zainul Yasni to chair the team.[35] Minister for Trade, Radius Prawiro, then established a

29 Pauker, "Indonesia in 1980: Regime Fatigue?" 233.

30 Hein, "Indonesia in 1981: Countdown to the General Elections," 207.

31 Grant, "Indonesia 1978: A Third Term for President Suharto," 146.

32 OPEC members and Communist bloc countries were ineligible for the Generalized System of Preferences (GSP) at the time of its implementation in 1976. See Özden and Reinhardt, "The Perversity of Preferences: GSP and Developing Country Trade Policies, 1976–2000," 6, footnote 12. However, Indonesia, Ecuador and Venezuela became eligible in 1980 through an amendment that extended GSP eligibility to OPEC countries that entered into a bilateral trade agreement with the United States. See Trade Partnership, "The U.S. Generalized System of Preferences Program: An Update," 3, footnote 4.

33 Hein, "Indonesia in 1981: Countdown to the General Elections," 206.

34 *Presidential Decree No. 36/1977 on Pembentukan Team Koordinasi Kegiatan Ekspor Timur Tengah.*

35 *Presidential Decree No. 127/M/78 on Pengangkatan Ketua Team Koordinasi Kegiatan Ekspor Timur Tengah*; Machmudi, "Islamising Indonesia: The Rise of Jemaah Tarbiyah and the Prosperous Justice Party (PKS)."

structure that initially focused on tradable goods and services but would later come to accommodate labour.[36]

It was at this uncertain moment that policymakers came to see international labour migration as a potential solution to Indonesia's foreign exchange problems. By the early 1980s the global economy had started to move into recession, which had devastating consequences for Indonesia.[37] International oil prices dropped as demand for other export commodities tapered off.[38] Economic policymakers reacted by escalating the search for alternatives to oil exports. The Indonesian leadership was reluctant to invite greater foreign direct investment to help balance the books, not least because the collective memory of the 15 January Incident (Malapetaka Limabelas Januari, Malari) of 1974, in which street demonstrations against Japanese interests turned into riots against foreign capital in Indonesia.[39] The search for other alternatives identified labour migration as an area of activity that the state could encourage. Following these discussions, Prawiro expanded the taskforce to include the Ministry of Manpower. A committee was then established to work out precisely how international labour migration could better serve that purpose.[40]

With a view to channelling migrant labour to Saudi Arabia, the working group brainstormed ideas about the necessary mechanisms for sourcing migrant labour in a more organized way.[41] The Ministries of Manpower, Foreign Affairs, Defence and Security and Religion were invited to join the deliberations.[42] A representative from the Saudi Arabian embassy was also included to provide advice on policy directions to which the Middle Eastern kingdom might be amenable.[43] Around 35,000 Indonesian citizens had reportedly already responded to Saudi Arabia's call for labour, and many were believed to remit part of their wages, which gave the team some confidence about the

---

36 *Ministerial Decree (Trade) No. 242/KP/III/78 on Susunan Organisasi Dan Tata Kerja Team Koordinasi Kegiatan Ekspor Timur Tengah.*

37 Ramcharran, "OPEC's Production under Fluctuating Oil Prices: Further Test of the Target Revenue Theory," 670.

38 Hill, *The Indonesian Economy*; Booth, *The Oil Boom and after: Indonesian Economic Policy and Performance in the Soeharto Era.*

39 Mackie, "Indonesia: Economic Growth and Depoliticization," 129–130.

40 *Chair Decree No. 6/SK/TT/VIII on Pembentukan Gugus Kerja Pembinaan Tenaga Kerja Indonesia.*

41 Team Koordinasi Kegiatan Ekspor Timur Tengah, "Gugus Kerja Pembinaan Tenaga Kerja Indonesia Di Timur Tengah," 5.

42 *Chair Decree No. 6/SK/TT/VIII on Pembentukan Gugus Kerja Pembinaan Tenaga Kerja Indonesia*, menimbang d.

43 Interview data, Pekanbaru, 21 April 2010.

programme's potential as a solution to Indonesia's economic problems.[44] Participants talked about necessary mechanisms to move even more Indonesians to the Middle East, including a formal proposal by the Ministry of Defence to send an army officer with each group of 50 migrants to survey the host environment and guide them during their time abroad.[45] Ultimately, the organizers decided that the state ought to set a limit on the cost of migration, produce standards for recruitment and develop a system of sanctions to manage the industry from within Indonesia.[46]

The fact that discussions around the expansion of international labour migration emerged as a response to far broader questions on economic policy contributed to a blurring of the boundary between migration and trade, as Indonesian companies became increasingly involved in both activities. Goods and people at times moved through similar – if not the same – transnational networks, as private individuals overseas used business partners in Indonesia to source goods and workers on their behalf. For example, in 1979 the Saudi Arabia-based Al-Basri Trading Establishment appointed Eldy International to liaise with state institutions in Indonesia for the purpose of procuring the necessary authorization for workers to leave the country.[47] Eldy International was first and foremost a commodity export company that traded in spices and wood.[48] With time, however, their business activity came to include labour recruitment services for business partners overseas. A ministry official assigned to the labour division in the export taskforce recalls that then migrant workers were also frequently used to transport goods for sale in Saudi Arabia, complicating efforts to distinguish between international migration and trade. Policymakers' first reaction was in fact not to separate migration and trade matters, but rather to increase migrants' export allowance to USD 2,000.[49]

One of the major obstacles to the development of the large-scale programme imagined by policymakers was the fact that there were no criteria for specialized migrant labour recruitment companies.[50] In 1982 the labour

44 Team Koordinasi Kegiatan Ekspor Timur Tengah, "Gugus Kerja Pembinaan Tenaga Kerja Indonesia Di Timur Tengah," 2 of the foreword.

45 Departemen Pertahanan Keamanan, "Berbagai Usaha Pembinaan Dan Pengamanan Tenaga Kerja Indonesia Di Luar Negeri Khususnya Di Timur Tengah," 2: point b(3).

46 Team Koordinasi Kegiatan Ekspor Timur Tengah, *Hasil Diskusi Panel: Peningkatan Usaha Pengiriman Tenaga Kerja Indonesia Ke Timur Tengah*, 5: points 6, 10, 11.

47 Al-Basry Establishment, "Letter of Authorization."

48 Embassy of Indonesia (Canada), "Company Profile: Eldy International, PT."

49 Interview data, Pekanbaru, 21 April 2010.

50 Direktur Jenderal Pembinaan dan Penggunaan Tenaga Kerja, "Garis-Garis Besar Antar Kerja Antar Negara," 26–35.

division in the Ministry of Trade taskforce produced a list of companies approved to recruit labour, showing that many businesses were involved in sourcing Indonesian workers for hospitality, construction or shipping employment. Indonesia's decision to enter the international labour market came late compared to that of other labour exporting countries, such as Pakistan and The Philippines.[51] Furthermore, the timing was not in the country's favour, as migrant labour demand from Saudi Arabia had already started to decline as a result of the oil glut and the reduction in foreign exchange revenue that it caused. The programme needed a niche in the international labour market, and private capital was necessary to help it get a foothold.[52] With this in mind, policymakers debated the need to overhaul the labour recruitment company licensing system in a way that would create a recruitment industry that made finding work for Indonesians overseas their main business rather than treating it as a side venture, as had been the case.

The Rise of Labour Recruitment Companies

The Ministry of Manpower started to seriously consider international labour migration as a potential solution to Indonesia's labour market problems towards the end of Professor Harun Rasjid Zain's years as minister (1978–1983). An intellectual-cum-administrator, Zain's loyalty to the regime partly earned him the country's first promotion from provincial governor of West Sumatra to minister in the New Order period.[53] The fact that he had a long academic engagement with labour, including study in the United States, made him a suitable candidate for the manpower portfolio. But he was also hired based on his achievements in West Sumatra with the transmigration programme, which President Suharto described as a major government initiative in the meeting where he informed Zain of the appointment. The task of finding employment outside Indonesia had already been outsourced to labour recruitment companies. But the programme was administered from within a section that itself was a sub-division of the directorate-general that was responsible for regulating the way in which labour was utilized. At the time of Zain's appointment, then, the programme was a relatively insignificant initiative.

This changed under Zain, who signed the country's first ministerial regulation on licensing labour recruitment companies in recognition of how

51 Cremer, "Deployment of Indonesian Migrants in the Middle East: Present Situation and Prospects," 74.

52 For a discussion of New Order attempts to develop an indigenous capital class that could help bankroll these kinds of endeavours, see Robison, *Indonesia, the Rise of Capital*.

53 Yusra, *Tokoh Yang Berhati Rakyat: Biografi Harun Zain*, 282.

significantly the programme had grown in importance to policymakers.[54] It required that recruiters pay a Rp. 100,000 (USD 100) application fee, have capacity to finance the migration process for at least 500 workers a year and possess office infrastructure, personnel and other necessary facilities.[55] He also introduced a strategic dimension to the industry, requiring that labour recruitment companies submit an annual plan for their job-matching business.[56] This and the introduction of mandatory overseas identity cards for migrant labour, which cost Rp. 1,000 (USD 1) each,[57] expanded the ministry's administrative role in the programme. As a result, the ministry reengaged in administrative processes that had come to be largely managed by the Ministry of Trade's taskforce.[58] Licensing of labour recruitment companies was a significant regulatory achievement that paved the way for the programme's eventual return to the Ministry of Manpower.

This regulatory amendment was partly responsible for the increase in recorded departures over ensuing months. When Zain left office, only around 20 companies were authorized to recruit migrant labour for work overseas. However, the number of migrant workers departing under the programme rose by almost 40 per cent on the previous year, with the increase in those heading for Saudi Arabia compensating for the 30 per cent decline in those bound for Malaysia and Singapore.[59] That rate of increase was maintained in 1984–1985 following a structural reorganization that shifted administration of the programme to the Overseas Employment Centre (Pusat Antar Kerja Antar Negara, Pusat AKAN).[60] In part, the reorganization was inspired by efforts in The Philippines that created a purpose-specific agency for the migration business.[61]

---

54 *Ministerial Regulation (Manpower) No. 1/MEN/1983 on Perusahaan Pengerahan Tenaga Kerja Indonesia Ke Luar Negeri.*

55 Ibid., article 3(b).

56 Ibid., article 5(d).

57 *Ministerial Regulation (Manpower) No. 128/MEN/1983 on Penggunaan Kartu Identitas Tenaga Kerja Indonesia Yang Bekerja Di Luar Negeri.*

58 The taskforce's mandate had been only temporary, as its primary objective was to coordinate and refine programmes that could potentially help Indonesia generate more foreign exchange.

59 Hugo, "Population Movement in Indonesia since 1971," 243.

60 *Presidential Decree No. 15/1984 on Susunan Organisasi Departemen*, article 178.

61 *Presidential Executive Order (The Philippines) No. 797 on Reorganizing the Ministry of Labor and Employment, Creating the Philippine Overseas Employment Administration, and for Other Purposes.* Indonesian and Philippines officials had also started to share information about systems as early as 1982. See "Indonesia-Pilipina Bekerjasama Dalam Penyaluran Tenaga Kerja Di Timur Tengah."

But in Indonesia, Pusat AKAN, along with five other centres and a special committee, was made directly responsible to Minister for Manpower. Pusat AKAN was assigned 11 personnel, which, according to a ministry official engaged there at the time, was sufficient because they were expected to perform few administrative roles.[62]

When Zain took office, the ministry already had records of Indonesian women migrating for work in the Persian Gulf. Requests for this category of migrant labour were usually communicated to the ministry via the consular office in Jeddah, which reported that migrant workers frequently sought consular assistance having experienced severe forms of exploitation.[63] It is presumably for this reason that the ministry began to reject authorization to recruit female labour migrants for jobs there.[64] To increase the viability of the potentially lucrative business, the ministry first sought to address some of the issues that led Indonesian domestic workers to seek assistance through bilateral channels. In response to the Saudi government's position that it was under no legal obligation to implement the principles of the International Labour Organization (ILO),[65] Zain imposed a total ban on migration for domestic work to the country.[66] His intention in doing so was to put pressure on recruiters to find alternative destinations for migrant workers, but it simply had the effect of driving the business underground.[67]

This restriction on Saudi Arabia was lifted as an outcome of the Ministry of Trade taskforce's involvement in reworking the overseas labour migration programme. In March 1982 the team published a document that highlighted policies and standards that needed clarification.[68] Within a relatively short

62 Interview data, Pekanbaru, 21 April 2010.

63 Yusra, *Tokoh Yang Berhati Rakyat: Biografi Harun Zain*, 285.

64 In 1977 the ministry turned down an attempt by an Indonesian entrepreneur to register the recruitment of 20 women for employment as domestic workers in Saudi Arabia. See Silvey, "Gender, Difference, and Contestation: Economic Geography through the Lens of Transnational Migration," 422. Saleh Alwaini would later become the chairperson of the government recognized association of employment companies, the Indonesian Manpower Supply Association (IMSA). For this entrepreneur's foreword as chairperson of the association, see Wirasmo, *Buku Panduan Tenaga Kerja Indonesia Di Arab Saudi*.

65 Yusra, *Tokoh Yang Berhati Rakyat: Biografi Harun Zain*, 285.

66 RDCMD-YTKI, *Prospek Pasar Kerja Di Arab Saudi Bagi Tenaga Kerja Indonesia*, 129.

67 Another consideration may have been related to the fact that the migrants were women. Some states attempt to prevent women from responding to opportunities for employment in the international labour market. Such restrictions or bans are also difficult to enforce when the measures are unilateral. For a discussion of 'value-driven emigration policies', see Nana Oishi, *Women in Motion*, 12.

68 Team Koordinasi Kegiatan Ekspor Timur Tengah, "Gugus Kerja Pembinaan Tenaga Kerja Indonesia Di Timur Tengah."

period, the Ministry of Manpower produced a document it described as a first step (*langkah awal*) to working out the necessary procedures and standards.[69] The push toward enabling more kinds of labour migration also came from external sources, including requests from the royal family in Saudi Arabia, which sought to have restrictive policies such as the ban on overseas domestic work revised.[70] Zain then wrote to the Indonesian consular office in Jeddah to explain that Saudi royals, senior government officials, and executives of ten companies were classified as eligible employers.[71] In Indonesia, Islamic boarding schools expressed concern about plans to target female students already trained to speak Arabic for recruitment.[72] In order to pre-empt this kind of resistance, a ministry spokesperson clarified that unmarried women could only take up a position in Saudi Arabia if they were over the age of 30 and not 'beautiful and sexy'.[73] Unsurprisingly, given the repressive, political climate of the early 1980s, statements of this kind effectively foreclosed further public debate.[74]

As part of these revisions, Zain imposed the requirement that either the employer or an Indonesian labour recruitment company must deposit a bond with the Indonesian government for each domestic worker employed. In addition to providing Indonesian authorities with an alternative source of funds with which to buy return tickets for Indonesian migrant workers,[75] the bond also served to prevent Saudi Arabia from dominating the programme.[76] Meanwhile, the re-election of Suharto to his fourth term as president a few months earlier had refocussed attention on the objective in the Third Five Year Development Plan (1979–1984) to achieve 100,000 departures at a time when the programme was struggling to even make 50 per cent of its annual target.[77] Following a conversation with the relevant director-general in the ministry,[78]

69 Direktur Jenderal Pembinaan dan Penggunaan Tenaga Kerja, "Garis-Garis Besar Antar Kerja Antar Negara," i.

70 "Sending of Women Workers Abroad Allowed Now."

71 Menteri Tenaga Kerja dan Transmigrasi, "Pengiriman Tenaga Kerja Rumah Tangga Ke Arab."

72 "Tolak Pengiriman Tenaga Kerja Wanita Ke Luar Negeri."

73 "Sending of Women Workers Abroad Allowed Now."

74 Robinson, "Gender, Islam, and Nationality: Indonesian Domestic Servants in the Middle East," 267–270.

75 Menteri Tenaga Kerja dan Transmigrasi, "Pengiriman Tenaga Kerja Rumah Tangga Ke Arab," point 4(b).

76 RDCMD-YTKI, *Prospek Pasar Kerja Di Arab Saudi Bagi Tenaga Kerja Indonesia*, 131.

77 Hugo, "Population Movement in Indonesia since 1971," 243.

78 *Chair Decree (Trade) No. 1/SK/TT/I/83 on Penyelenggaran Diskusi Panel Mengenai Usaha-Usaha Pengembangan Pengiriman Tenaga Kerja Indonesia Ke Timur Tengah*, memperhatikan.

the taskforce convened a discussion panel that included over 50 participants from the recruitment industry and a wide range of government agencies.[79] The purpose of this meeting was to work out a road map for producing further systems and procedures to help the recruitment industry compete on a larger scale with other countries exporting labour to the Middle East.[80]

The establishment of Pusat AKAN marked an end to the Ministry of Trade's involvement in the programme, in line with a broader shift that had taken place. With the establishment of the Fourth Development Cabinet (1983–1988), new ministers were able to adjust institutional arrangements put in place by their predecessors. The new Minister for Trade, Rachmat Saleh, disbanded the taskforce, noting that it had already served its purpose. Members, including officials on secondment, were sent back to the Ministry of Trade to work on new initiatives. The taskforce's labour division had become very profitable for those involved, a fact brought to the attention of the new Minister for Manpower, Admiral Sudomo, who recalled officials on his ministry's payroll. Sudomo then used his connections with the president to wrest control over the programme away from the Ministry of Trade.[81] Having reclaimed the migration business for the Ministry of Manpower, Sudomo stationed the activity on the seventh floor of a privately-owned building.[82] It was with this change that the programme's purpose shifted from generating foreign exchange to focusing more exclusively on servicing labour recruitment companies.

Maximizing Economic Benefits for the Recruitment Industry

The appointment of Sudomo to the manpower portfolio marked a shift towards a more authoritarian approach to migrant labour, as indeed was the case for labour relations more generally.[83] Sudomo was a retired Navy officer whom Suharto had entrusted to manage the intelligence and surveillance body called the Operational Command for the Restoration of Security and Order (Komando Operasi Pemulihan Keamanan dan Ketertiban, Kopkamtib). Sudomo's defence force background positioned him well to help suppress social

79 Team Koordinasi Kegiatan Ekspor Timur Tengah, *Hasil Diskusi Panel: Peningkatan Usaha Pengiriman Tenaga Kerja Indonesia Ke Timur Tengah.*

80 *Chair Decree (Trade) No. 1/SK/TT/I/83 on Penyelenggaran Diskusi Panel Mengenai Usaha-Usaha Pengembangan Pengiriman Tenaga Kerja Indonesia Ke Timur Tengah*, menimbang b.

81 President Suharto announced Sudomo's appointment as Minister for Manpower on 19 March 1983, and enacted the decree that formally ensconced the programme in the ministry on 14 March 1984 through Presidential Decree No. 15/1984.

82 Interview data, Pekanbaru, 21 April 2010.

83 Ford, *Workers and Intellectuals: NGOs, Trade Unions and the Indonesian Labour Movement.*

discontent in line with the New Order's commitment to providing political stability for foreign and domestic capital. This orientation was reflected in his approach to international labour migration.

After two years in the minister's seat, Sudomo passed a law that defined labour recruitment companies' responsibilities concerning migrant workers.[84] The Ministry of Trade had suggested a regulation of this kind before Sudomo took office. However, it had been deprioritized, only to be reconsidered when a spate of cases involving Indonesian labour migrants in Saudi Arabia put pressure on the ministry intervene.[85] Sudomo attempted to overcome this problem by requiring that labour recruitment companies take responsibility for resolving problems that arose overseas.[86] To strengthen the state's capacity to intervene more directly, Indonesia's first labour attachés were posted to the capital cities of the programme's two biggest destination countries, Saudi Arabia and Malaysia. One of the duties of those labour attachés was to monitor migrant workers with left-wing political tendencies.[87] Day-to-day, the Ministry of Manpower expected that the postings would prevent Indonesian consular offices from gate-keeping access to the local labour market by only approving the applications of particular companies.[88]

Desire on the part of Indonesian bureaucrats to exercise greater control over access to Indonesian migrant labour grew alongside their commercial interests. The ministry beseeched Indonesian embassies to use their diplomatic clout with host governments to restrict work permits to Indonesian migrants registered with Indonesian authorities.[89] Policymakers' interest in the control of Indonesian migrant labour from overseas was partly motivated by the distribution of financial rewards associated with the migration business. However, it can also be explained by the New Order regime's shifting orientation. The early 1980s were an uncertain period for the New Order leadership, as popular support for the regime began to wane. During this period, the international migration programme became increasingly oriented towards bureaucratic ends,

84 *Ministerial Decree (Manpower) No. 420/MEN/1985 on Persyaratan Dan Kewajiban Perusahaan Pengerahan Tenaga Kerja Indonesia Ke Luar Negeri.*

85 "12 Ormas Islam Mendesak Penghentian Pengiriman TKW."

86 *Ministerial Decree (Manpower) No. 420/MEN/1985 on Persyaratan Dan Kewajiban Perusahaan Pengerahan Tenaga Kerja Indonesia Ke Luar Negeri*, article 2(g).

87 *Chair Decree No. 6/SK/TT/VIII Pembentukan Gugus Kerja Pembinaan Tenaga Kerja Indonesia*, 12: point f.

88 For a report on this matter, see "Rejection of Labour Placement in Saudi Arabia Regretted."

89 Direktur Jenderal Pembinaan dan Penggunaan Tenaga Kerja, "Garis-Garis Besar Antar Kerja Antar Negara," 4.

such as achieving targets and helping the recruitment industry turn a greater profit.[90]

Sudomo became increasingly concerned with the consequences that migrant workers' actions had for Indonesia's international image.[91] In an attempt to control migrant workers, he introduced a requirement that they sign a declaration to the effect that they would abstain from talking about their labour migration experiences with the mass media or non-governmental organizations (NGOs).[92] Sudomo was concerned about the negative publicity that these groups could generate in Indonesia.[93] He also feared that news of exploitation of Indonesian labour migrants by Saudi employers could jeopardize Jakarta's bilateral relationship with Riyadh. This requirement reflected a general consensus among Indonesian policymakers that the rights and welfare of labour migrants were a lower priority than the programme's economic and political objectives. In line with this view, they also blamed labour migrants for their own exploitation, arguing that Indonesian migrants could be lackadaisical and undisciplined, which in turn damaged the country's good name.[94]

Sudomo also took the opportunity to require migrant workers to remit at least 50 per cent of their wage to Indonesia via the formal banking system.[95] Part of an attempt to make remittances of foreign currency to Indonesia legible to state institutions, this policy mirrored an attempt by The Philippines government to do so a year earlier.[96] The Philippines decree, which required

---

90 Spaan, "Taikongs and Calos: The Role of Middlemen and Brokers in Javanese International Migration"; Lindquist, "Labour Recruitment, Circuits of Capital and Gendered Mobility: Reconceptualizing the Indonesian Migration Industry."

91 Asyari, "Indonesia's Administrative and Legislative Measures on Labor Migration from a Rights-Based Perspective." He was not alone. Many officials had expressed the same concern before Sudomo became minister, as indeed they would decades later.

92 This declaration read 'I will not say anything to newspapers at home or abroad or to those who are not authorities concerned with my problems, if any, that I experience while working abroad, because I am fully aware that these problems are sensitive ones that could jeopardize friendly relations between Indonesia and the country where I am employed'. See *Ministerial Decree (Manpower) No. 420/MEN/1985 on Persyaratan Dan Kewajiban Perusahaan Pengerahan Tenaga Kerja Indonesia Ke Luar Negeri*, appendix 2, point 2.

93 Robinson, "Gender, Islam, and Nationality: Indonesian Domestic Servants in the Middle East."

94 *Ministerial Decree (Manpower) No. 420/MEN/1985 on Persyaratan Dan Kewajiban Perusahaan Pengerahan Tenaga Kerja Indonesia Ke Luar Negeri*, appendix 2, point 5.

95 Ibid., appendix 2, point 4.

96 *Presidential Executive Order (The Philippines) No. 857 on Governing the Remittance to the Philippines of Foreign Exchange Earnings of Filipino Workers Abroad and for Other Purposes.*

overseas contract workers to show evidence of their remittances when extending their passports, was cancelled following a campaign against forced remittances.[97] No such campaign emerged in Indonesia. In part, this was because the ministry did not establish administrative systems to enforce the requirement. As a result, Indonesian labour migrants continued to remit money through informal intermediaries or brought their total earnings with them on the flight home.

Further attention to state involvement in the administration of international labour migration in Indonesia reveals some of the ways in which the system helped generate greater profits for intermediaries. The ministry attempted to increase demand from employers by adjusting the division of recruitment costs. As part of a promotion strategy, the Indonesian government supported the decision to transfer the cost of recruitment from employers to workers with the justification that it would make Indonesian migrant labour more competitive.[98] In Sabah, for example employers had been asked to cover the entire cost of recruitment in 1978.[99] After the ministry changed its position, employers were allowed to pay the fee and then deduct it from migrants' wages under an agreement signed by the minister. Sudomo reaffirmed Indonesia's commitment to this financing arrangement at the end of 1983, helping Indonesians overtake Filipinos as the largest group of foreign workers in that state.[100] Such agreements not only changed existing arrangements so that they made more economic sense to employers but also inserted the ministry into the migration process.

The Presidential Office also intervened to make the business more profitable for labour recruitment companies by exempting intending migrant workers from an international departure tax charged to Indonesian citizens and expatriates known as *fiskal*.[101] In theory, the exemption helped make Indonesian migrant labour more competitive in the international labour market. In practice, it meant that labour recruitment companies generated higher profits, as the cost reduction was not passed on to clients. Efforts to make the business more profitable also benefited low-level bureaucrats. For example,

---

97 *Presidential Executive Order (The Philippines) No. 1021 on Encouraging the Inward Remittances of Contract Workers Earnings through Official Channels.*

98 RDCMD-YTKI, *Prospek Pasar Kerja Di Arab Saudi Bagi Tenaga Kerja Indonesia.*

99 Departemen Tenaga Kerja, *Perluasan Kesempatan Kerja Melalui Antar Kerja Antar Negara Ke Malaysia Timur.*

100 Kurus, "Migrant Labor: The Sabah Experience," 288.

101 *Presidential Decree No. 84/1982 on Kebijaksanaan Pemberian Surat Keterangan Fiskal Luar Negeri*, article 2(e).

one ministry official recalls that servicing labour recruitment companies in the early 1980s as a junior clerk provided him with extra income. His official salary was around IDR 18,000 (USD 17) each month, but the extra income from 'consultancies' for labour recruitment companies helped him make five times that much.[102]

Sudomo also restricted access to labour recruitment company licences, which made it even easier for licensed recruiters to maximize their profits. In 1986 a Pusat AKAN team revoked over 80 per cent of recruitment licences from labour recruitment companies that supplied migrant labour to the Middle East and forced other businesses into merger arrangements.[103] Companies that emerged intact from this first round of evaluations and supplied migrant labour to the Middle East were told whether they could recruit men or women. An overhaul on this scale would not be seen again until the mid-1990s, when Minister for Manpower, Abdul Latief (1993–1998), reversed the more liberal regime that his predecessor Cosmas Batubara (1988–1993) introduced as a correction to Sudomo's downsizing.[104] Companies that supplied migrants to non-Middle Eastern destinations were not subject to either round of evaluations, demonstrating the relatively lower priority that the ministry placed on the Asia-Pacific region at the time. The decision to focus on the Middle East and the identification of companies that retained their licences took into account a mix of technical and political factors, including whether the outcome would affect the business interests of officials in the ministry or in other government agencies.

A Different Kind of Intervention

By the mid-1980s, departures to the Middle East had steadily increased and neighbouring countries in Southeast Asia emerged as popular destinations. The numbers of labour migrants travelling through the formal programme to Malaysia and Singapore were unstable. The ministry registered between five and eight thousand departures each year between 1982 and 1986, but that figure leaped to 20,000 in 1988.[105] In part, this jump is attributable to a shift in the purpose of the programme, which policymakers increasingly saw as a mechanism for making Indonesian labour migration in the region more orderly.

102 Interview data, Pekanbaru, 21 April 2010.

103 Yusak, "Mekanisme Pengiriman Tenaga Kerja Indonesia Ke Luar Negeri," 10.

104 Batubara, *Cosmas Batubara, Sebuah Otobiografi Politik*, 278.

105 Idrus, "Makkunrai Passimokolo': Bugis Migrant Women Workers in Malaysia."

Indonesian labour migrants frequently crossed international borders in the region without passports or the need for an employment permit.[106] Moreover, administrative systems in the region were weak, which enabled Indonesians to acquire local identity documents.[107] It was this situation that the programme increasingly sought to address.

Pusat AKAN's re-evaluation of the recruitment industry in 1986 had not been entirely driven by domestic political concerns. The greater numbers of Indonesians leaving the country under the programme had caught the attention of policymakers in intergovernmental organizations, including the United Nations Development Programme (UNDP) and the ILO. In that circle, the prevailing view was that the poor were migrating in search of work because economic development had failed to generate the opportunities those people needed to remain at home.[108] Around the same time, wealthier states became more interested in the idea of controlling labour migration, which some attempted to achieve by promoting more targeted economic development in countries of origin. The logic followed that the economic incentives for migration would disappear once differences in the standard of living between countries diminished. On the other hand, however, these same states implemented migration policies that enabled their citizens to hire labour migrants for the purpose of performing work that was unattractive to local workers.

In Indonesia, international agencies sought to influence policy in ways that supported global processes in an orderly way. In the early 1980s the UNDP funded a project to help Indonesia refine its technical processes and better market Indonesian labour to the Middle East.[109] The initiative started off as a joint project between the ILO and the International Trade Centre under the General Agreement on Tariffs and Trade (GATT).[110] An ILO consultant employed on the project recalls recommending that Indonesia treat migration and trade separately,[111] perhaps influencing Sudomo's 1983 decision to reintegrate the international migration programme into the manpower portfolio.

---

106 Spaan, "Taikongs and Calos: The Role of Middlemen and Brokers in Javanese International Migration"; Kaur, "Indonesian Migrant Workers in Malaysia: From Preferred Migrants to 'Last to Be Hired' Workers."

107 Lyons and Ford, "The Chinese of Karimun: Citizenship and Belonging at Indonesia's Margins"; Sadiq, *Paper Citizens: How Illegal Immigrants Acquire Citizenship in Developing Countries.*

108 Massey, "Economic Development and International Migration in Comparative Perspective," 383.

109 Yusak, "Mekanisme Pengiriman Tenaga Kerja Indonesia Ke Luar Negeri," 2.

110 Email correspondence with ILO consultant, Terence Kelly, 1 July 2009.

111 Email correspondence with ILO consultant, Terence Kelly, 9 July 2009.

The employment dimension of the joint project was gradually shifted to the ILO, which engaged a former Philippines Overseas Employment Office employee to work with Indonesian government personnel to straighten out technical aspects of the programme.[112] The ILO Office in Jakarta has since destroyed the policy documents that this team of consultants produced.[113] However, a later document that draws on direct experience with this project indicates that a primary focus at that time was refining systems with the view to expanding the supply of migrant labour.[114]

In conjunction with Pusat AKAN, ILO consultants produced a list of recommendations for modifying institutional and legal structures concerning the programme. The report was ultimately authored by Pusat AKAN bureaucrat, Yusak Masduki, the centre's head of promotion.[115] Masduki examined 39 substantive weaknesses in the programme's institutional and legal architecture. He reported, for example, that the centre was seriously under-resourced with only 52 personnel – in The Philippines, 520 officials were assigned to the same kind of work.[116] The report also lamented that the centre was inappropriately located in a vocational training centre, 12 kilometres away from the ministry's main administrative seat. The physical distance might not have been a serious problem except that Pusat AKAN lacked even basic communication infrastructure, such as a telephone or facsimile machine. This serious lack of resources impeded the centre's capacity to communicate effectively with stakeholders in Indonesia and in destination countries.[117] Major recommendations also included simplifying bureaucratic procedures to develop a competitive edge on other labour sending countries, such as India, Pakistan, The Philippines and South Korea.[118]

ILO involvement in the reforms was part of an international push to make human movement to the global north more legible to administrators. France, Spain, Italy, The United Kingdom and The United States had all passed legislation by the mid-1980s that sought to regularize foreign nationals working

112 Email correspondence with ILO consultant, Terence Kelly, 27 June and 1 July 2009.

113 Email correspondence with the ILO library liaison officer in Jakarta, Ariel Golan, 13 February 2013. There was no written rule for archiving policy documents at the time but this project can be identified with this reference: INS/82/013 (country/starting year/document number).

114 Juridico, "Overseas Employment and Recruitment Practices of Asian Labour-Sending Countries."

115 Yusak, "Mekanisme Pengiriman Tenaga Kerja Indonesia Ke Luar Negeri," 2.

116 Ibid., 4.

117 Ibid., 5.

118 Ibid., 34.

without passports and/or work permits. In Southeast Asia, the push for regularization is illustrated by the part that Malaysian authorities played in negotiating bilateral labour agreements with neighbouring countries in those years. In 1982 Malaysia established a cross-sectoral committee to coordinate recruitment of foreign workers for employment in the country.[119] Two years later, it signed what came to be known as the Medan Agreement with Indonesia, outlining mechanisms for sourcing migrant labour.[120] Indonesia's Ministry of Manpower then implemented the agreement through a regulation that mapped out the necessary procedures for migration.[121] Ultimately, however, this attempt to include Malaysia in the programme's scope failed, reportedly due to a lack of appropriate administrative systems in Indonesia.[122]

Opening Up to Criticism from Within

In the late 1980s, the New Order government introduced a policy of 'openness' (keterbukaan), a kind of political liberalization. Economically, the regime had already started to move away from centralized control to a more liberal way of managing foreign investment.[123] As a consequence, Indonesia's middle class had grown significantly.[124] The Indonesian Democratic Party (Partai Demokrat Indonesia, PDI) had also become more of an opposition force to reckon with. Further complicating matters for the president, trusted men like Ali Moertopo had died or retired. Others, like Benny Moerdani, who had taken a critical stance on the business activities of Suharto's children, and Yusuf Wanandi, who had suggested to Suharto that he start planning for succession, had fallen

119 Peng, "Migration Issues in the Asia Pacific: Issues Paper from Malaysia."

120 Malaysia then entered into similar arrangements with The Philippines (1985) and Bangladesh (1986), two other source countries for foreign workers. Ibid.

121 *Ministerial Decree (Manpower) No. 408/MEN/1984 on Pengerahan Dan Pengiriman Tenaga Kerja Ke Malaysia.* For critical analysis of the implementation, see Ford, "After Nunukan: The Regulation of Indonesian Migration to Malaysia," 235.

122 Jones, *Making Money off Migrants*, 16. Employers and recruiters in Malaysia also resisted the new procedures because they interfered with an established way of doing business. See Tirtosudarmo, *Mencari Indonesia: Demografi-Politik Pasca-Soeharto*, 267. Indonesia had proposed using systems developed for administering extended migration to the Middle East, including the requirement that all departures leave on commercial aircraft from Jakarta, which was inappropriate for migration to the adjacent Malaysian Peninsula. For a discussion of the policy orientation at the time that focused on Jakarta, see Ford, "After Nunukan: The Regulation of Indonesian Migration to Malaysia," 229. For broader context, see Hugo, "Indonesian Labour Migration to Malaysia: Trends and Policy Implications."

123 Hein, "Indonesia in 1989: A Question of Openness," 221.

124 Aspinall, *Opposing Suharto: Compromise, Resistance and Regime Change in Indonesia*, 261–263.

out of favour.[125] The regime also became increasingly sensitive to media coverage, which had become increasingly strident as media outlets grew more confident publishing critical articles about formerly taboo matters.[126]

These changes in the broader political landscape had implications for the ministry and the implementation of its programmes. Following the 1987 elections Suharto loyalist Sudomo was given oversight of the portfolio that coordinated politics, law and security, partly in recognition of his successes as Minister for Manpower. His replacement, Cosmas Batubara – who in 1966 had been at the front line of the pro-Suharto student movement[127] – started to reverse the corporatist labour relations policies of the Sudomo period.[128] His approach to the overseas labour migration programme was also much more liberal than that of his predecessor. Batubara revised restrictions on the number of labour recruitment companies involved in recruitment.[129] In response to mass media reports that Malaysian authorities had progressively adopted a tougher stance in dealing with unlawful migrants, Batubara made trips to Sabah and Sarawak to see first-hand the severity of the situation.[130] On that trip, he signed a bilateral agreement, which was followed by the first of a series of regularization programmes in Sabah.[131]

Batubara writes in his autobiography that he saw this and the liberalization of the licensing system as serious attempts to tackle Indonesia's high level of underemployment.[132] Like Zain, Batubara claims to have tightened selection criteria to prevent migrants with poor skills from leaving under the

---

125 Wanandi, *Shades of Grey: A Political Memoir of Modern Indonesia, 1965–1998*, 231–232, 233–238.

126 Emmerson, "A Foreshadow Play," 182.

127 Aspinall, *Opposing Suharto: Compromise, Resistance and Regime Change in Indonesia*, 117. Batubara was rewarded for his support in 1967 when Suharto organized for him and 17 other student activists from his association to replace lawmakers associated with the Indonesian Communist Party (Partai Komunis Indonesia, PKI) who were suspended following the failed coup in 1965. See n.d., "History Perlawanan."

128 Ford, *Workers and Intellectuals: NGOs, Trade Unions and the Indonesian Labour Movement.*

129 Batubara, *Cosmas Batubara, Sebuah Otobiografi Politik*, 278–279.

130 Jones, *Making Money off Migrants*, 20. For a discussion of events that led up to the crackdown, see Liow, *The Politics of Indonesia-Malaysia Relations: One Kin Two Nations*, notes 98–104. For example, there was a public outcry in Malaysia in response to a case where three Indonesian males held a female Malaysian magistrate hostage in Kuantan prison. Following this incident, Malaysian authorities then rounded up 800 Indonesians without valid migration documents, put them on eight boats and abandoned them in international waters. See "Malaysia Acts to Stem Tide of Illegal Immigrants."

131 Jones, *Making Money off Migrants*.

132 Batubara, *Cosmas Batubara, Sebuah Otobiografi Politik*, 278.

programme.[133] It was at this time that the ministry introduced higher standards for mandatory training and certification. Domestic workers had to be taught to cook, iron and how to use a washing machine, while nannies needed to learn how to watch, wash, feed and put children to sleep.[134] Batubara also required that Indonesian migrant workers had to have a minimum competency in the target language to enable communication with employers, obliging labour recruitment companies to teach them at least 200 words. In practice, however, these policies were not consistently enforced. The mandatory training requirement thus in fact helped rogue labour recruitment companies charge migrants for services they did not receive.

As part of an attempt to expand the formal role of labour recruitment companies into other geographical areas, Batubara positioned them as programme partners (*mitra kerja*).[135] He required these companies to perform more administrative roles to help the ministry respond to complicated problems, such as the non-payment of wages overseas. Mention of the government-recognized Indonesian Manpower Supply Association (IMSA) was included in regulations, where it was charged with helping communicate policy and monitoring implementation among members.[136] The ministry under Batubara also took advantage of the fact that the association had formed informal groupings around destination regions and cities to better target its monitoring role. As these examples suggest, the principle that informed many of Batubara's policy choices was that government ought 'to steer rather than row'.[137] In the context of the overseas labour migration programme, this and poor implementation meant that labour recruitment company owners were frequently free to decide their own course.

A Step Backwards

After Suharto's re-election to the presidency in 1992, another businessman, Abdul Latief, was appointed as Minister of Manpower in the Sixth Development Cabinet (1993–1998). Before the election, international commentators had stepped up their criticism of the New Order regime, claiming that it was

---

133 Ibid., 279.

134 Ibid., 280.

135 Ibid., 279.

136 *Ministerial Regulation (Manpower) No. 01/MEN/1991 on Antar Kerja Antar Negara; Ministerial Decree (Manpower) No. 195/MEN/1991 on Petunjuk Pelaksanaan Antar Kerja Antar Negara; Ministerial Decree (Manpower) No. 196/MEN/1991 on Petunjuk Teknis Pengerahan Tenaga Kerja Indonesia Ke Arab Saudi.*

137 Batubara, *Cosmas Batubara, Sebuah Otobiografi Politik*, 282.

falling short of its economic reform programmes because of red tape and corruption.[138] During the campaign, critics – and even other members of government – described Pusat AKAN as a den of thieves (*tempat maling*).[139] These accusations were not without reason: an official who worked there at the time recalls the comfortable lifestyle he and his colleagues were able to finance through the collection of bribes. A portion was handed over to senior officials but the junior bureaucrats pocketed the rest. It is this corrupt culture of administration that reportedly prompted Latief to move Pusat AKAN's operations to the ministry's main building, where their work could be monitored more easily. Formalizing Latief's move through a decree six months later, the president approved his proposal to fold Pusat AKAN into the Directorate-General of Guidance of Labour Placement.[140]

The following year, Latief instituted a mechanism that would allow the ministry to perform the kind of ad hoc evaluations of labour recruitment companies that Sudomo had used to restrict the industry in 1986. Evaluations could be undertaken periodically or at random by the Evaluation Team.[141] Labour recruitment companies could be given verbal or written warnings, have their licences temporarily suspended or permanently cancelled.[142] The criteria for performance were based on four main areas: quality of management, human resources, capital and promotion of migrant labour.[143] The minister also defined the team's role as helping with the technical aspects of assessing applications for licences.[144] In terms of its structure, the team was intended to include other individuals, such as accountants and an industry representative from IMSA.[145] In practice, however, the committee only included ministry personnel. As in 1986 the ministry revoked the majority of labour recruitment company licences in line with the new standards for licensing. This predictably had the effect that survivors would be more

138 MacIntyre, "Indonesia in 1992: Coming to Terms with the Outside World," 209.

139 Interview data, Pekanbaru, 21 April 2010.

140 *Presidential Decree No. 104/1993 on Perubahan Atas Keputusan Presiden Nomor 15 Tahun 1984 Tentang Susunan Organisasi Departemen Sebagaimana Telah Duapuluh Kali Diubah, Terakhir Dengan Keputusan Presiden Nomor 83 Tahun 1993*, article 176(5).

141 *Ministerial Regulation (Manpower) No. 2/MEN/1994 on Penempatan Tenaga Kerja Di Dalam Dan Ke Luar Negeri*, article 38(2).

142 Ibid., article 39.

143 Ibid., article 37.

144 *Ministerial Decree (Manpower) No. 44/MEN/1994 on Petunjuk Pelaksanaan Penempatan Tenaga Kerja Indonesia*, article 75(b).

145 Ibid., article 76.

amenable to Latief's requests that they channel formal fees to his private account.[146]

The ministry delegated some of the administrative roles of the former Pusat AKAN to its regional implementation units, instituting an internal reporting mechanism that enabled the compilation of statistics on a national scale.[147] The units were recast in a subordinate relationship to the Ministry of Manpower's provincial offices, where they were then authorized to assess labour recruitment companies' requests to recruit labour migrants.[148] Unit personnel were required to witness the signing of employment contracts and furnish labour migrants with the necessary note exempting them from *fiskal*.[149] In Jakarta, most of these roles gradually returned to the ministry in response to complaints by labour recruitment companies that implementation unit staff were not adequately trained.[150]

A state-owned company called Binajasa Abadikarya (Bijak) was established to ostensibly introduce competition into the recruitment industry, which was dominated by privately owned labour recruitment companies that had come to specialize in overseas domestic work.[151] Bijak was set up as a subsidiary of Jamsostek, another state-owned company that provided employment insurance to workers in Indonesia. The Indonesian state involved itself in a wide range of commericial businesses through such arrangements. In this case, Latief was chairperson of the board of directors and a career bureaucrat, Soeramsihono – who would later rise to the senior-most position in relation to the programme – was the president director. Statistics for this government-to-government scheme were kept separate from the private-to-private scheme

146 Latief established a foundation to collect the levy that employment companies were required to pay for each migrant worker. The foundation's bank accounts were in the private names of Latief, the Director General for Guidance and Placement of Labour and the treasurer. It collected USD 11 million before Latief transferred the role to a consortium of insurance companies. Latief is rumoured to have misused ministry resources to pay for a private jet, the construction of hotels in Padang, the purchase of land and refurbishment of his office. See "Ke Mana Rp 1 Triliun Duit TKI," 1; n.d., "Latief Curi Uang TKI."

147 *Director General Decree (Guidance and Placement of Labour) No. 15/BP/1995 on Petunjuk Teknis Pelaksanaan Penempatan Tenaga Kerja Ke Luar Negeri*, article 1(g); Indrawati, "Agus- Sorot- Depnaker."

148 *Director General Decree (Guidance and Placement of Labour) No. 15/BP/1995 on Petunjuk Teknis Pelaksanaan Penempatan Tenaga Kerja Ke Luar Negeri*, article 11.

149 Ibid., 16(3) and 18(3).

150 Interview data, Pekanbaru, 21 April 2010.

151 Setiawati, "The Demographic and Socio-Economic Characteristics of Overseas Contract Workers (OCWs) from Indonesia," 89.

because although labour recruitment companies sometimes supplied labour, Bijak worked through a government appointed taskforce.

Latief also negotiated a deal with the Directorate-General of Immigration that would enable the ministry to open a 'one stop shop'. The special unit, which formerly operated in Halim,[152] took up occupancy in the ministry's main building on the mezzanine floor between its first and ground levels, adjacent to the minister's quarters. This arrangement was short-lived due to allegations of corruption. Despite being under-staffed, the immigration unit would sometimes produce up to 500 passports a day. Ministry personnel defended the extra fees the immigration officials charged as compensation for unpaid overtime. However, public censure by Latief prompted the Directorate-General of Immigration to move the special unit to office space in Cikokol, West Jakarta, where it gradually abandoned its collaboration with the ministry. In retrospect, one ministry official who worked closely with the special unit then believes that Latief sacrificed it to shift attention from corrupt practices in areas of the overseas labour migration programme that could be directly linked to him.[153]

Public criticism mounted as details surfaced that ministry officials siphoned off revenue for their own purposes. Nevertheless, between 1996 and 1997 the ministry achieved a 75 per cent rise in departures.[154] This dramatic increase put pressure on departure and arrival services at Jakarta International Airport, to which Latief responded by issuing decrees that directed migrants away from the general return hall. In 1993 Latief gave Oring Jabu Jaya, a company that would later provide skills training for migrants with jobs in the Middle East, the exclusive right to transport returned migrant workers to their villages.[155] Oring Jabu Jaya failed to do so in a timely way, forcing some migrant workers to wait in its Jakarta compound for days while passengers were sorted according to their destination.[156] Following these failures, Latief cancelled the appointment in 1994, instead requiring individual labour recruitment companies to organize the transportation.[157] The system was also not entirely effective: long-term taxi drivers recall that passengers could bribe gatekeepers in return for

152 Yusak, "Mekanisme Pengiriman Tenaga Kerja Indonesia Ke Luar Negeri," 15.

153 Interview data, Pekanbaru, 21 April 2010.

154 Badan Nasional Penempatan dan Perlindungan Tenaga Kerja Indonesia, *Data Penempatan TKI Ke Luar Negeri: Tahun 1994–2007*.

155 *Ministerial Decree (Manpower) No. 141/MEN/1993 on Penunjukan PT. Oring Jabu Jaya Sebagai Pelaksana Jasa Pelayanan Angkutan Pumulangan TKI Ke Daerah Asal.*

156 Raharto et al., "Kebutuhan Informasi Bagi Tenaga Kerja Migran Indonesia."

157 *Ministerial Decree (Manpower) No. 137/MEN/1994 on Pelayanan Angkutan Pemulangan TKI Ke Daerah Asal.*

access to new arrivals. Nevertheless, it would later constitute one of the mandatory services in the controversial migrant worker arrival hall.[158]

Stymied Reform after the Asian Financial Crisis

1997 and 1998 turned out to be turbulent years in Indonesia, as the Asian Financial Crisis set in motion events that would unseat the president and bring an end to his 32 years of autocratic rule.[159] Before those events unfolded, President Suharto replaced Latief with Theo Sambuaga in the short-lived Seventh Development Cabinet (March-May 1998).[160] President Suharto resigned following massive riots in Jakarta in May 1998,[161] and vice president Bacharuddin Jusuf Habibie, assumed the top job. Habibie replaced Sambuaga with Fahmi Idris, Sambuaga's immediate successor as vice secretary to the Golkar Advisory Council. Like Batubara, Idris had supported Suharto's rise to power while a student activist.

Upon Idris' appointment to the manpower portfolio in the Development Reform Cabinet (1998–1999), questions were raised about whether he could deliver a reformist programme. But despite his strong association with the New Order, Idris pushed through a series of important reforms.[162] On his ninth day in office, Idris cancelled the decree on mandatory insurance for migrant workers – which Sambuaga had passed just a few weeks earlier – because he deemed it inappropriate that the Ministry of Manpower selected insurers when the Ministry of Finance had the expertise to do so.[163] Idris followed through by declaring void related administrative decisions, such as the appointment of a consortium of insurers to handle migrants' claims by the Director-General for Guidance of Overseas Labour Placement. In line with broader policy, Idris

158 For an ethnography of the data collection, see Silvey, "Unequal Borders: Indonesian Transnational Migrants at Immigration Control"; Hugo, "Information, Exploitation and Empowerment: The Case of Indonesian Overseas Workers," 449–451; Kloppenburg and Peters, "Confined Mobilities: Following Indonesian Migrant Workers on Their Way Home."

159 Hill, "The Indonesian Economy: The Strange and Sudden Death of a Tiger"; Suryadinata, "A Year of Upheaval and Uncertainty: The Fall of Soeharto and Rise of Habibie."

160 Sambuaga was considered to be one of Golkar's prominent public figures at the time, serving as vice secretary to the Golkar party in the national legislature and headed parliamentary missions overseas. Tirtosudarmo, *Mencari Indonesia: Demografi-Politik Pasca-Soeharto*, 272.

161 Suryadinata, "The Decline of the Hegemonic Party System in Indonesia: Golkar after the Fall of Soeharto," 337.

162 Hadiz, "Reformasi and Changing State and Labour Relations in Indonesia and Malaysia," 109.

163 "Mantan Menteri Soalkan Monopoli Asuransi TKI."

removed New Order-style officials from executive positions and replaced them with public figures from outside the bureaucracy. For example, he appointed Professor Din Syamsuddin as Director-General for the Guidance of Overseas Labour Placement partly because he had a public reputation for siding with migrant workers over labour recruitment companies.

With time, it became clear that the ministry needed a cross-sectoral structure to coordinate other state agencies' involvement in the administration of the overseas labour migration programme.[164] The concept was not new: ministry officials had proposed it as early as 1988.[165] Habibie issued a presidential decree that established such a coordinating agency involving seven ministers, head of the police and governor of the Bank of Indonesia, while leaving the day-to-day administration to the ministry's Directorate-General of Guidance of Overseas Labour Placement.[166] The coordinating agency partly served its purpose, using quarterly meetings to work out how different state organizations could align their administrative work to speed up processing. However, the structure was largely ineffective for two main reasons. First, the administrative expenses were taken from the Ministry of Manpower's budget, making proposals for initiatives subject to internal ordering of priorities. Second, it was staffed by members with responsibilities in their own portfolios rather than by dedicated personnel, which complicated efforts to negotiate and implement policy.

Idris also decreed a range of other changes to the programme in the weeks before the 1999 legislative elections.[167] He obtained permission to reorganize the infrastructure formerly established by Pusat AKAN in the regions to include sections for preparation and guidance, protection and evaluation and a division for managing units' administrative, financial and human resources. To administrators in areas such as East Java, this initiative was experienced as little more than a change in name.[168] However, the internal restructuring would become important in the context of decentralization. Before this change, the units were subordinate and responsible to the ministry's regional offices, which would be reorganized into the provincial government under decentralization.

---

164 *Presidential Decree No. 29/1999 on Badan Koordinasi Penempatan Tenaga Kerja Indonesia.*

165 Yusak, "Mekanisme Pengiriman Tenaga Kerja Indonesia Ke Luar Negeri," 3.

166 *Presidential Decree No. 29/1999 on Badan Koordinasi Penempatan Tenaga Kerja Indonesia*, article 7.

167 For details about how Habibie sought to bolster his reformist credentials in the lead up to the 1999 election, see Mietzner, "The Ambivalence of Weak Legitimacy: Habibie's Interregnum Revisted."

168 Dinas Tenaga Kerja Transmigrasi dan Kependudukan, "Sejarah Lembaga Pelayanan Penempatan TKI Di Jatim."

Pre-empting this, Idris made the units responsible to the ministry in Jakarta but left them under the coordination of local manpower offices. This dealt with the growing concern that once regional autonomy was implemented the ministry would need its own institutional infrastructure outside the capital city to administer the overseas labour migration programme.

Fallout of the Asian Financial Crisis complicated Idris' reform agenda, as it motivated greater numbers of Indonesians to migrate. The unemployment rate rose as companies laid off workers, and the cost of living increased due in part to the higher cost of importing goods with a much weaker rupiah. At the same time, overseas employment appeared more attractive than ever before, as the wages in places like Hong Kong, Malaysia and Singapore increased in rupiah value. In one prominent case, the leader of an Indonesian migrant worker organization in Hong Kong recalls that economic hardship compelled her to drop out of university and register for overseas employment.[169] She was not alone, as the number of departures to Hong Kong in that period rose from 3,142 (1996) to 19,531 (1998).[170]

This speedy rise in migrants' earnings overseas has been described by some as a 'blessing'.[171] More critical observers found that those who responded to the change still spent the bulk of their income paying off recruitment debts and the consumption needs of their families in Indonesia. Before the crisis, foreign domestic workers in Hong Kong earned the equivalent of IDR 700,000. By 1998 they made IDR 3,500,000 a month, five times more in nominal terms. Simultaneously, however, indebtedness became an even stronger feature of the programme. For recruitment to Hong Kong, the Association of Indonesian Labour Service Companies (Asosiasi Perusahaan Jasa Tenaga Kerja Indonesia, APJATI), formerly IMSA, lobbied the Minister for Manpower to authorize the charging of fees in pre-crisis foreign currency values.[172] The request was approved with only minor revisions, allowing recruiters to collect the equivalent of seven months' salary from Hong Kong-based workers.[173] This practice would continue despite repeated attempts by the ministry to lower the fee in later years.[174]

---

169 Palmer, "Learning to Lead (interview with Eni Lestari)."

170 Badan Nasional Penempatan dan Perlindungan Tenaga Kerja Indonesia, *Data Penempatan TKI Ke Luar Negeri: Tahun 1994–2007*.

171 Ananta and Arifin, "Should Southeast Asian Borders Be Opened?" 12.

172 Asosiasi Perusahaan Jasa Tenaga Kerja Indonesia, "Biaya Penempatan TKI Ke Hong Kong."

173 Direktur Jenderal Pembinaan dan Penempatan Tenaga Kerja, "Struktur Biaya Penempatan TKI Ke Hong Kong."

174 For example, see *Director General Decree (Guidance of Labour Placement) No. 186/PPTK/VI/2008 on Komponen Dan Besarnya Biaya Penempatan Calon Tenaga Kerja*

Changes in employer company practice in Asian destination countries further exacerbated the situation. In Hong Kong, labour recruitment companies also discovered a market for 'discounted' workers, promoting Indonesian labour migrants at below the legal minimum rate.[175] In other destinations, such as Malaysia and Singapore, labour recruitment companies began advertising zero cost services, which transferred fees from employers to Indonesian migrant workers. This was largely possible because in these countries the law enabled labour recruitment companies to charge migrants' fees to future employers, who would in turn deduct them from their workers' wages. As a consequence, the crisis made the service cheaper for employers without diminishing returns to recruiters.

The Long Reform

In 1999 President Habibie pushed through an ambitious decentralization programme that promised to fundamentally change centre-periphery relations in Indonesia. Laws were introduced in the May of that year that transferred a greater proportion of the national budget to local government as well as authority to regulate all matters except for foreign affairs, defence, justice, monetary or fiscal policy, religion and other specified activity.[176] The implementation of this law was of course not immediate. The legislature delegated much responsibility to outline the process and systems for transferring administrative authority and the associated budget. By 2001 the executive branch had still not yet produced all of the necessary regulations to implement the programme, and administrators sometimes found that articles in the decentralization laws conflicted with other laws.[177] As this suggests, the years immediately following the promulgation of the decentralization programme were shrouded in a great deal of legal uncertainty. While this was particularly the case for groups seeking to form new sub-national units of government, the

---

Indonesia Penata Laksana Rumah Tangga, Perawat Bayi, Dan Perawat Orang Tua/jompo Untuk Negara Tujuan Hongkong; *Director General Decree (Placement and Protection of Overseas Labour) No. 653/DP2TKLN on Biaya Penempatan Calon Tenaga Kerja Indonesia Informal Ke Hong Kong*; Government of Indonesia et al., *Memorandum of Understanding: Struktur Biaya Penempatan TKI Ke Hong Kong.*

175 Palmer, "Public-Private Partnerships in the Administration and Control of Indonesian Migrant Labour in Hong Kong," 5.

176 *Law No. 22 on Regional Governance*, article 7(1).

177 SMERU, "Pelaksanaan Desentralisasi Dan Otonomi Daerah: Kasus Tiga Kabupaten Di Sulawesi Utara Dan Gorontalo," 38.

same problems faced those with the task of sorting out how to divide up administrative activity that had previously been handled exclusively by central government agencies.

Habibie's party, Golkar, only won 120 seats in the June 1999 legislative election. In October the People's Consultative Assembly (Majelis Permusyawaratan Rakyat, MPR) rejected his accountability speech. Sensing that his bid for the presidency was no longer a realistic goal, Habibie then withdrew his candidacy for the presidency, which at that time was still determined by members in the assembly, comprised of all 560 parliamentarians in the People's Representative Council (Dewan Perwakilan Rakyat, DPR) and the 132 members of the Regional Representative Council (Dewan Perwakilan Daerah, DPD). As a result in 1999, Megawati Sukarnoputri missed out on the presidency even though the Indonesian Democratic Party of Struggle (Partai Demokrasi Indonesia–Perjuangan, PDIP) held the largest number of seats in the DPR. A coalition of Muslim parties called the Poros Tengah alliance, backed Nahdlatul Ulama figurehead Abdurrahman Wahid, the leader of the National Awakening Party (Partai Kebangkitan Bangsa, PKB). Golkar then also threw its weight behind Wahid, which gave him enough votes to win against Megawati. This controversial start to Indonesia's return to democratic rule led observers to question whether the political system would support the substance of the reform package introduced in the Habibie Interregnum.[178]

President Wahid replaced Idris with Bomer Pasaribu, a Golkar cadre and chairperson of the Confederation of All Indonesia Workers Unions (Konfederasi Serikat Pekerja Seluruh Indonesia, KSPSI),[179] as Minister for Manpower in the National Unity cabinet (1999–2001). In this period, administration of the overseas labour migration programme progressively departed from the intention to reform it.[180] For the entire year that Pasaribu spent in the position, he was busy dealing with the politics of negotiating the content of Law No. 21/2000 on Trade Unions. He also instructed the ministry's legal bureau to produce decrees and regulations that would strengthen the position of workers against employers.[181] As part of this initiative, a study was conducted of the 197 decrees and regulations issued during the New Order years, which found

178 Mackie, "Indonesia's New 'National Unity' Cabinet."

179 Pasaribu continued to be chairperson of KSPSI until he finished his five year term in 2000. See Caraway, "Explaining the Dominance of Legacy Unions in New Democracies: Comparative Insights from Indonesia," 1382.

180 Tirtosudarmo, *Mencari Indonesia: Demografi-Politik Pasca-Soeharto*, 273.

181 Caraway, "Explaining the Dominance of Legacy Unions in New Democracies: Comparative Insights from Indonesia," 38.

that they all favoured employers and government. It is during this time that Pasaribu passed a decree that reduced labour flexibility by making it more expensive to hire and fire workers. During this time, the reformist bureaucrat, Syamsuddin, who was tasked with reforming administration of the overseas labour migration programme, tendered his resignation three times partly out of frustration with the lack of support he received from the minister.[182]

The receding drive to reform the overseas labour migration programme continued after Wahid replaced Pasaribu with Al Hilal Hamdi through a cabinet reshuffle in August 2000, during which the ministry was re-amalgamated with the transmigration portfolio.[183] In the following month, the Indonesian Council of Islamic Scholars (Majelis Ulama Indonesia, MUI) issued a fatwa that sending women to work overseas without making arrangements to guarantee their honour and safety was forbidden under Islamic law.[184] Hamdi responded that he was sympathetic to their concern but that there were simply not enough jobs in Indonesia.[185] This policy position found traction among his senior-most staff. Soeramsihono, the career bureaucrat who had formerly held the programme's top post under Latief, replaced Syamsuddin as director-general. Soeramsihono is on the public record for supporting the labour recruitment companies' push to reverse reforms to the programme that required them, not migrants, to pay for mandatory pre-departure training.[186]

In 2001 Hamdi finalized the process for redistributing administrative roles between the three tiers of government under Law No. 22/1999 on Regional Governance. In line with the law, the ministry decentralized much of the administration relating to the selection of migrant workers to the city/district level. Lawmakers imagined a much less autonomous role for provincial authorities, which were expected to act as an administrative extension of the centre.[187] However, an implementing regulation complicated the division of labour by allowing central authorities to directly provide services related to national scale programmes. For these reasons, the ministry retained control over licensing of employment and insurance companies, granting permission

182 "Bomer: Minggu Ini Ada Pergantian Eselon I Depnaker."

183 The last time Manpower and Transmigration were managed by the same minister was under Harun Zain (1978–1983).

184 Majelis Ulama Indonesia, "Fatwa: Pengiriman Tenaga Kerja Wanita (TKW) Ke Luar Negeri."

185 "Dilarang Merekrut TKI Hingga Desember 2000."

186 "Dana Pungutan TKI Diusut Kejaksaan Agung."

187 *Governmental Regulation No, 25/2000 on Kewenangan Pemerintah Dan Kewenangan Propinsi Sebagai Daerah Otonom*, elucidation.

to recruit migrant labour, providing pre-departure training and finalizing the administrative process for labour migrants ready to leave Indonesia.

The redistribution of assets and personnel to the sub-national level complicated matters for staff assigned to the implementation units. Unit staff complained about reduction in prestige, the loss of earning power and the lack of work after the ministry's offices were turned over to the provincial government.[188] Those officials, along with labour recruitment companies, successfully lobbied the ministry to recentralize the units under the Directorate-General of Guidance of Overseas Labour Placement. Where the unit occupied a separate office or building, the ministry simply assumed control of the assets and personnel. This was the case, for example, in Nunukan in East Kalimantan.[189] Frequently, however, the process was more complex, as most units relied on the resources of provincial authorities for office space and other basic infrastructure. The ministry gradually acquired land and built stand-alone offices as agreements between the ministry and provincial authorities expired, as was the case in Yogyakarta.[190] In all locations, central and provincial officials were responsible to managers who worked for different tiers of government, which did not always share priorities or purposes. Collegiality initially prevented conflict between them, but legal and political developments over the ensuing five years sorely tested their willingness and capacity to cooperate.

The transition to decentralized government was an uncertain period for labour recruitment companies. In particular, they were confused by the laws produced by hundreds of districts and cities on the costs and procedures for setting up recruitment infrastructure and registering residents for international labour migration. Predictably, this created competition between local governments.[191] For example, Kediri District made it easier to obtain the required documents if labour recruitment companies established subsidiary offices in its jurisdiction.[192] Patterns of recruitment changed as a consequence of these local government policies, shown by reduction of recruitment in less profitable areas of the business, such as males for employment in Malaysia, which declined by 30 per cent in comparison to the previous three years.[193] Conversely, more profitable segments of the market, such as the recruitment of women

188 Interview data, Jakarta, 26 January 2011.

189 Interview data, Nunukan, 3 June 2010.

190 Interview data, Yogyakarta, 10 October 2010.

191 Schleifer and Vishny, "Corruption."

192 Interview data, Malang, 28 September 2009.

193 Badan Nasional Penempatan dan Perlindungan Tenaga Kerja Indonesia, *Data Penempatan TKI Ke Luar Negeri: Tahun 1994–2007*.

for employment in Hong Kong and Singapore, increased. In Jakarta, where the majority of migrants were processed, the central and provincial government authorities attempted to address competition in the system by introducing an informal division of administrative labour according to destination country. Whereas the ministry finalized the administrative process for migrants bound for the Middle East and Taiwan through a unit in East Jakarta, the provincial government did so for the rest of the Asia-Pacific region in South Jakarta.[194]

This reorganization may have helped to prevent competition between state agencies, but did little to improve conditions for the migrant workers participating in the state-sponsored system. As noted earlier, recruiters in Hong Kong, Malaysia, Singapore and other destination countries had arrangements with labour recruitment companies in Indonesia that enabled women in particular to register for migration without paying upfront fees. In Hong Kong, the administration took action against employers who paid the fee directly to recruiters, prompting them to design alternative methods, such as through loans from public finance companies.[195] Malaysia and Singapore had no such laws, so labour recruitment companies there continued with arrangements whereby employers recouped the expense from workers' wages. In all cases, labour recruitment companies continued charging for sub-standard services in an attempt to protect their investment in expenses, such as food and accommodation. The immediate reform period thus delivered little in the way of substantive change.

When 'Reformists' Lose Their Drive for Reform

In 2001 the MPR impeached Wahid and installed Megawati Sukarnoputri as president, a position she held until 2004.[196] Megawati appointed loyal supporter Jacob Nuwa Wea as Minister of Manpower and Transmigration. Nuwa Wea had held leadership positions in the PDI since 1981, but his close relationship with Megawati can be traced back to 1993 when he derailed Suharto's attempts to marginalize Megawati at the PDI's fourth congress by organizing cars and jeeps to crash into the Hotel Tiara auditorium, where party cadres were

---

194 Badan Pemeriksa Keuangan, "Hasil Pemeriksaan Atas Pengelolaan Dana Pembinaan Dan Penyelenggaraan Penempatan Tenaga Kerja Indonesia Dan Pelaksanaan Penempatan Tenaga Kerja Indonesia Ke Luar Negeri Tahun Anggaran 2004 Dan 2005 Pada Ditjen Pembinaan Dan Penempatan Tenaga Kerja Luar Negeri, Dinas Tenaga Kerja, Balai Pelayanan Dan Penempatan Tenaga Kerja Indonesia Serta Instansi Terkait Lainnya Di Surabaya, Pekanbaru Dan Batam," 8.

195 See Chapter 5. See also Palmer, "Public-Private Partnerships in the Administration and Control of Indonesian Migrant Labour in Hong Kong," 6.

196 Tan, "Anti-Party Reaction in Indonesia: Causes and Implications," 484.

voting.[197] A few months later Megawati was appointed leader at an extraordinary congress. But Nuwa Wea also had over 30 years' experience in labour matters and was chairperson of KSPSI (2000–2005) at the time of his appointment. Nuwa Wea's background made him a suitable candidate for the manpower portfolio. But it was his decision to distance KSPSI from his predecessor's political party, Golkar, and ally the trade union with PDI that convinced Megawati that he was the most suitable candidate for the job.[198]

Nuwa Wea soon came under pressure to orient the country's overseas labour migration programme more toward providing fully documented workers to neighbouring countries. At the beginning of 2002 Indonesian factory workers in Malaysia rioted, prompting authorities to adopt a 'Hire Indonesians Last' policy.[199] It was following these sorts of developments that Nuwa Wea sought to at least reduce the number of Indonesians working in Malaysia without valid migration documents. He instructed officials to draft a new decree to introduce ambitious, pro-migrant standards, such as the capping of recruitment fees. In the case that migrants had to pay the fee, Nuwa Wea limited it to the equivalent of one month's wages and forbade post-deployment payment schedules that required migrants to hand over more than 25 per cent of their income at any time.[200] However, the decree failed to effect change partly because Nuwa Wea refused to compromise with labour recruitment companies regarding the limits it imposed on financing labour migration. Recruiters of course preferred the status quo and the ministry was unable to control the sum that they, financiers and employers in destination countries charged to Indonesian migrant workers.

The situation quickly worsened after Malaysian authorities started deporting what would soon amount to over 400,000 people to various ports in Indonesia in August.[201] Almost 70 people died in camps in East Kalimantan, which came to be known as the Nunukan Tragedy. By and large, the deaths were caused by the failure of Indonesian authorities to coordinate an appropriate

197 Wanandi, *Shades of Grey: A Political Memoir of Modern Indonesia, 1965–1998*, 271.

198 Caraway, "Explaining the Dominance of Legacy Unions in New Democracies: Comparative Insights from Indonesia," 1382.

199 Kaur, "Indonesian Migrant Workers in Malaysia: From Preferred Migrants to 'Last to Be Hired' Workers," 26.

200 *Ministerial Decree (Manpower) No. 104A/MEN/2002 on Penempatan Tenaga Kerja Indonesia Ke Luar Negeri*, articles 54 and 55(2).

201 Tirtosudarmo, *Mencari Indonesia: Demografi-Politik Pasca-Soeharto*; Ford, "After Nunukan: The Regulation of Indonesian Migration to Malaysia"; Probokusumo, "Kondisi Dan Pelayanan Pekerja Migran Di Daerah Transit: Studi Kasus Di Kabupaten Nunukan Kalimantan Timur."

response despite knowing for some time that an influx of return migrants was inevitable. At the heart of the problem was the fact that central government agencies in Jakarta, including the manpower portfolio, refused to commit resources to handling it. The local government in Nunukan had set up a repatriation taskforce as part of its response, but quickly stepped back after realizing that a large proportion of deportees had no interest in going back to their province of origin.[202] The ministry's labour recruitment companies stepped in, seeking to make a profit out of deportees' desire to return to Malaysia for work. It was in these recruiters' camps where so many people died. Mounting public pressure around the deaths compelled the central government to intervene by acquiring land to construct temporary barracks. However, these were never fully built and national, provincial and local authorities stopped coordinating their efforts, leaving the military with the task of feeding the deportees.[203]

This administrative debacle became the basis of a class action against the government. In January 2003 a group of 53 people filed a citizen's lawsuit against nine senior government officials, who had authority to respond to the humanitarian crisis, including Megawati and Nuwa Wea.[204] In May the Central Jakarta court accepted the case for hearing based on the finding that Indonesian law permitted citizens who were not directly aggrieved to sue the government for negligence. The court decided in December that the government had failed to act appropriately, ordering the enforcement and ratification of all relevant laws.[205] The Jakarta High Court would annul that order a year later, but not before four alternative bills concerning the overseas labour migration programme and migrant workers were tabled in the national legislature. Nuwa Wea represented the government in meetings with lawmakers, who decided that migrant labour was a complex governance problem that deserved a separate law.[206] Two months after the citizen's lawsuit was registered, the president signed into law the statute on labour that paved the way for one of the migrant labour bills to itself become law some eighteen months later.[207]

202 "Tragedi Nunukan: Enggan Pulang Kamupng, 17,600 Bertahan Di Nunukan."

203 "4.300 TKI Masuk Penampungan Baru."

204 The other seven officials were the vice president, the Coordinating Minister for People's Prosperity, the Minister for Foreign Affairs, the Minister for Welfare, Minister for Health, the Ambassador to Malaysia and the Director-General for Immigration in the Ministry of Justice and Human Rights. See hukumonline.com, "Pro-Kontra Citizen Law Suit: Belajar Dari Kasus Nunukan."

205 Santosa, Khatarina, and Assegaf, "Indonesia."

206 *Law No. 13 on Labour*, articles 33–34.

207 *Law No. 39 on Placement and Protection of Indonesian Workers Overseas.*

The following year would prove to be a particularly difficult time at which to push through legislative change. Counter-terrorism measures dominated in the aftermath of the Bali Bombings in October 2002 and the resumption of conflict in Aceh well into 2004.[208] Economically, the balance of domestic and foreign investment was lower than expected partly because textile, footwear and other light manufacturers had started to relocate to other countries, such as China, which had a stronger reputation for containing labour costs.[209] Other internal developments indicate that 2003 was a significant 'detour, if not a setback', concerning the reform agenda.[210] The rise of military power, the ability of New Order cronies to regain influence, an increase in the number of people prosecuted for insulting the president and the ease with which the wealthy and well-connected avoided legal sanction are all cited as evidence of a widening cleft between reformist rhetoric and implementation of the reform agenda. These developments successfully sidelined the Nunukan Tragedy in the mass media and forced the proposal to introduce legislation that dealt with migrant workers' needs to be put on the back-burner.

It was not until the bill became part of the president's effort to get re-elected that parliamentarians recommenced deliberations. Campaigns in the lead-up to the March 2004 legislative elections did not take up the issue of migrant workers. In May, however, the high profile case of Nirmala Bonat, an Indonesian domestic worker who was tortured by her employer in Malaysia, caught the attention of Indonesia's presidential hopefuls. Candidates had just started campaigning for the first round of the country's first direct presidential elections set for early July. Megawati invited Bonat's mother to her private residence in Jakarta for a 15 minute meeting, and then Amien Rais also met with her, offering moral and financial support.[211] She was then chaperoned to Kuala Lumpur by the Minister for Manpower and the chairperson of APJATI to visit her teenage daughter in hospital. One week later, the government announced the intention to sign a bilateral agreement with Malaysia concerning Indonesian workers in the formal sector, just one month before the election.[212] The following month the minister was instructed to represent the government in the legislature to develop a law on overseas labour migration.

208 Malley, "Indonesia in 2002: The Rising Cost of Inaction"; Kipp, "Indonesia in 2003: Terror's Aftermath."
209 Kipp, "Indonesia in 2003: Terror's Aftermath," 64.
210 Ibid., 68–69.
211 "Presiden Megawati Akan Menemui Keluarga Nirmala."
212 "Indonesia-Malaysia Tandatangani MoU Perlindungan"; "Malaysia's Draft MoU One-Sided, Unrealistic."

A Migrant Worker Law Focussed on Recruitment

Megawati would ultimately lose the presidency in the September 2004 election, but not before signing a migrant worker bill into law. The legislative process took longer than anticipated partly because the government was at times uncooperative, refusing to attend meetings to discuss the bill.[213] The process was complex and difficult, reflected in the fact that four draft bills were registered with the legislature.[214] The Consortium for the Defence of Indonesian Migrant Workers (Konsorsium Pembela Buruh Migran Indonesia, KOPBUMI) had already tabled a bill for consideration that used as its basis the 1990 International Convention on the Protection of the Rights of All Migrant Workers and Members of their Families.[215] The other three drafts consisted of versions authored by the law faculty at Brawijaya University, the legislature's own legislation division and the ministry's legal bureau.[216]

Migrant worker groups lobbied intensively against the ministry's draft, arguing that it offered an elaborate system of administrative procedures for recruitment in Indonesia but was vague about what the state would do to improve the weak position of labour migrants overseas.[217] This draft was nevertheless eventually chosen as a starting point for deliberation. According to an ILO official, the decision to use the government draft was made during backroom deals in which ministry officials, labour recruitment companies and lawmakers, whose interests are not easily disentangled, exchanged political and financial favours.[218] For example, an all-expenses paid trip to Bali financed using the ministry's off-budget funds succeeded in securing lawmakers' support for

---

213 One of the sticking points was an attempt by lawmakers to dismantle the monopoly that employment companies had over recruitment of migrant labour in Indonesia by enabling individuals and companies from overseas to recruit directly with permission from an Indonesian consular office. The Minister for Manpower eventually spoke out on the matter, claiming that it would further complicate efforts by the ministry to monitor recruitment practices. "Batas Usia Calon TKI Minimal 18 Dan 21 Tahun"; hukumonline.com, "RUU Perlindungan Tenaga Kerja Diharapkan Hapus Monopoli PJTKI."

214 hukumonline.com, "RUU Buruh Migran Versi Depnakertrans Dinilai Tidak Berorientasi Perlindungan."

215 "Kebijakan Penempatan Pekerja Indonesia Cuma Memosisikan TKI Sebagai Komoditas." Incidentally, Megawati would sign the international convention on 22 September, two days after the presidential election, but the legislature would not ratify the instrument until 31 May 2012.

216 hukumonline.com, "RUU Buruh Migran Versi Depnakertrans Dinilai Tidak Berorientasi Perlindungan."

217 "Koalisi Buruh Migran Menolak RUU PTKLN."

218 Interview data, Jakarta, 16 December 2010.

the ministry bill over their own. Critical observers claim that the legislature simply upgraded the status of Nuwa Wea's ministerial decree. In fact, one ministry official goes as far to say that the content was simply copy-pasted (*dikopipaste*).[219] As a result of this process, the ministry acquired significant discretionary power to set standards and procedures that, according to them, needed to be flexible in order to respond appropriately to developments concerning recruitment.

The logic informing the law was that practices within Indonesia were in a large part to blame for migrant workers' problems overseas, and that the ministry was best positioned to intervene to improve these practices.[220] Attention to the parliamentary debates, however, confirms that migrant worker support groups were excluded from the conversation about what the emphasis of the law should be. The legislature would learn to invite migrant worker advocacy groups in the capacity of experts, as was the case for deliberations concerning Law No. 21/2007 on the Eradication of the Crime of Trafficking in Persons, but deliberations for the migrant worker law were a classic case of 'jobs for the boys', including only senior government officials and academics on the state's payroll. Lawmakers, too, had little sense of the migrant perspective so focused instead on processes concerning the business activities of recruiters.

Tough criminal sanctions were introduced for recruiters who circumvented procedures. This predictably drove much of the frequent illegal activity underground. Criminalization raised the stakes for recruiters who still aspired to do business the old way by using real but fake (asli tapi palsu, aspal) documents, such as birth certificates that contained false data.[221] A former company employee recalls making alterations to ages recorded on state documents on a daily basis.[222] However, after the police began pursuing cases of falsification more aggressively, labour recruitment companies came to fear the demands for bribes and threats of prosecution that followed. In response, the industry outsourced the responsibility to intermediaries who ensured that recruits arrived with a full set of documents. Women and men were treated differently, not least because there is more competition for 'men's jobs', such as

219 Interview data, Jakarta, 16 December 2010.

220 A frequently cited figure is that 80 per cent of migrant workers' problems overseas not only have their origins in Indonesia. See, for example, "80% Masalah TKI Di Luar Negeri Berawal Dari Kampung Halaman"; "80 Persen Masalah BMI Terjadi Di Dalam Negeri"; "Menlu: Moritorium Penempatan TKI."

221 For a detailed discussion of the 'real but fake' phenomenon, see Ford and Lyons, "Travelling the Aspal Route: 'Grey' Labour Migration through an Indonesian Border Town."

222 Interview data, Blitar, 17 March 2010.

employment on construction sites. By contrast, demand for female workers often outstrips supply so networks of intermediaries with access to migrant labour source areas (*kantong TKI*) became more necessary.[223] Before the law intermediaries were paid IDR 500,000 (USD 50) for the service, but within a year collected up to IDR 5,000,000 (USD 500) to partly compensate for the greater risk involved in ensuring recruits were fully documented.

When Susilo Bambang Yudhoyono won the 2004 presidential election, he reappointed Idris as Minister for Manpower. Within a few months, the ministry had produced a string of implementation regulations based on authority delegated to it under the overseas migration law. Among them was a regulation that formalized a more elaborate version of the system of administrative sanctions that the ministry already had in place.[224] It outlined procedures for applying those sanctions, which were formerly not clear to those outside the ministry. Another regulation set standards for accommodation facilities, requiring labour recruitment companies to provide recruits with at least 2,500 calories of food and two litres of water a day.[225] These two regulations were among the first that Idris signed into law because the systems and standards they mandated were more or less already developed. In other words, they required little in the way of further negotiation with recruiters. In fact, the ministry already had a reputation for using its control over other administrative roles, such as issuing recruitment certificates, to punish unruly recruiters.

As one of his first acts upon his return to office, Idris re-established the inter-departmental network for coordinating state responses to migrant workers' problems, first established by the president when Idris was Minister for Manpower in 1999. Idris issued a decree calling on this inter-departmental network to support an effort to suppress recruitment for 'non-procedural' migration.[226] The decree also emphasized the provision of return services to migrants re-entering Indonesia, complementing activities of the team.[227] However, a cursory examination of the list of state organizations included in the taskforce reveals

223 Lindquist, "Labour Recruitment, Circuits of Capital and Gendered Mobility: Reconceptualizing the Indonesian Migration Industry."

224 *Ministerial Regulation (Manpower) No. 5/MEN/III/2005 on Ketentuan Sanksi Administratif Dan Tata Cara Penjatuhan Sanksi Dalam Pelaksanaan Penempatan Dan Perlindungan Tenaga Kerja Indonesia Di Luar Negeri.*

225 *Ministerial Regulation (Manpower) No. 7/MEN/IV/2005 on Standar Tempat Penampungan Calon Tenaga Kerja Indonesia.*

226 For the use of the term 'non-procedural' in relation to labour migration in formal state documents, see *Ministerial Decree (Manpower) No. 14/MEN/I/2005 on Tim Pencegahan Pemberangkatan TKI Non-Prosedural Dan Pelayanan Pemulangan TKI.*

227 *Presidential Decree No. 106/2004 on Tim Koordinasi Pemulangan Tenaga Kerja Indonesia Bermasalah Dan Keluarganya Dari Malaysia.*

a greater interest in uncovering and intercepting recruitment that circumvented the official system. The team included just one official from the Coordinating Ministry of People's Prosperity, and none from the Ministries of Health or Welfare, which would be necessary partners for providing quality return service to the large number of migrant workers who re-entered Indonesia each day.

Opportunities for Career Advancement

Under the 2004 law, this coordinating mechanism was reorganized into an independent agency tasked with taking responsibility for operational aspects of the migration programme, to be known as the BNP2TKI. However, by mid-2006 the technical team within the Ministry of Manpower had made little progress on the draft regulation for the president to formally establish such a body. The legislature delegated the responsibility to flesh out the detail concerning its form, function and operating procedures in an implementation regulation to the president in October 2004.[228] During an official visit to Kuala Lumpur in December 2005 and a visit to Qatar in May 2006, the president had the opportunity to talk with migrant workers about the overseas labour migration programme. Common themes emerged that indicated a serious problem with the system was its unnecessarily complicated processes.[229] Upon returning to Indonesia, the president instructed the Minister for Manpower to organize a high level technical coordination meeting that included a session personally chaired by the president in which targets were set to reform the programme's administration.

One week before he left for Kuala Lumpur in December 2005, the president appointed Erman Suparno as Minister for Manpower as part of an attempt to include at least one representative from each major faction within PKB in cabinet. In order to make room for Suparno, Idris was moved to the Ministry of Industry. At the same time, Alwi Abdurrahman Shihab, who had been Coordinating Minister for People's Prosperity, was dropped from cabinet and made special emissary to the Middle East. By this appointment, the president hoped to capitalize on the networks that Shihab developed during his time serving as Minister of Foreign Affairs (1999–2001). In addition to being treasurer of PKB, Suparno had formerly chaired Commission V in the national legislature, which focused on trade, industry and investment matters. He had a Masters of Business Administration from the United States and would later complete a PhD and write two books on Indonesian labour.[230]

228 *Law No. 39 on Placement and Protection of Indonesian Workers Overseas*, article 97.

229 Krisnawaty, "Reformasi Dibelenggu Birokrasi," 9.

230 Suparno, *National Manpower Strategy: (Strategi Ketenagakerjaan Nasional)*; Suparno, *Grand Strategy: Manajemen Pembangunan Negara Bangsa.*

In March 2006 Suparno followed up on his predecessor's ministry-wide reorganization with a regulation that took account of the programme's infrastructure outside the capital city, including its implementation units.[231] However, the momentum to establish the BNP2TKI did not gain pace until after August, when the president issued an instruction to 11 ministers, the head of police, all governors, district heads and mayors to take action.[232] Finally, a draft regulation, which outlined the form and function of the agency, was produced for the president to sign into law.[233] The ministry-authored draft specified that a bureaucrat be appointed as head of the new agency, a condition that was dropped in the regulation's final form.[234]

In principle, regulatory functions were to stay with the ministry, while operational activity fell within the BNP2TKI's mandate; however, the Directorate-General of Guidance of Overseas Labour Placement was abolished.[235] The minister followed up with a regulation that folded residual domains of activity, such as policymaking and standard setting, into a more general division whose mandate included administering the recruitment activity of labour recruitment companies that supplied labour internally and overseas.[236] The ministry also retained authority to license and discipline labour recruitment companies, which the ILO rightly predicted would complicate the relationship between the ministry and the new agency in years to come.[237]

Conclusion

Attention to policy direction in the historical overview of Indonesia's overseas labour migration programme presented in this chapter has revealed congruencies and inconsistencies within particular periods of Indonesia's political

231 *Ministerial Regulation (Manpower) No. 6/MEN/III/2006 on Organisasi Dan Tata Kerja Unit Pelaksana Teknis Di Lingkungan Departemen Tenaga Kerja Dan Transmigrasi*; *Ministerial Regulation (Manpower) No. 14/MEN/VII/2005 on Organisasi Dan Tata Kerja Departemen Tenaga Kerja Dan Transmigrasi.*

232 *Presidential Instruction No. 6/2006 on Kebijakan Reformasi Sistem Penempatan Dan Perlindungan Tenaga Kerja Indonesia.*

233 *Presidential Regulation No. 81/2006 on Badan Nasional Penempatan Dan Perlindungan Tenaga Kerja Indonesia.*

234 Ibid., article 36(2).

235 Ibid., article 48.

236 *Ministerial Regulation (Manpower) No. 5/MEN/IV/2007 on Organisasi Dan Tata Kerja Departemen Tenaga Kerja Dan Transmigrasi.*

237 Interview data, Jakarta, 16 December 2010.

history. During the New Order era, bureaucrats more or less administered programmes in line with the wishes of the president and his allies. The resignation of Suharto did not significantly interrupt the provision of services: the immediate post-New Order period was one of business as usual for the recruitment industry, not least because of the demand generated by the 1997 Asian Financial Crisis. The five ensuing Ministers for Manpower implemented reforms, but those alterations effected little change in the day-to-day management of migration. The decentralization programme produced equally disappointing results, with significant changes to the institutional structures of the overseas labour migration programme delayed until after the passage of the overseas migration law in 2004. This law paved the way for the establishment of the BNP2TKI in 2007.

Over this period, what began as a technical solution to the challenges of shrinking foreign income gradually developed into a strategy to address Indonesia's labour market problems. To further interrogate the claim that the programme effectively deals with the country's 'labour surplus', an examination of the population segment that obtains overseas employment under it is necessary.[238] But, for the purpose of this book, it is sufficient to note that policy directions in the 1980s and 1990s created a system that enabled private intermediaries – both public and private, which was typical of the New Order era – to maximize their ability to profit from their involvement in recruitment. These years saw the rise of a dedicated recruitment industry, concentrated by periodic re-evaluations that culled non-compliant labour recruitment companies. It is in this period too that many of the challenges that complicated matters for administrators decades later have their roots. This narrative provides the background necessary to make sense of the conflict that was to develop between the ministry and the BNP2TKI and its impact on the management of overseas labour migration, described in the chapters that follow.

238 As a next step, research must critically assess what segment of society the Indonesian government refers to with the term 'labour surplus'. See Pye et al., "Precarious Lives: Transnational Biographies of Migrant Palm Workers."

CHAPTER 3

Contestation at the Centre

Intra-state conflict around the administration of the overseas labour migration programme emerged after the BNP2TKI was established in 2007. The President of Indonesia appointed a non-career bureaucrat to lead the agency instead of senior officials in the Ministry of Manpower who had years of experience with the programme. The appointment caused concern for the Minister for Manpower and senior officials, which was not without basis. Policy-making authority was to remain in the ministry, but the newly established agency was slated to assume authority over operational aspects of the programme, such as the provision of pre-departure training and finalization of administration. This textbook division of labour separated the operational and regulatory dimensions of administration concerning migrant workers, which partly addressed an old criticism that handling both matters in a single agency posed a conflict of interest. However, there was no precedent for sharing control. For this reason, senior ministry bureaucrats entered the relationship anxious about the fact that while the BNP2TKI was required to coordinate with them, it was not subordinate to the ministry.

The relationship quickly descended into a spate of conflicts around the way in which migrant workers ought to be administered. The ambiguity of the systems in place created a fertile field in which the BNP2TKI could use 'symbolic politics'[1] to pursue aims and objectives contrary to the immediate concerns of the ministry. The BNP2TKI used its operational mandate to enforce a number of procedures and standards that had formerly been neglected, and which the ministry was reluctant to see implemented. Conflict concerning the BNP2TKI's enforcement policy gradually resulted in the ministry revising the division of labour that gave the BNP2TKI power to do so by first reducing its role and then abolishing it altogether. The processes for handling these conflicts laid bare the troubled nature of interactions between the executive, judicial and legislative branches of government in post-New Order Indonesia. The immediate effect did not result in a compromise between the ministry and the BNP2TKI. Rather, the processes served to shift public opinion, raising awareness of power relations between the various branches of government.

1 Matland, "Synthesizing the Implementation Literature: The Ambiguity-Conflict Model of Policy Implementation," 169–170.

 | DOI 10.1163/9789004325487_004

The sum of these parts reveals a use of law that emphasizes the place of procedure and authority over other considerations such as legal substance and intention. Emphasis on procedure over substance is not unique to Indonesia, as bureaucrats in a wide variety of states are encouraged to prioritize a procedural approach, which entails 'formalized repetition', over empathy and 'individual justice'.[2] But in Indonesia, this disjuncture is the source of a great number of intra-state conflicts, which have led many observers to claim that Indonesian administrators and politicians have little respect for law.[3] In a high profile case, the Indonesian government has been criticized for permitting a mayor to stop the construction of a Christian church in his jurisdiction despite instructions by the Ministry of Internal Affairs and Supreme Court to the contrary.[4] However, as this chapter shows, through attention to the inter-agency contest for control over administration of the overseas labour migration programme, there is another parallel narrative: rather than simply using law as a prescription of what they must do, officials also use it as a resource for justifying what they want to do.

The first section of the chapter analyses the main sources of conflict that pushed the ministry and the BNP2TKI into a competitive relationship despite aspirations that they would share control of the programme. Disagreement about scope of authority, access to labour recruitment companies' economic resources and the career ambitions of senior ministry officials all contributed to the development of that conflict. The next section examines the different spaces in which the BNP2TKI contested the legitimacy of the ministry's push to reclaim the BNP2TKI's main administrative roles. This discussion draws attention to the complex environment in which Indonesian administrators work, where narratives of legality and political legitimacy are frequently harnessed as resources to support or undermine their authority. The final section focuses attention on the factors and developments that motivated stakeholders within these government agencies to end the most aggressive aspects of the conflict. Compromise only became a possibility, however, after a shift in the political context and once obstacles, such as senior government officials with an interest in maintaining the status quo, had been removed.

2 Massaro, "Empathy, Legal Storytelling, and the Rule of Law: New Worlds, Old Wounds?" 2100.

3 For an historical analysis of why this might be the case, for example, see Cribb, "A System of Exemptions: Historicizing State Illegality in Indonesia." For a contemporary examination which argues that they law does matter in Indonesia and provides a detailed account of when and how, see Butt, *Corruption and Law in Indonesia*.

4 Minako Sakai and Amelia Fauzia, "Islamic Orientations in Contemporary Indonesia: Islam on the Rise."

Conflict

Within a few months of the BNP2TKI's establishment in March 2007, its relationship with the ministry had started to break down. From the outset, those not transferred to the BNP2TKI resented the missed opportunity to take up more senior positions in the new agency.[5] The Minister for Manpower, Erman Suparno, had reservations about the BNP2TKI because his preferred candidate for the agency's top position was overlooked by the president, who appointed Jumhur Hidayat, a non-career bureaucrat with an activist background.[6] Soon after the appointment, rumours began circulating that those to be reassigned to the BNP2TKI were paying for management positions. Those seeking specific appointments were expected to make up-front payments – unlike some other government positions, where appointees could pay retrospectively.[7] Appointment to the most senior posts was not an entirely internal process in the BNP2TKI, as a special committee involving many other agencies makes such decisions. But the second tier is more or less appointed at the discretion of the agency manager. According to a senior official in the BNP2TKI, positions in the placement and protection divisions, which interact directly with employment and insurance companies, were the most costly, not least because of the opportunities they offer for greater rent-seeking.

As an ILO official remarked a few years later, it was thus inevitable BNP2TKI officials would attempt to recoup the investment through illegal means, such as manipulating the budget under their control.[8] However, the appointment process also had an impact on relations between the BNP2TKI and the ministry. Flows of 'fees' between different levels within the BNP2TKI bureaucracy created strong vertical relationships with the agency managers at the expense of horizontal relationships with former ministry colleagues, reducing their capacity to cooperate. The situation was further exacerbated by the fact that Suparno believed that the BNP2TKI was first and foremost intended to implement the ministry's policies. To his mind, coordination entailed following

5 They were also eager to criticize its head, Hidayat, for *faux pas* such as parking in areas that were dedicated for ministers at official events.

6 See "Sekilas Mohammad Jumhur Hidayat." Shortly after the surprise appointment was made public, Suparno told the mass media that Hidayat had made a political contract with the president. The president, in turn, attempted to reassure him by explaining that Hidayat would only remain in place if he performed his public function appropriately. See "Penempatan TKI: PPTKIS Berharap BNP2TKI Terbuka Terhadap Masukan."

7 For a discussion of this phenomenon more broadly, see Kristiansen and Ramli, "Buying an Income: The Market for Civil Service Positions in Indonesia."

8 Interview data, Jakarta, 16 December 2010.

instructions, an interpretation that foreclosed any possibility that the BNP2TKI might hold different views about how the international migration programme should be handled. This combination of factors produced an institutional context in which neither agency had a formal mechanism to coerce the other into cooperation, and in which an informal command structure evolved to keep staff in line with the policy direction set by their respective institutions regardless of its legal status.

The break down in the relationship became quite public by early July 2007, when the BNP2TKI's policies concerning the recruitment of migrant labour for employment in South Korea came into effect. A coalition of non-governmental organizations wrote to the president, the head of the national legislature and the Minister for Manpower complaining that the BNP2TKI had outsourced operational activity to an ad hoc committee that involved a large number of labour recruitment company owners.[9] The ministry instructed the BNP2TKI to revise the decree and exclude private individuals from the committee, arguing that the scheme was a government-to-government only initiative.[10] Previously, the ministry had involved private recruiters in the programme as part of an attempt to meet the bilaterally agreed quota, but the system had quickly gained a reputation for charging illegal fees to migrants and routinely fell short of the target nonetheless. Those who were cut out of the business lobbied against the BNP2TKI, writing to the Minister for Manpower to report nepotism, such as the requirement that Hidayat's brother handle international ticketing.[11] In spite of this and the resulting formal censure from the ministry, Hidayat persevered, based on the belief that policymaking within the BNP2TKI's area of activity was his prerogative.[12] This provided yet more evidence that Hidayat had little patience for the Ministry of Manpower's culture of procedure (*budaya prosedural*).[13]

Such experiences reaffirmed the ministry's decision to limit the administrative responsibilities to the BNP2TKI. According to the presidential regulation that established the new agency, the ministry was to hand over full

9 Agency Decree (BNP2TKI), "Komite Pelaksanaan Penempatan Tenaga Kerja Indonesia Ke Korea Dalam Rangka Program G to G."

10 Secretary General Memorandum (Ministry of Manpower) No. 34/MEN-SJ/V/2007, 31 May 2007 cited in Ministry of Manpower, "Penjelasan Komite Pelaksanaan Penempatan TKI Ke Korea." Government-to-government refers to initiatives in which the BNP2TKI holds an agreement with a foreign government agency to supply migrant labour.

11 "BNP2TKI Tangani TKI Ke Korsel."

12 "BNP2TKI Diminta Benahi Komite Korea."

13 Nasution et al., "Blunder Jumhur Hidayat (Kepala BNP2TKI): Amburadulnya Pengelolaan TKI Dan Suburnya Praktik Percaloan Di BNP2TKI."

responsibility for administration of the overseas labour migration programme. This was not what happened in practice. Authority to provide the full suite of administrative services to finalize the pre-departure process was also specifically mentioned in the law.[14] But the ministry downgraded the BNP2TKI's role from one of setting standards to one of fleshing out procedures for implementation.[15] Anticipating the imminent transfer of administrative control, the ministry had already upgraded authority to issue recruitment certificates from the Directorate-General of Guidance of Overseas Labour Placement to the minister,[16] arguably because the law stipulated that this was a function for the minister to delegate.[17] The ministry also retained other administrative roles, such as licensing labour recruitment companies, appointing insurers and issuing administrative sanctions against them. The official reason given was that they pertained to the set-up and regulation of the programme's wider infrastructure, whereas the BNP2TKI's mandate involved administration of the migrant workers it registered.

Operator versus Regulator

The ministry's manoeuvring irritated senior officials in the BNP2TKI, prompting them to quickly establish control over the operational dimension of the programme. The BNP2TKI sought to intervene in a range of situations, for example, responding to evidence that ineffective systems were partly responsible for the large number of Indonesian migrant workers returned by employers with the explanation that they were 'unfit' for employment.[18]

14 *Ministerial Regulation (Manpower) No. 18/MEN/IX/2007 on Pelaksanaan Penempatan Dan Perlindungan Tenaga Kerja Indonesia Di Luar Negeri*, n.d., article 95(2b).

15 *Ministerial Regulation (Manpower) No. 19/MEN/V/2006 on Pelaksanaan Penempatan Dan Perlindungan Tenaga Kerja Indonesia Di Luar Negeri*, article 28; *Ministerial Regulation (Manpower) No. 18/MEN/IX/2007 on Pelaksanaan Penempatan Dan Perlindungan Tenaga Kerja Indonesia Di Luar Negeri*, 2007.

16 *Ministerial Decree (Manpower) No. 104A/MEN/2002 on Penempatan Tenaga Kerja Indonesia Ke Luar Negeri*, article 38; *Ministerial Regulation (Manpower) No. 19/MEN/V/2006 on Pelaksanaan Penempatan Dan Perlindungan Tenaga Kerja Indonesia Di Luar Negeri*, article 2(2).

17 *Law No. 39 on Placement and Protection of Indonesian Workers Overseas*, article 32.

18 The president issued a regulation concerning physical and psychological fitness in September 2011 although Law No. 39/2004 stipulated that the Minister for Manpower was required to do so with the expectation that the BNP2TKI would implement it. But the president often intervenes in this way when the office comes under pressure because two or more of the cabinet's ministers – in this case those in charge of the Manpower and Health portfolios – cannot work out how to cooperate in pursuit of a government objective. See *Presidential Regulation No. 64/2011 on Pemeriksaan Kesehatan Dan Psikologi Calon Tenaga Kerja Indonesia*.

It also introduced a rating system to evaluate the work of mandatory training centres with a reputation for providing competency certificates without the necessary courses, putting them on notice of its intention to follow up with a crackdown.[19] In addition, the BNP2TKI intermittently took action against medical clinics that issued health certificates without undertaking the full suite of examinations.[20] Causing a row with the ministry, the BNP2TKI blacklisted negligent clinics and then launched a computerized system that made it more difficult for labour recruitment companies to register their recruits without first presenting the necessary health certificates. Their rigid enforcement of these requirements upset labour recruitment companies, which were accustomed to meeting administrative obligations shortly before departure, something made possible by the manual system formerly used by the ministry.

The BNP2TKI also used its operational role to level sanctions against insurance companies that the Ministry of Manpower had failed to discipline. In June 2007 the agency took action against the state owned enterprise Jasindo for holding up the payment of migrant workers' insurance claims. Hidayat informed labour recruitment companies that the BNP2TKI would temporarily cease to accept the insurer's policy.[21] Following procedure, he reported Jasindo to the ministry, which had authority to impose administrative sanctions such as warning letters, moratoria and retraction of the right to participate in the business.[22] However, the BNP2TKI deemed that the ministry's response was too lenient. One week after the BNP2TKI claims to have sent a warning letter to Jasindo, the insurer posted an announcement on its website to the effect that it would finalize claims within seven days when all the necessary documents were submitted.[23] But Jasindo denied receiving the warning letter on that date, citing this as a reason why the company was unable to come good

---

19 Badan Nasional Penempatan dan Perlindungan Tenaga Kerja Indonesia, "Ade Adam Noch: Rating BLK LN Akan Dilakukan Tiap Tahun"; Badan Nasional Penempatan dan Perlindungan Tenaga Kerja Indonesia, "BNP2TKI Juara II Anugerah Media Humas Pemerintah 2010"; Badan Nasional Penempatan dan Perlindungan Tenaga Kerja Indonesia, "Drs Nurfaizi MM Terpilih Sebagai Ketua APJATI 2008–2012."

20 Badan Nasional Penempatan dan Perlindungan Tenaga Kerja Indonesia, "Kepala BNP2TKI Sidak Tempat Pelayanan Kesehatan TKI"; Badan Nasional Penempatan dan Perlindungan Tenaga Kerja Indonesia, "Kasubdit Fasilitas Kesehatan BNP2TKI: Pemeriksaan Kesehatan TKI Harus Serius, Bukan Formalitas"; Badan Nasional Penempatan dan Perlindungan Tenaga Kerja Indonesia, "BNP2TKI Segera Sidak Sarkes."

21 "Ijin Operasional Jasindo Dibekukan BNP2TKI."

22 *Ministerial Regulation (Manpower) No. 23/MEN/V/2006 on Asuransi Tenaga Kerja Indonesia*, article 18.

23 Asuransi Jasindo, "Jasindo Bayar Klaim 4.985 TKI."

on its promise to meet the deadline set for it to start paying claims on time.[24] In addition to these failures, the BNP2TKI justified taking action against Jasindo for procedural reasons such as having ignored calls to enter policy details in the BNP2TKI's data management system.

Acquiescing to the view that the BNP2TKI had in this case overstepped its mandate, Hidayat reversed the moratorium.[25] However, the issue of insurance continued to be a major irritant in the relationship between the BNP2TKI and the ministry.[26] The ministry justified setting the price above the market rate and forcing insurers into a consortium on two grounds. First, the arrangement is said to prevent price competition that leads to the offering of bare-bones cover, and second, it ensures that the industry had sufficient resources to handle expensive items such as hospitalization. However, according to labour recruitment company owners, the ratio of payouts is so low that insurers offer to channel part of the policy cost back to recruiters through kickbacks.[27] Insurers and recruiters cooperate to further reduce the probability of pay outs by concealing the fact that migrant workers have insurance policies.[28] Labour recruitment companies have an interest in hiding claimable items from the state that could result in legal sanctions (which also frequently entailed some form of extortion) such as incidents that occur during the pre-departure phase.[29] When incidents occur overseas, migrants frequently return home without all of the necessary documents for a successful claim, such as a cover letter from the closest consular office. As this suggests, payment of compensation is generally not a high priority for insurers.

A key problem with the system was the way in which insurance companies were appointed. In 1998 the Minister for Manpower turned over authority to appoint insurers to the Ministry of Finance, which managed the licensing system.[30] But by 2006 the Ministry of Manpower had returned to the New Order practice whereby the minister decided which insurance companies

24 Asuransi Jasindo, "Tanggapan Atas Pemberitaan 'Pembekuan Asuransi TKI Jasindo.'"

25 Asuransi Jasindo, "Pembekuan Asuransi TKI Jasindo Dicabut"; Asuransi Jasindo, "BNP2TKI Akan Cabut Pembekuan Jasindo."

26 Following a meeting about the consortium, Hidayat made a widely quoted statement outside the Minister for Manpower's office those insurers were 'all assholes' that could not be trusted to come good on their policies. See "Jumhur: Asuransi TKI Berengsek Semua."

27 Interview data, Malang, 28 September 2009.

28 Palmer, "Discretion and the Trafficking-like Practices of the Indonesian State."

29 Hernawan and Supriyadi, "Penerapan Sanksi Terhadap Pelanggaran PPTKIS Dalam Pra Penempatan TKI Di Luar Negeri."

30 See Chapter 2.

could provide mandatory cover to migrant workers.[31] Consistent with the relevant ministerial regulation, a selection team sought applications from insurers claiming to meet the minimum criteria. As the most important criterion was that the company had a licence to insure from the Ministry of Finance, a list of applicants was sent to the relevant division there to seek confirmation. A bureaucrat from the ministry's selection team recalls that he then helped to organize applications from most to least qualified, according to the ministry's technical criteria.[32] After doing so, however, he was asked to leave the room by the 'boys club',[33] which included Director General for Guidance of Overseas Labour Placement, Gusti Made Arka, Director for Placement, Abdul Malik Harahap, and the head of the legal bureau, Sunarno.[34] In conjunction with the minister, this team then worked out between themselves which companies to appoint.

Similarly, although the ministry maintained formal authority to set migrant wages, the BNP2TKI intervened with the intention of challenging the status quo. In the first 100 days of operation, the BNP2TKI sought wage rises for Indonesian migrant workers in eight countries. For employment in Singapore, labour recruitment companies in Indonesia were told that the BNP2TKI would only process recruits for whom employers in Singapore had agreed to pay twenty per cent more than the going rate, raising monthly wages from SGD 280 (USD 188) to SGD 350 (USD 226).[35] In another example, recruiters dealing in migrant labour for Saudi Arabia were given two years to comply with a larger increase from SAR 600 (USD 156) to SAR 800 (USD 208),[36] the first pay rise the migrant workers had received in more than two decades.[37] These higher wages enabled recruiters to collect more fees, as the recruitment charge is generally calculated as months of salary rather than a set figure. In principle, the ministry was supportive of the BNP2TKI's initiative because Indonesians' wages are relatively

31 *Ministerial Regulation (Manpower) No. 23/MEN/V/2006 on Asuransi Tenaga Kerja Indonesia.*

32 Interview data, Jakarta, 9 June 2010.

33 This term was used in English by my informant.

34 In a later role, he could honestly say to colleagues in other agencies, such as the Ministry of Foreign Affairs, that he only knew from hearsay that the team exchanged appointment for a combination of financial contributions to the Minister's for Manpower political party and the ministry's off-budget account as well as that they gave preferential treatment to an insurer which was closely associated with the minister's son.

35 "Upah Minimum TKI Di Singapura Naik 20 Persen."

36 Badan Nasional Penempatan dan Perlindungan Tenaga Kerja Indonesia, "Gaji TKI PLRT Singapura Dan Hong Kong Naik Pada 2012."

37 Damayanti, "Arab Saudi Tunda 50 Ribu Visa Calon TKI."

low compared to those of other nationalities doing the same work. Nonetheless, officials in the ministry expressed frustration at BNP2TKI circulars, released without prior consultation, instructing them, for example, to reduce the proportion of wages that the migration industry collects from migrant workers each month for repayment of recruitment debts.[38]

As these examples suggest, in seeking to establish a pro-worker image for the BNP2TKI, Hidayat acted in ways that exacerbated tensions in the agency's relationship with the ministry. The ministry responded by progressively excluding the BNP2TKI from direct involvement in administration of the private-to-private scheme.[39] In the case of insurance, the ministry reduced the BNP2TKI's role to that of monitor and reporter in an amendment to the law in September 2007, a few months after the Jasindo débâcle.[40] The ministry then overrode the BNP2TKI's authority to finalize the migration process in March 2008 after labour recruitment companies complained that rigid enforcement of procedures was causing a bottleneck in the system.[41] Ultimately, these different understandings of what constituted operation and regulation culminated in decisions on the part of the ministry to cut the BNP2TKI out of processes involving labour recruitment companies altogether. To those in the ministry, the BNP2TKI's pro-migrant posturing further complicated their already complex relationships with the migration industry.

Labour Recruitment Companies as an Economic and Political Resource

Another factor that complicated the relationship was competition over access to the recruitment industry's economic resources. The ministry has a long history of outsourcing financial responsibility for problems encountered

---

38 *Agency Circular Memorandum (BNP2TKI) No. B.307/BNP2TKI/VI/2007 on Pemotongan Upah TKI Dan Penindakan Terhadap Agency Di Hong Kong.*

39 Private-to-private describes the scheme in which private employment company owners supply Indonesian workers directly to employers or through partner recruiters overseas.

40 *Ministerial Regulation (Manpower) No. 20/MEN/X/2007 on Asuransi Tenaga Kerja Indonesia*, articles 16(1) and 24. The amendment was made when the minister revised the law before the administrative court was set to hear make a decision about whether it contravened the constitution as claimed by one of the country's associations of employment companies. The Government rarely wins these cases so the minister is thought to have sought to pre-empt the court with a revised law. See "Perlindungan TKI, Antara Asuransi Dan Jaminan Sosial."

41 *Director General Decree (Guidance of Labour Placement) No. 68/PPTK/III/2008 on Pembentukan Tim Pelaksana Pembekalan Penempatan Tenaga Kerja.*

by migrant workers to labour recruitment companies.[42] Insurance companies covered the cost of handling frequent incidents such as death and sickness. However, labour recruitment companies generally footed the bill for costs that require immediate payment.[43] The budget cycle invariably allocates inadequate funds for flights and other expenses, which puts consular offices in a difficult position given that the law increasingly requires them to handle those issues regardless of their financial capacity to do so.

Labour recruitment companies also bankroll government agency activities.[44] In 2009 for example, the Secretary-General of APJATI accompanied the ministry's Directorate-General Secretary for Guidance of Labour Placement on an official trip to Malaysia for the purpose of working out a new bilateral agreement on recruitment with the Malaysian Ministry of Internal Affairs.[45] An informant in the Indonesian Ministry of Manpower explained that the initiative on this particular occasion came from Indonesian labour recruitment companies wanting the Indonesian delegation to demand a larger cut of the fees that their Malaysian business partners charge to migrant workers.[46] The association covered the cost of international travel, hotel accommodation, entertainment and even paid the delegation a per diem. The close relationship between Indonesian officials and labour recruitment companies has not gone unnoticed by Malaysian recruiters, who suspect that Indonesian officials and recruiters work together to maximize their ability to privately profit from the business.[47] But while labour recruitment companies in Indonesia appear keen to subsidize the state's political work, there is a strong feeling of resentment among them that the state's administrative apparatus is oriented to first and foremost serve the private interests of government officials.[48]

The motivation to compete for access to the economic resources of labour recruitment companies is partly tied to the patronage that government officials offer. In the ministry, the relationship is expressed in terms of patrons

42 Palmer, "Public-Private Partnerships in the Administration and Control of Indonesian Migrant Labour in Hong Kong."

43 Palmer, "Discretion and the Trafficking-like Practices of the Indonesian State."

44 Employment companies' involvement in the migration business has grown at the expense of opportunities for defence personnel, which were greatest when Admiral Sudomo was Minister for Manpower. However, the 2002 establishment of the police as a separate institution from the defence forces took with it jurisdiction over law enforcement, which strategically positioned police officers to grant exemptions from the law.

45 Interview data, Kuala Lumpur, 21 December 2009.

46 Interview data, Jakarta, 17 February 2010.

47 Interview data, Kuala Lumpur, 7 September 2010.

48 Interview data, Jakarta, 3 December 2009.

and 'protégés' (*binaan*). In practice, this relationship enables labour recruitment companies to negotiate exemptions from the law and avoid sanctions for illegal behaviour. Government officials in strategic positions can make other such interventions, as indicated by the line-up for the election of APJATI's chairperson in 2008.[49] Two contending police officers (an Inspector-General and a Grand Commissioner) had come to own labour recruitment companies in retirement and promised to use their clout with the state to further the industry's interests. The winner was formerly the head of a police division that investigated evidence of illegality and compiled cases for prosecution. Prior to that, he was the head of Jakarta's metropolitan police office, in whose jurisdiction the majority of labour recruitment companies are formally registered. As this suggests, relevant administrative and law enforcement roles can bring government officials to become privately involved in the recruitment industry.

Close association with labour recruitment companies has also helped bureaucrats and recruiters with political leadership ambitions win elections. There are rumours that those who profit from the business occupy positions in the national legislature. However, their presence is much more obvious at the sub-national levels. In 2000 Masduki Yusak, who was Pusat AKAN's contact person for the ILO in the 1980s,[50] was elected vice regent by the Kendal District legislature in Central Java. His campaign was in part funded using wealth that he accumulated during his time working in the Ministry of Manpower.[51] In another example, a labour recruitment company owner from PKB – the party of the Minister – was elected to the Surabaya City legislature in 2009. The same man was subsequently appointed secretary for the East Java chapter of the government-recognized labour recruitment companies' association APJATI in 2011.[52] APJATI's chairperson ran as a Great Indonesia Movement Party (Partai Gerakan Indonesia Raya, Gerindra) candidate in the 2010 election for Vice Regent of Malang District. Ultimately, he lost the election but then convinced the victor to switch parties and take over his role as head of the local Gerindra chapter. As demonstrated by these examples, competitive elections

---

49 Badan Nasional Penempatan dan Perlindungan Tenaga Kerja Indonesia, "Drs Nurfaizi MM Terpilih Sebagai Ketua APJATI 2008–2012."

50 See Chapter 2.

51 Masduki Yusak was unseated two years into the position on the basis of irregularities in his report of personal wealth. See "Di Balik Pelengseran Wakil Bupati Kendal (2-Habis): Bagaimana Tanggung Jawab Panitia Pemilihan Dulu?"; "Wakil Bupati Kendal Diberhentikan: Putusan Aklamasi Dewan"; "Kilas Balik Perjalanan Masduki Yusak."

52 Dinas Tenaga Kerja Transmigrasi dan Penduduk, "Mundur Dari APJATI, Deklarasikan IEMSA."

have installed those who profit privately from the recruitment industry in positions of power that span the executive and legislative branches of government.

Labour recruitment company owners without political aspirations have been known to make financial contributions to political parties that control strategic government agencies, including the Ministry of Manpower.[53] It is common practice for leaders of political parties to solicit financial support from such interest groups.[54] Suparno and his successor, Muhaimin Iskandar – both cadres of the PKB and who served as Minister for Manpower – are no exception. Bureaucrats within the ministry claim that labour recruitment companies made all manner of contributions to the party as part of an attempt to secure benefits for their businesses in amendments to regulations pertaining to migrant labour. These contributions reportedly grew under Suparno as part of a lobby to have the ministry curtail the BNP2TKI's role.[55] Later BNP2TKI staff were not surprised when Suparno's successor, Iskandar, announced that he would continue with the controversial curtailments immediately after taking over the leadership of PKB. Even ministry officials believed that Iskandar's position was inevitable given the large number of labour recruitment company owners who attended the national congresses of PKB and its affiliated organization, Nahdlatul Ulama, the following year. As party chairperson, Iskandar was largely responsible for securing the funds necessary to hold the conventions; and, as is the case with so many other government officials in this area of administration, labour recruitment companies sought, and may have even responded to opportunities to exchange money for, more influence over the overseas labour migration programme.

Career Advancement and Personalities

These structural forms of competition were complicated by institutionalized corruption. The New Order regime bequeathed a generation of officials to post-authoritarian Indonesia that expected to secure appointments and

---

53 For a detailed analysis of how and why political parties are predatory and offer patronage that would otherwise be provided by the state, see Mietzner, *Money, Power, and Ideology: Political Parties in Post-Authoritarian Indonesia.*

54 Indonesian political leaders are well known for using private resources to finance party activity. See for example Jusuf Kalla's admission that he distributed money to party cadres to pay for the national congress in which he was elected chairperson. See "Jusuf Kalla Akui Bocoran Wikileaks Benar." There is a positive correlation between this and corruption cases involving governors, mayors, district heads and legislators. See Mietzner, "Funding Pilkada: Illegal Campaign Financing In Indonesia's Local Elections."

55 "Erman Suparno Siap Lepas Posisi Bendahara Umum PKB."

promotions through financial contributions in addition to merit.[56] Appointment processes always have a political dimension, but never more so than in New Order Indonesia, where President Suharto introduced a 'franchise' system in which officials could buy promotions.[57] In addition to making him and his family wealthy, this system had the effect of instituting a strong but informal command structure that sought to maintain compliance within the rank and file. Political leaders and senior bureaucrats often paid the highest fees in return for appointment to positions that would give them power to bestow privileges on clients, who are involved in the business of migration.[58] During the New Order era, this system encouraged government officials to seek rents in their relationships with business or 'privately tax' the economy.[59]

These practices have continued in the ministry since that time. What has changed is that political parties rather than an autocratic president have come to determine who is appointed to most positions in the executive branch. By the end of 2009, the ministry had had six different ministers, originating from four different parties, under just as many presidents since Suharto's resignation in 1998. Bureaucrats lament that the political parties have effectively hollowed out the ministry's human resources division, which does little more than rubber-stamp appointments upon the minister's recommendation.[60] Although successful candidates had previously been expected to make financial contributions in exchange for appointments, the formal process included a performative dimension, where personnel made presentations in a tender-like system. Although it was clear that this aspect had not counted for more than financial contributions, bureaucrats appreciated the ritual, which has since disappeared. Those who experienced that system directly were flummoxed to learn that political parties allowed payments to be made in instalments after taking up the new posts.[61]

---

56 McLeod, "Institutionalized Public Sector Corruption: A Legacy of the Soeharto Franchise"; Kristiansen and Ramli, "Buying an Income: The Market for Civil Service Positions in Indonesia."

57 On this phenomenon in Indonesia, see McLeod, "Institutionalized Public Sector Corruption: A Legacy of the Soeharto Franchise"; McLeod, "Soeharto's Indonesia: A Better Class of Corruption." For a comparative perspective, see this article on the Ukraine: Darden, "The Integrity of Corrupt States: Graft as an Informal State Institution."

58 See Chapter 1 for a discussion of how decentralization may have created a local oligarchy and encouraged the development of patron-client relationships in relation to management of the overseas migration programme outside the state's centre.

59 McLeod, "Government-Business Relations in Indonesia," 148.

60 Interview data, Jakarta, 9 February 2010.

61 Interview data, Kuala Lumpur, 10 February 2011; Interview data, Singapore, 25 January 2011.

Those who were inducted into the bureaucracy during the 'thuggish days' (*hari preman*) of the New Order period quickly discovered that bureaucrats had to be less brazen when seeking rents in the post-authoritarian context. Under the New Order, one low-ranking official reported being required to collect contributions for his directorate-general's off-budget account.[62] Kickbacks became more prevalent in the post-New Order period, as these officials grew less convinced that their managers could guarantee immunity to criminal punishment after anti-corruption laws were introduced in 1999.[63] Senior ministry bureaucrats convicted of corruption in the years following the rise of political parties are also partly a symptom of financially driven appointments. At least two former directors-general were convicted of corruption between 2007 and 2010.[64] As this suggests, the post-authoritarian years have presented a much more complicated – but not impossible – context in which to encourage bureaucrats to toe the line.

Individuals with personal ambition to hold top posts have nonetheless taken advantage of the opportunities that this institutional context continues to offer. In 2007 Arka, for many years the most senior executive official in the overseas labour migration programme, was appointed caretaker for the Directorate-General of Guidance of Labour Placement in a move that was widely understood as compensation for the fact that he missed out on the top

62 This official worked in the directorate that authorized foreign nationals to work in Indonesia, would collect part of the Rp 7,000,000 (USD 700) fee was paid to the Ministry of Manpower, Directorate-General for Immigration and the police, and then deposit the rest of it in the off-budget account each week.

63 *Law No. 31 on Eradication of the Crime of Corruption*. This law mandated the creation of the Corruption Eradication Commission (Komisi Pemberantasan Korupsi, KPK), which was established in 2003. The commission uses 'aggressive tactics' in the investigation of corruption. See Horowitz, *Constitutional Change and Democracy in Indonesia*, 230. It has had a high success rate securing conviction of corruption cases relative to the attorney-general. See Butt, *Corruption and Law in Indonesia*. Although these anti-corruption measures have targeted the big fish (*ikan kakap*), the conviction of senior government officials has sent a clear message to more junior staff that they might sooner or later be held accountable for corrupt behaviour. See, for example, Interview data, Jakarta, 21 December 2010.

64 "Eks Pejabat Depnakertrans Divonis 3 Tahun Bui"; Komisi Yudisial, "Mantan Pejabat Depnakertrans Divonis 4 Tahun Penjara." One of those found guilty lamented that the courts showed little understanding of how the budgeting process worked in practice, while another complained that Jacob Nuwa Wea, who was Minister for Manpower at the time, was not interrogated, although only he could have authorized the corrupt activity. See hukumonline.com, "Mantan Dirjen Depnakertrans Divonis Tiga Tahun Penjara."

position in the BNP2TKI.[65] That position remained in caretaker mode for the next four years, attracting the attention of other bureaucrats who, like Arka, aspired to hold a top post before retirement. Abdul Malik Harahap and then Sunarno would later be appointed to the position by Iskandar. In part, the fact that none of these bureaucrats made a successful bid for a full appointment is a consequence of the role each had played in shoring up greater control for the ministry over the overseas labour migration programme at the expense of the BNP2TKI between 2007 and 2010.

One official who succeeded in advancing his career in this institutional context was Harahap. He had gained a reputation for being competent and forceful after ending an industrial relations dispute between the state owned enterprise Pertamina and workers during a two and a half year assignment to Bengkalis District in Mainland Riau as head of the ministry's regional office between 1999 and 2001.[66] It is as a consequence of this experience – and wealth that he accumulated there – that Harahap was then appointed as Labour Attaché to the Embassy of Indonesia in Malaysia, a post in which he served from 2002 to 2005. During this overseas assignment, he was involved in an informal system that collected illegal fees from Indonesian migrants through intermediaries in exchange for services such as issuing passports.[67] Harahap emerged from the scandal unscathed, although a former Suharto financial advisor claims to have seen boxes of Malaysian currency in the official's office at the time. Harahap subsequently secured appointment as secretary-general to assist Arka with management of the Directorate-General of Guidance of Overseas Labour Placement uncharacteristically soon after returning to Indonesia (2005–2007).

Contestation

At the time of the BNP2TKI's establishment, Arka and Harahap held the highest positions in the overseas labour migration programme. They were most

65 Arka had replaced Soeramsihono as Director General for the Guidance and Placement of Overseas Labour in 2003. The position was left vacant largely because the Minister for Manpower was unable to put forward a suitable candidate for consideration by the Presidential Office and a string of other government organizations, such as the National Intelligence Agency. See "Indonesia Siapkan Evakuasi TKI Dari Timur Tengah."

66 Interview data, Kuala Lumpur, 14 September 2009.

67 In a particularly high profile case, his Ambassador was later convicted for permitting the Embassy to charge these fees to migrant workers who sought to take advantage of the Malaysian government's amnesty for unlawful migration status. Harahap's involvement is based on discussions with his former colleagues. For detail about the corruption case, see hukumonline.com, "RUU Perlindungan Tenaga Kerja Diharapkan Hapus Monopoli PJTKI."

aggrieved when Hidayat and Edi Sudibyo were given the equivalent positions within the BNP2TKI.[68] Arka and Harahap lobbied the Minister for Manpower to move them to another division in the ministry before the automatic transfer of officials in the Directorate-General of Guidance of Overseas Labour Placement to the BNP2TKI, scheduled for 1 March 2007.[69] The Human Resources Bureau reassigned them to the Directorate-General of Guidance of Internal Labour Placement as general staff with no executive authority. This in itself was not unusual, as other senior officials frequently spend some time in limbo between appointments. The Directorate-General of Guidance of Overseas Labour Placement was abolished six months later and its residual domains of activity, such as policymaking and standard setting, were organized into the newly-minted Directorate of Overseas Placement, charged with overseeing the country's various labour placement programmes.[70] Harahap was immediately appointed Director for Overseas Placement. Arka had to wait for Tjetje Al Anshori, who had served as director-general in their temporary division, to serve a term as director-general in the new division before Arka was given the post.

This disgruntlement effectively made a bad situation even worse in terms of the agencies' institutional capacity to share control. By the end of 2008, the uncooperative relationship between the ministry and the BNP2TKI was openly antagonistic. In March, the ministry had intervened against the BNP2TKI in response to complaints from the recruitment industry that BNP2TKI's policies had prevented 8,000 Indonesians from leaving the country for jobs overseas. Harahap, now Director for Overseas Placement, announced plans to temporarily take control of the BNP2TKI's administrative roles in an urgent meeting with labour recruitment company owners.[71] In April, the minister met with the head of the BNP2TKI to discuss an alternative division of labour in which the ministry would administer the private-to-private scheme and the BNP2TKI would administer government-to-government arrangements.[72] Hidayat disagreed, but by May it became clear that the ministry had no intention of disbanding the ad hoc team it had set up in March. In response, Hidayat and his Deputy for Placement, Ade Adam Noch, discussed legal measures that

68 Interview data, Kuala Lumpur, 21 December 2009; Singapore, 31 December 2009; Jakarta, 9 February 2010.

69 Interview data, Jakarta, 10 June 2009.

70 *Ministerial Regulation (Manpower) No. 5/MEN/IV/2007 on Organisasi Dan Tata Kerja Departemen Tenaga Kerja Dan Transmigrasi.*

71 Direktur Penempatan Tenaga Kerja Luar Negeri, "Undangan."

72 *Agency Regulation (BNP2TKI) No. 31/KA/V/2008 on Prosedur Tetap Pelayanan Penerbitan Surat Izin Pengerahan Dan Persetujuan Penempatan Tenaga Kerja Indonesia Untuk Kepentingan Perusahaan Sendiri.*

would stall the ministry's attempt to do so. The result was a BNP2TKI regulation in which the agency claimed authority to issue recruitment certificates.[73] The BNP2TKI justified the measure on the grounds that the minister had been required to appoint an official for the purpose since promulgation of the overseas migration law in 2004 but had not yet done so. In this way, the BNP2TKI compensated for loss of control over administrative functions at the end of the pre-departure process by claiming legal authority to permit recruitment of labour migrants.

As part of the ministry's attempt to reclaim control, the Directorate-General of Guidance of Labour Placement set up a sub-unit on ministry owned land behind the BNP2TKI's technical implementation office in East Jakarta. In September 2008, the Minister for Manpower decreed that Harahap would assume responsibility for issuing recruitment certificates.[74] Within the next month the director general, Anshori, launched operations, moving to the role of service provision, instructing labour recruitment company associations to inform members that the BNP2TKI had been called on to cease activity. The ministry also announced that any recruitment certificates issued by the BNP2TKI had to be re-registered with their office in East Jakarta.[75] Anshori threatened labour recruitment companies with penalties under the overseas migration and anti-trafficking laws.[76] The director general sent a carbon copy to the Indonesian National Police (INP) to inform them of the policy shift. However, the BNP2TKI continued to communicate with the police primarily through the Director for Security, who was a seconded police officer.[77] In response, the minister followed up by requesting the police to limit coordination concerning private labour recruitment companies to his portfolio. Labour recruitment companies were given until the beginning of February 2009 to redirect their business to the ministry.

Hidayat and senior officials in the placement division of the BNP2TKI greeted this policy shift in high dudgeon. They publicly accused the ministry

---

73 Ibid., menimbang b.

74 *Ministerial Decree (Manpower) No. 200/MEN/IX/2008 on Penunjukan Pejabat Penerbitan Surat Izin Pengerahan*; *Ministerial Decree (Manpower) No. 201/MEN/IX/2008 on Penunjukan Pejabat Penerbitan Persetujuan Penempatan Tenaga Kerja Indonesia Di Luar Negeri Untuk Kepentingan Perusahaan Sendiri.*

75 *Director General Memorandum Circular (Guidance of Labour Placement) No. 14/PPTK-TKLN/X/2008 on Penerbitan Surat Ijin Pengerahan (SIP) Dan Surat Persetujuan Penempatan (SPP) Tenaga Kerja Indonesia Untuk Kepentingan Perusahaan Sendiri.*

76 *Law No. 21 on Eradication of the Crime of Trafficking in Persons*; *Law No. 39 on Placement and Protection of Indonesian Workers Overseas.*

77 Badan Nasional Penempatan dan Perlindungan Tenaga Kerja Indonesia, "Jumhur: Penempatan TKI 2008 Lebih Banyak."

of letting labour recruitment companies dictate policy direction and subvert the law. A strong political motivation for establishing the BNP2TKI had been a drive for improvement (*semangat perbaikan*),[78] which the ministry had proved incapable of delivering. The overseas migration law mandated that the BNP2TKI provide all public services that migrant workers required, which further strengthened their officials' refusal to accept the substance of the ministry's new regulation. The BNP2TKI even refused to acknowledge the new regulation in formal correspondence with provincial governors and local government manpower offices.[79] Labour recruitment company owners were wary of the BNP2TKI's approach because they wanted the valid regulation to form the basis of administration, since it gave them legal access to the system. However, company owners in Jakarta and Malang admitted to obtaining recruitment certificates from both government agencies in order to avoid creating the impression that they supported one group of officials over the other while the policy shift remained contested.[80]

The Minister for Manpower, meanwhile, claimed that its attempts to cut the BNP2TKI out of the private-to-private scheme were motivated by a commitment to the government's ongoing decentralization programme. In 2007 the government issued a detailed regulation that mapped out a division of labour for all policy sectors, identifying the principal roles that each tier of government was expected to perform.[81] The overseas labour migration programme was one of seven areas that required intervention within the Manpower portfolio.[82] Using these principles as a justification for amendment, the ministry removed any mention of the BNP2TKI, which it claimed was out of step with the decentralization agenda, having maintained its implementation units in the provinces. The minister reserved authority to issue recruitment certificates but left open the possibility of delegating the provision of pre-departure training and finalization of the pre-departure processes to provincial authorities.[83] Ministerial Regulation No. 23/MEN/XII/2008 on Overseas Indonesian Workers Insurance, issued a few days later, required local government to help organize

78 Interview data, Jakarta, 21 December 2010.

79 hukumonline.com, "PPTKIS Siap Mengirim TKI Meski Tanpa BNP2TKI."

80 Interview data, Malang, 11 August 2009.

81 *Ministerial Regulation (Manpower) No. 18/MEN/IX/2007 on Pelaksanaan Penempatan Dan Perlindungan Tenaga Kerja Indonesia Di Luar Negeri*, n.d.

82 *Governmental Regulation No. 38/2008 on Pembagian Urusan Pemerintahan Antara Pemerintah, Pemerintahan Daerah Provinsi, Dan Pemerintahan Daerah Kabupaten/Kota*, appendix N5.

83 *Ministerial Regulation (Manpower) No. 22/MEN/XII/2008 on Pelaksanaan Penempatan Dan Perlindungan Tenaga Kerja Indonesia Di Luar Negeri.*

migrants' insurance claims.[84] Together these regulations offered a new division of labour in which sub-national governments were called on to play a much larger role in the administration of the private-to private scheme, and the BNP2TKI no role at all.

Negotiation in the Regions

The ministry claimed that the reorganization of authority was necessary to bring the overseas labour migration programme's institutional structure into line with the decentralization agenda. However, the fact that the ministry as a central government agency had taken on the BNP2TKI's administrative roles in the Jakarta Special Region reveals a different motivation. Labour recruitment company owners immediately understood that the ministry's main target was to take control of the overseas labour migration programme in Jakarta. After all, they had successfully lobbied for the ministry to intervene against the BNP2TKI to expedite finalization of the pre-departure process in March 2008. By contrast, mid-career bureaucrats in the ministry took a little longer to understand the complex motivations behind the policy shift. One official who was reassigned to the unit in East Jakarta operation left the ministry under the impression that the arrangement was only temporary.[85] However, as months passed she grew increasingly uncomfortable meeting BNP2TKI officials at the front gate because by then it was clear to all that the ministry had no intention of relinquishing control to Jakarta's provincial government.

The ministry could intervene directly in Jakarta because it already had structures in place to provide the services that were needed. The ad hoc committee, which was established to take control of BNP2TKI's administrative roles in March 2008, was never disbanded. The Directorate of Overseas Placement had subsumed BNP2TKI's roles into its placement section and officials had already set up systems to verify necessary documents, such as health and training certificates. The minister never entertained the idea of delegating authority to issue recruitment certificates to provincial governments mostly because he wanted to maintain centralized control of authorization to recruit migrant workers. But by December 2008, the ministry had promulgated a regulation that enabled the minister to delegate authority to provide pre-departure training and finalize the pre-departure process. However, the minister never formalized the delegation of authority through a ministerial decree, largely because he had no intention of doing so in Jakarta, where the ministry was still

84 *Ministerial Regulation (Manpower) No. 23/MEN/XII/2008 on Asuransi Tenaga Kerja Indonesia.*

85 Interview data, Jakarta, 17 February 2010.

embroiled in a struggle with the provincial government.[86] After all, one of the reasons for the ministry's March intervention had been to shield labour recruitment companies that sent around 20,000 migrant workers to Saudi Arabia through Jakarta each month from interference by other state agencies.[87]

The ministry was far less interested in administration of labour migrants leaving regional centres. It had lost the best part of its foothold outside Jakarta after assets were transferred to sub-national governments and the BNP2TKI. The land and buildings that the ministry retained in regional centres were generally located far from the major embarkation points. It was politically difficult to negotiate the acquisition of new buildings to directly perform administrative roles, first because the BNP2TKI had assets and staff in place, and second because the ministry would have to make a case for why the administration could not otherwise be carried out by a sub-national authority. With little chance of performing these roles itself, the ministry approached provincial governments with the proposal that it assume responsibility for the processing of recruits in the province's jurisdiction.[88] The ministry outreach team began working out arrangements with provincial government authorities that would enable informal delegation of responsibility to perform the administrative roles, starting in Yogyakarta.[89]

The outreach team used a range of strategies to disseminate the new procedures and standards through what bureaucrats in Indonesia refer to as *sosialisasi*, which includes public hearings, announcements in the mass media, technical coordination meetings and negotiations that involve some form of horse-trading in order to secure compliance. Negotiations were difficult, as the ministry was effectively asking provincial governments to take on responsibility for elements of the overseas labour migration programme without a formal budget allocation. The 2009 budget for providing pre-departure training, verifying migration documents and producing overseas identity cards was allocated to the BNP2TKI by the president in 2008.[90] The ministry reclaimed

86 See Chapter 4.

87 This is not to say that these workers are from Jakarta. The opposite is in fact true, as the majority come from provinces in Java and the Lesser Sunda Islands and only transit there. By contrast, the major destination for workers transiting through regional centres is frequently Malaysia. See Badan Nasional Penempatan dan Perlindungan Tenaga Kerja Indonesia, *Data Penempatan TKI Ke Luar Negeri: Tahun 1994–2007*, 10–23.

88 The major destination for workers transiting through regional centres is most often Malaysia.

89 hukumonline.com, "PPTKIS Siap Mengirim TKI Meski Tanpa BNP2TKI."

90 *Presidential Regulation No. 72/2008 on Rincian Anggaran Belanja Pemerintah Pusat Tahun Anggaran 2009.*

the BNP2TKI's roles on 9 December before securing the Minister for Finance's support for a budget amendment to bankroll the program. From the BNP2TKI's perspective, the budgeting cycle had already begun. The budget would not be accessible until 1 January 2009 but, as is common practice in Indonesia, the BNP2TKI had already started arranging expensive procurements from 29 November 2008, the date on which it was formally announced. As this suggests, any attempt by the ministry to appropriate that allocation would be met with fierce resistance from the BNP2TKI. The ministry outreach team, therefore, sought to convince provincial governments to assume responsibility without a formal budget allocation in that budget cycle in exchange for promises of compensation in the future.

Outside Jakarta, the outreach team was forced to be more tentative in its approach because it had to work through governors, who are line managers for the provincial manpower office. This particularly frustrated the team leader, Director for Overseas Placement, Harahap, who had headed a regional manpower office in the final years before decentralization.[91] By contrast, the BNP2TKI was still able to directly perform its administrative roles in the regions through its implementation units. Through strategic appointments, these units sought to cultivate working relationships with relevant sub-national government units in each location, whose cooperation was key to achieving their objectives. The quality of these relationships differed from site to site, and the BNP2TKI frequently recalled staff who had failed to build strong links with the local officials who controlled civil administration, labour and immigration matters. In 2009 for example, the head of the BNP2TKI unit in Pekanbaru was replaced by a colleague from Jakarta because relationships with the provincial manpower office had deteriorated to such an extent that the units rarely communicated.[92] In more successful sites, manpower staff were frequently quite happy with the status quo, whereby the BNP2TKI office performed the administration with its own formal budget allocation, and were thus reluctant to respond to the ministry's urgings for them to assume control.[93]

The outreach team used technical coordination meetings as a forum through which to sell the new procedures to stakeholders in the regions – an initiative that quickly gained a reputation for falling short of its objectives. At one such meeting in Pekanbaru, the heads of relevant local government agencies were invited to a two day event that included payment for return transportation, two nights' accommodation and a per diem as permitted by the

91 See Chapter 2.

92 Interview data, Pekanbaru, 21 April 2010.

93 See Chapter 4.

law.[94] The meeting was cut short after the first day, ostensibly because agencies had sent officials who not only lacked understanding of context beyond the narrow focus of their own responsibilities but also were too junior to influence internal policymaking processes. This problem was partly due to the fact that attendance at such meetings is never strictly determined by rank. Rather, officials are sent based on consideration of other principles that help manage relationships within individual agencies, such as ensuring that everyone gets their turn. Such meetings are important financially not just for individuals given the opportunity to participate, but for their institutions. Participants attend with the expectation that they will sign invoices for expenses in excess of what they receive, as it is understood that the kickbacks are a way of funding government activity for which there is not an adequate budget allocation.

The technical coordination meetings were just one of many strategies used by the ministry to generate funds to support their attack on the BNP2TKI. In Jakarta, the Directorate of Overseas Placement charged labour recruitment companies for the inclusion of each recruit in the pre-departure seminars at its unit in East Jakarta. The revenue it earned contributed around USD 100,000 to government coffers each month, creating a source of income to finance the provision of other services, such as the production of overseas identity cards.[95]

From the perspective of provincial agencies critical of this approach, the issue was not so much the backstage forces that motivated policy change. The stronger consideration was a matter of legitimacy, as they doubted whether they could justify the new policy direction in ways that allowed them to claim that they were acting within the boundaries of the law (*jalur hukum*). The argument that provincial authorities could point to another political objective in the system – decentralization – did not allay their concerns that the Ministry of Manpower's regulation conflicted with a presidential regulation and the overseas migration law. Furthermore, the fact that the BNP2TKI was in a position to provide the services free of charge also meant the proposal was very difficult to justify.

Provincial authorities generally preferred the status quo for these reasons. Equally important, however, was the fact that the contest had not yet produced a clear victor. As a consequence, they were reluctant to choose sides, hedging their bets on whatever the outcome might be. Shortly after the contested ministerial regulation came into force, a trade union, whose advisory council

---

94 Participant observation at the BNP2TKI's Technical Coordination Meeting in Pekanbaru, April 2010.

95 See the BNP2TKI's PowerPoint slides at the Open Hearing Meeting in Jakarta at the People's Representative Council, 14 February 2010.

Hidayat chaired, filed a judicial review that challenged the legality of sidelining the BNP2TKI.[96] Harahap was in Tanjung Pinang, the provincial capital of Riau Islands province, when the court ordered the Minister for Manpower to cancel the regulation. Incidentally, only a day earlier, Harahap had told the head of the BNP2TKI's technical implementation unit there privately that the ministry had taken the necessary measures to ensure victory. But after the verdict, Harahap ended the ministry's mission prematurely, recognizing that the provincial manpower office would prove even more reluctant than before to agree to assume control of the BNP2TKI's roles. The team returned to Jakarta, where the relevant ministry officials presumably held conversations about what measures were necessary to maintain control in the interim.

Mediation by the Judicial and Legislative Branches

As this example suggests, the BNP2TKI involved the judicial and legislative branches of government in its attempt to erode support for the ministry. These interventions were ultimately ineffective because the ministry chose to ignore its intervention. However, it showed that the other branches of government deemed the minister's policy direction and treatment of the BNP2TKI to be illegal. As a consequence, the ministry became ensnared in an 'illegality trap',[97] which prevented the outreach team from framing the ministry's strategy in positive terms.

The first judgement, which the ministry ignored, was a Supreme Court decision in which the judiciary invalidated the content of the disputed ministerial regulation. Convinced that the judiciary would use its authority to invalidate the regulation, the BNP2TKI took the case to the Supreme Court. As soon as the regulation came into force, Hidayat coordinated the registration process for judicial review through his connections in the Amalgamated Free Trade Unions of Indonesia (Gabungan Serikat Pekerja Merdeka Indonesia, GASPERMINDO). The court immediately took on the case partly because of claims that the regulation was inconsistent with the principle of the hierarchy of laws, and because the decrees caused legal uncertainty. Just over a month later, the court invalidated the regulation, arguing that it contravened three higher level laws and indeed caused confusion.[98] The ministry was given 90 days to reverse the rules

96 Supreme Court, "Legal Decision No. 5 P/HUM/2009."

97 Jones-Correa and de Graauw, "The Illegality Trap: The Politics of Immigration & the Lens of Illegality."

98 Rajagukguk, "Teori Hukum Positif (Legal Positivism) 1: Kuliah 3 Firsafat Legal Positivism Menyangkut Ekonomi."

and realign the system with the law. Experience in post-New Order years has taught government to expect to lose cases in the Administrative Court (Pengadilan Tata Usaha Negara, PTUN).[99] Their experience in the Supreme Court has been no different. However, the ministry and associations of labour recruitment companies were surprised that the Supreme Court not only invalidated the laws but did so swiftly.

The judicial review process alerted the ministry to the tenuousness of the legal basis of the regulation. The ministry was given fourteen days to provide the Supreme Court with a written response to its query. In that response, the ministry's legal bureau head, Sunarno, reasoned that there were articles in the law that authorized the ministry to delegate administrative roles.[100] He also argued that the regulation was consistent with the objective of decentralizing administrative authority. Simultaneously, the legal bureau drafted a regulation that involved more ministry divisions in the programme's administration, serving to further ensconce it within the ministry's structures. In this draft, the Directorate-General of Guidance of Labour Placement retained control of the responsibility to provide pre-departure training, to finalize the administrative process and to issue overseas identity cards. The Directorate-General of Training and Productivity and the Agency for Research and Development were required to assist with vocational and data management aspects of their work.[101]

The ministry expected the Supreme Court to take this regulatory innovation into account when assessing the legality of its attempt to decentralize administrative authority at the expense of the BNP2TKI's mandate. Because the ministry had had advance warning, it had time to repeal and reissue the decree that authorized the Director-General for the Guidance of Labour Placement to issue recruitment certificates before the Supreme Court invalidated the regulation.[102] The minister then informed stakeholders that, as per the Supreme Court decision, the invalidated ministerial regulation would remain legally binding for the next 90 days or until the minister repealed it, whichever date is earliest. Almost 90 days later – on the day that the BNP2TKI was prepared

---

99 McLeod, "Soeharto's Indonesia: A Better Class of Corruption"; Bedner, *Administrative Courts in Indonesia: A Socio-Legal Study*.

100 hukumonline.com, "Depnakertrans Jawab Permohonan Uji Materi Permenakertrans No. 22/2008."

101 *Ministerial Regulation (Manpower) No. 5/MEN/II/2009 on Pelaksanaan Penyiapan Calon TKI Untuk Bekerja Di Luar Negeri*, article 3(3).

102 *Ministerial Decree (Manpower) No. 156/MEN/V/2009 on Penunjukan Pejabat Penerbit Surat Izin Pengerahan.*

to reassume control[103] – the ministry repealed the regulation and reissued the invalidated regulation's content in three new regulations. While procedurally legal, the widely held view was that this tactic was in fact an abuse of the law (*pelecehan hukum*).

In addition to further enhancing the BNP2TKI's political legitimacy, the ministry's failure to garner support from other arms of government emboldened the BNP2TKI to publicly announce its intention to duplicate the administrative roles that the ministry had reclaimed. The BNP2TKI's Director for Preparation and Departure, Arifin Purba, wrote to the ministry informing it that his division would continue providing the contested services, copying in the head of police investigations, immigration, airport management and all senior officials in the ministry and provincial manpower offices, as well as labour recruitment companies.[104] In it, he noted reports that ministry officials had threatened labour recruitment companies that were found using the BNP2TKI's services with blacklisting and, more drastically, cancellation of their recruitment licences. He also emphasized that labour recruitment companies using the BNP2TKI's services were doing so because only the BNP2TKI had the necessary infrastructure to issue overseas identity cards as required by the law, which stipulates punishments of up to five years in prison and/or five billion rupiah in fines for not arranging them.

In correspondence with the ministry, the head of the East Jakarta Tax Office questioned the legality of ministry issued exemption letters, which sought to replace the overseas identity cards issued by the BNP2TKI. The BNP2TKI interpreted this query to mean that other executive agencies were also critical of how the ministry had ignored the substance of the Supreme Court's decision. The BNP2TKI successfully lobbied the legislature for an open mediation session involving the BNP2TKI, the Ministry of Manpower and the Ministry of Foreign Affairs. To the national legislature's Commission IX, Director for Protection of Indonesians Abroad within the Ministry of Foreign Affairs gave evidence that the fact that the BNP2TKI and the ministry ran separate administrative systems and refused to share data with each other had complicated

---

103 The BNP2TKI had counted down from the day on which the judgment was finalized (8 May 2009), whereas the Ministry of Manpower started when the legal bureau received it (18 May 2009), which meant that they held different understandings about when the ministry's regulation would become void. As a result, the BNP2TKI announced plans to reassume control before the ministry was ready to cancel the invalidated regulation. See *Agency Circular Memorandum (BNP2TKI) No. 3/KA/VIII/2009 on Pelaksanaan Dan Perlindungan Tenaga Kerja Indonesia.*

104 *Director Memorandum Circular (Preparation and Departure) No. B. 539/PEN/VIII/2009 on Pelayanan Penempatan TKI.*

efforts by Indonesian consular offices to support migrant workers overseas.[105] Hidayat then presented a PowerPoint slideshow that explained the legal and political background to the conflict, pointing out policy concerns that might interest legislators, such as inefficiency and corruption involved with the ministry's handling of the programme.[106] When asked to explain the ministry's position, Arka delegated the task to the legal bureau head, Sunarno, who he argued could better clarify the legal reasoning.[107] Arka also refused to publicly divulge information about the ministry's political motivations after activists and news reporters heckled him from the observation deck.[108] He offered instead to send a written response, which was never provided.[109] The head of the commission expressed his disapproval, but acknowledged that they lacked a mechanism to force Arka to respond.[110] Commission members then passed a unanimous resolution instructing the ministry to return administration of the programme to the BNP2TKI. Unsurprisingly, the motion was ignored.

The hearing did, however, serve to make public the nature of the relationships between the key players in the conflict. Hidayat shouted that the 'purpose of the government is to govern' rather than in-fight for control of administration of the scheme and greater budget allocations.[111] In response, Arka and Harahap shook their heads, clearly seeing the outburst as yet another example of what happens when a non-career bureaucrat is given executive power.[112] Sunarno, the only other ministry representative present, was unresponsive, suggesting that he was not entirely comfortable with the ministry's tactics.

105 Personal observation of the Ministry of Foreign Affairs' Director for the Protection of Indonesian Citizens and Legal Entities Overseas at the Open Hearing Meeting in the People's Representative Council, Jakarta, 10 February 2010.

106 Personal observation of the head of the BNP2TKI at the Open Hearing Meeting in the People's Representative Council, Jakarta, 10 February 2010.

107 Personal observation of the Ministry of Manpower's head of the legal bureau at the Open Hearing Meeting in the People's Representative Council, Jakarta, 10 February 2010.

108 Arka asked for the lawmakers to exclude observers but was told that it was a public hearing and that observers were entitled to sit in. Personal observation of Arka and head of Commission IX at the at the Open Hearing Meeting in the People's Representative Council, Jakarta, 10 February 2010.

109 Personal observation of Arka at the Open Hearing Meeting in the People's Representative Council, Jakarta, 10 February 2010.

110 Personal observation of the head of Commission IX at the Open Hearing Meeting in the People's Representative Council, Jakarta, 10 February 2010.

111 Personal observation of the head of the BNP2TKI at the Open Hearing Meeting in the People's Representative Council, Jakarta, 10 February 2010.

112 Personal observation of the Open Hearing Meeting in the People's Representative Council, Jakarta, 10 February 2010.

In fact, Sunarno was seen to have an apologetic conversation with a BNP2TKI director and former ministry colleague during the hearing break.[113] When later prompted for details, that director recalled asking Sunarno to explain what was going on, as they had both been involved in the design of the BNP2TKI in 2006, at which time there was a strong consensus about the division of administrative labour between the two agencies. Sunarno apologized but explained that his job as legal bureau head was to justify the minister's policy choices.[114] These observations, along with the fact that BNP2TKI officials dominated the hearing in numbers, indicated to all present that the ministry was fighting an uphill battle in its attempts to regain control.

Engaging with the Public

The BNP2TKI's judicial and legislative strategies complemented other attempts to develop a stronger reputation for public accountability. In 2009 and 2010 the National Audit Agency (Badan Pemeriksa Keuangan, BPK) gave the BNP2TKI the highest award for integrity in managing public money – appropriate with no exception (*wajar tanpa pengecualian*).[115] The BNP2TKI publicized this significant achievement. The ministry, by contrast, consistently falls short of this assessment, receiving the middle ranking – appropriate with exception (*wajar dengan pengecualian*) – for its poor internal systems and non-compliance with the law.[116] The BNP2TKI also won an award for innovative public relations strategies in recognition of its use of multimedia to communicate their activities and convey relevant developments to the public.[117] This award was developed and presented by the Ministry of Communication and Information, which strongly encourages government agencies to increase

113 Personal observation of the Open Hearing Meeting in the People's Representative Council, Jakarta, 10 February 2010.

114 Interview data, Jakarta, 9 June 2010.

115 hukumonline.com, *Awas, Sesat Pikir Tentang Wajar Tanpa Pengecualian*; Badan Nasional Penempatan dan Perlindungan Tenaga Kerja Indonesia, "BNP2TKI Juara II Anugerah Media Humas Pemerintah 2010." Note that the designation does not necessarily indicate good public service or low levels of corruption. Rather, it is recognition that the agency has adhered to Indonesian accounting standards, produces the necessary reports and is not hiding anything. Moreover, convictions demonstrate that the National Audit Agency has accepted bribes in exchange for the most positive assessments.

116 "Muhaimin Target 'Lulus' Laporan Keuangan BPK: Pada 2009, Kemenakertrans Mendapat Label Wajar Dengan Pengecualian (WDP)."

117 Badan Nasional Penempatan dan Perlindungan Tenaga Kerja Indonesia, "BNP2TKI Juara II Anugerah Media Humas Pemerintah 2010."

the volume of information that they channel to the public.[118] In the Ministry of Communication and Information's citation, the BNP2TKI was praised as a model for public relations that enhances legitimacy by influencing public perception.

As these achievements suggest, the media was an important tool for the BNP2TKI. Hidayat hired journalists to develop the agency's capacity to produce and publish its own mass media-style reports, starting at the end of 2007. The career journalists instructed the BNP2TKI's public relations division in the format used by the mass media for delivering information to the public. At first, they attended formal events, such as technical coordination meetings and then supervised the write up of reports for publication on the BNP2TKI's official website. With time, however, BNP2TKI officials developed the capacity to do so independently and were soon publishing multiple reports every day. This mode of communication gave the BNP2TKI an advantage over the ministry's Directorate-General for Guidance of Labour Placement, which relied on more conventional public relations methods, such as making announcements in the ministry's press room. Hidayat's advisors, meanwhile, had recommended that the press room was an appropriate venue for question and answer events with executive level bureaucrats and specialists, but was less effective for channelling bite-size information to the public about daily activities. Statistics show that some of the reports produced by BNP2TKI attracted tens of thousands of hits, and the content is often reproduced in the mass media.[119]

Another media strategy used by the BNP2TKI to build a public profile was direct communication. Indonesian language media include almost daily reports on migrant worker matters, whereas the English language venues, such as *Jakarta Post* and *Jakarta Globe*, carry only occasional pieces. Partly, the reason for this discrepancy is perceived reader interest. Whereas the English language newspapers publish an occasional update, Indonesian language media report on the government's ongoing response to migrant worker matters.[120] These media, especially *Kompas*, *Republika* and *Detik.com*, regularly cite the BNP2TKI as a source of information about a wide range of issues. The reports sometimes claim that Hidayat passed on the information through an email or

118 Badan Nasional Penempatan dan Perlindungan Tenaga Kerja Indonesia, "Sesdirjen Kominfo Appresiasi Pemberitaan BNP2TKI."

119 Badan Nasional Penempatan dan Perlindungan Tenaga Kerja Indonesia, "Mengupayakan Peningkatan Pasar TKI-LN."

120 A comprehensive search of English newspapers (*Jakarta Post* and *Jakarta Globe*) showed that these outlets published significantly fewer articles on migrant workers between 2007 and 2010 than Indonesian media (*Kompas* and *Republika*).

by short message service (SMS), providing content that would otherwise be difficult to gather.[121] Indonesian media outlets rely heavily on such updates about the Indonesian government's activities in other countries due to limited resources. While many have foreign correspondents and agreements with media agencies in neighbouring Malaysia, fewer have a presence further abroad in regions such as the Middle East, where the Indonesian government is frequently involved in bilateral initiatives to do with Indonesian migrant workers.

Twitter has also helped to deliver the BNP2TKI's message in a country where the middle class eagerly engages in social media conversations. The BNP2TKI's public relations division maintains a Twitter account that tweets about the agency's activities and engages with those who re-tweet its content.[122] On occasion, followers have re-tweeted the updates along with critical comments. The BNP2TKI has found that this criticism provides a useful gauge of the public perceptions of their work. This complements perspectives that the BNP2TKI attempts to glean from the mass media through its daily compilation of reports that contain keywords that pertain to their mandate. In addition, Hidayat maintains his own Twitter account through which he communicates details about his schedule and interactions with ministers, sub-national government leaders, immigration officers and the police.[123] He has also used Twitter to inform the public that the BNP2TKI is waiting for the ministry to act on their reports that detail illegal behaviour of labour recruitment companies. This micro-blogging activity gradually created the impression that the BNP2TKI was doing its job while ministry officials were sitting on their hands.

The BNP2TKI also sought to establish links with the wider public through its relationships with civil society organizations. Through Hidayat, it maintained personal and mutually beneficial relationships with grass roots organizations that were traditionally natural enemies of the ministry, such as GASPERMINDO. In part, the president appointed Hidayat as head of the BNP2TKI in exchange for the support he garnered among these groups in the lead up to the 2004 Presidential Elections.[124] Critics argue that Hidayat provided patronage to some of these organizations, for example, giving them access to government assets, such as motor vehicles. One of the core motivations for developing these relationships was to build a broader base of support for the BNP2TKI. For example, the BNP2TKI invited over 50 faith-based groups to attend an overnight

121 See, for example, "Dualisme Kemenakertrans-BNP2TKI Berakhir."

122 The BNP2TKI public relations Twitter handle is @BNP2TKI.

123 Hidayat's personal and professional Twitter handle is @jumhurhidayat.

124 Aditjondro, *Membongkar Gurita Cikeas: Di Balik Skandal Bank Century.*

event at a hotel in the hills outside Jakarta, where they were given a night's accommodation in exchange for listening to the BNP2TKI's version of the conflict with the ministry and their ideas for future policy direction.[125] This kind of patronage was crucial for managing anti-BNP2TKI sentiment, which could potentially stack odds in favour of the ministry if the mass media switched sides, as it widened the BNP2TKI's support base.

Towards a New Deal

The BNP2TKI's success in developing a popular public image and pro-BNP2TKI coverage of the dispute undermined the public's view of the ministry. Ultimately, however, the ministry won the battle, if not the war. By February 2010, Hidayat conceded that control had effectively been prised away from the BNP2TKI, ending the period of duplication in services. The BNP2TKI's doors were still open for provision of pre-departure training, finalization of administrative processes and issuance of overseas identity cards. But the ministry's threat of administrative sanctions on labour recruitment companies using the BNP2TKI's services was simply too great to ignore. The ministry's threats, if carried out, would have directly affected the ability of labour recruitment companies to participate in the industry and to earn significant profits from it. Although the BNP2TKI offered free service provision and the ministry charged labour recruitment companies a combination of formal and informal fees, the savings the BNP2TKI promised paled in comparison to the losses recruiters would make if the ministry cancelled their licences.

By December 2009 it was clear to the BNP2TKI that the ministry had succeeded in reorienting the recruitment industry towards its own implementation unit in East Jakarta. In a last-ditch attempt to direct some of that business to its unit, the BNP2TKI announced a crackdown on labour recruitment companies that failed to arrange overseas identity cards for migrant workers, starting on 11 January 2010.[126] In response, the ministry's Director for Overseas Placement declared that the BNP2TKI was acting beyond its authority because, according to Ministerial Regulation No. 18/MEN/VIII/2009 on the Criteria and Procedure to Obtain an Overseas Workers Identity Card, it was the ministry's

125 Participant observation, Bogor, 30 April 2010.

126 The consequences of this policy for administration of the overseas migration programme in the regions are explored in Chapter 4.

right to issue – or delegate the issuance of – the card.[127] Hidayat countered that the BNP2TKI was simply implementing the law, which stipulated that migrant workers must hold overseas identity cards. The ministry's technical implementation unit in East Jakarta had been issuing exemption letters instead of cards, as the data management system that the ministry's Agency for Research and Development was instructed to develop ten months earlier was still not in place.

These conflicting instructions left other agencies very confused. On the day that BNP2TKI's policy came into force, the police unit at Jakarta International Airport was hesitant to comply, explaining to the media that law enforcement agencies preferred to proceed with caution. Previous experiences with infighting executive agencies had caused them to look incompetent when they followed the executive's instructions blindly.[128] In this case, the officer pointed out that the ministry, as the state's primary labour agency, would be asked for a legal opinion in prosecutorial proceedings and, given its relationship with the BNP2TKI, would predictably recommend dropping charges against anyone arrested for not carrying a migrant labour identity card. A legislator joined the conversation in response to the police's expression of confusion, calling on the president to intervene.[129] To outsiders, the solution seemed simple: call the government agency managers into the presidential office and make them resolve their differences. However, a resolution was going to require a much more complex set of interventions. First, the motivation to compromise and negotiate a new division of labour required some change in political context: amendments to the law and judgements concerning it had thitherto proved to be ineffective. Second, movement towards any such compromise was going to require the removal of officials with interests in maintaining the conflict. The discussion that follows offers an explanation for why the president may not have intervened when coordination had visibly broken down in 2007, and for most of 2009, when the agencies duplicated public services, seriously damaging the government's public image.

The President's Silence

President Yudhoyono never intervened publicly in the conflict. Unlike direct interventions in other areas, such as creating ad hoc taskforces to deal with rogue officials (*oknum*) in law enforcement agencies, his response to this

127 *Ministerial Regulation (Manpower) No. 18/MEN/VIII/2009 on Bentuk, Persyaratan, Dan Tata Cara Memperoleh Kartu Tenaga Kerja Luar Negeri.*

128 "Polres Bandara Bingung Soal KTKLN."

129 "Anggota DPR Desak SBY Atasi Konflik BNP2TKI & Depnakertrans."

governance problem offered no such spectacle. The president's silence on the matter indicates that he decided the conflict was simply not important enough to demand his attention. More pressing was the fallout from the Bank Century scandal, in which the president's former and current vice presidents were key protagonists, the legislature's threat to impeach him following media coverage of massive corruption cases that involved the Tax Office, and dealing with a skirmish between his Minister for Finance, Sri Mulyani, and another minister, Aburizal Bakrie, over the Bakrie family conglomerate's tax obligations. Rather than intervene in the relatively inconsequential conflict between Suparno and Hidayat, the president opted to sit back and let the state's internal systems handle it.

The president's muted support for Hidayat was also partly a strategy to avoid alienating potential political opponents.[130] Yudhoyono has been criticized for his reluctance to make public his position concerning activity that enjoys the support of politically powerful groups. For example, the government has been criticized internally and internationally for its response to acts of intimidation by the Islamic Defender's Front (Front Pembela Islam, FPI), and, as mentioned earlier, to the refusal by a Muslim mayor to allow the construction of a Christian church to proceed despite an instruction to permit it from the Supreme Court. In the particular case of the conflict between the ministry and the BNP2TKI, the president's first and foremost consideration was his rainbow cabinet that included five major political parties,[131] one of them PKB – the party chaired by Muhaimin Iskandar, who had replaced Suparno as Minister for Manpower in 2009. The heavily factionalized party had two ministers in cabinet and 29 party cadres in the legislature. The president was predictably reluctant to force the minister to reverse changes that his predecessor had put in place for two reasons. First, Iskandar's predecessor, Suparno, had hailed from the same party and, second, had most likely made ministry appointments in return for financial contributions to PKB. Instructing the minister to undo Suparno's system

130 Interview data, Jakarta, 28 April 2010.

131 The president's coalition included give political parties, excluding only one after it chose to sit in opposition. These coalition parties are: the Democratic Party (Partai Demokrat, PD), the Prosperous Justice Party (Partai Keadilan Sejahtera, PKS), the National Mandate Party (Partai Amanat Nasional, PAN), the United Development Party (Partai Persatuan Pembangunan, PPP) and the National Awakening Party (Partai Kebangkitan Bangsa, PKB). The coalition did not include the Indonesian Democratic Party of Struggle (Partai Demokrat Indonesia Perjuangan, PDIP). For an analysis of President Susilo Yudhoyono's inclusive government cabinets, see Slater, "Indonesia's Accountability Trap: Party Cartels and Presidential Power after Democratic Transition."

risked damaging the party's public image, which could result in retaliation against Yudhoyono's government.

Another criticism of the president concerning this conflict has been his decision – noted earlier – to appoint a non-bureaucrat to lead the BNP2TKI. According to Suparno, the appointment was partly repayment to Hidayat for the services he rendered in the lead-up to the 2004 Presidential Election.[132] This may well have been the case. However, Hidayat's appointment was also part of a much larger strategy, which sought to unsettle networks and ways of doing things that were deeply entrenched in the system; New Order legacies that persisted despite frequent changes in political leadership since 1998. Establishment of the BNP2TKI in 2007 dispersed power and drew the Ministry of Manpower into competition with it. In theory, intra-state competition should keep executive agencies in check, motivate them to seek popular support for their policy direction, and ultimately drive them to improve the quality of their work. In the contest that emerged between the ministry and the BNP2TKI, both sets of officials sought to expose flaws in their competitor's systems leading to problems with mandatory health checks, insurance and training, thus putting them under pressure to make refinements.

It is difficult, then, to imagine that the president expected Hidayat's relationship with Suparno to be harmonious, especially given public knowledge about his background and character. Hidayat's public identity was closely associated with his involvement in anti-regime protest in 1989, when he and five other students led a demonstration against the Minister for Internal Affairs who was on an official visit at the Bandung Technology Institute.[133] The incident landed Hidayat in prison for three years. In the post-Suharto years, Hidayat became involved in labour organizing, taking on a leadership role in his union. His curriculum vitae did not promise a candidate for the leadership of the BNP2TKI who would help maintain the status quo. In appointing Hidayat, the president presumably wanted the kind of 'transformational leadership'[134] that individuals like Islamic leader Din Syamsuddin as Director-General for the Guidance of Overseas Labour Placement had delivered following the resignation of Suharto. It is predictably for this reason that a ministry official was not appointed to the role, as the BNP2TKI was established to help reform the ministry programme.

---

132 "Penempatan TKI: PPTKIS Berharap BNP2TKI Terbuka Terhadap Masukan."

133 "Sekilas Mohammad Jumhur Hidayat." Also see the memoir that Hidayat's mother wrote on his student days: Amiati, *Memoir Bunda Seorang Aktivis*.

134 This leadership is expected to enhance performance in the bureaucracy by introducing an external, formerly excluded set of values. See Bass and Riggio, *Transformational Leadership*.

In April 2010 the president did, however, act to create an opportunity for the ministry to solve its coordination problems with the BNP2TKI. In Presidential Instruction No. 3/2010 on a Fair Development Programme, the president called on his ministers and agency heads to tackle intra-state disagreements in the provision of almost fifty public programmes. Under the instruction, the ministry was required to refine systems for implementing the overseas labour migration programme by working out a more appropriate division of administrative labour. To complement this measure, the BNP2TKI was given the task of coordinating the development of a series of standard operating procedures. Better coordination would arguably translate to better service provision to migrant workers, the supply of better quality migrant labour to international labour markets and a reduction in number of migrants with problems overseas. But whatever the objective may have been, the action to be taken, result that it ought to achieve and the deadline for achieving it, were clear. By the end of 2010, the Minister for Manpower was to have introduced a new division of administrative labour between the ministry, the BNP2TKI and provincial governments that would end the public conflict.

A Human Resources Legacy

Following the presidential instruction, the minister reshuffled staff as part of his effort to solve coordination problems with the BNP2TKI. First, Iskandar split up Arka and Harahap, appointing Arka as caretaker of another division in the ministry's portfolio.[135] This move was relatively simple because Arka was already seen to have made sufficient money (*kenyang,* lit. to be sated), having held a top post in four different directorates-general over seven years. This gave him sufficient opportunities to recoup the significant financial investment that bureaucrats make to advance their career. Arka was reasonably accepting of the minister's plan to transplant him from the troubled Directorate-General of Guidance of Labour Placement to a neighbouring division, where he remained until retirement one year later. Dealing with Harahap proved to be slightly more complicated. Like Arka, he was also set to retire. But he was still eager to attain a top level appointment before doing so. In the reshuffle, Iskandar appointed Harahap to fill the void that Arka left, making him caretaker Director-General for the Guidance of Labour Placement. According to a senior official in the BNP2TKI, Harahap entered the position seeking to become a fully fledged director-general, and was led to expect that the minister would support his candidacy. This posed a problem from the perspective of the

135 Arka was appointed to manage the Directorate General of Guidance of Labour Monitoring in 2010.

minister: how to accommodate Harahap's career ambitions when he was so invested in maintaining the status quo?

The minister also dealt with older but more junior officials in the reshuffle. Iskandar reassigned the Director for Overseas Placement, Maula, who helped manage the ministry's transition back into direct administration of the programme, to a higher-level position in another directorate-general. His replacement, Roostiawati, who was one of the four bureaucrats who headed a section in his directorate, had a strong reputation for toeing the line. Colleagues expressed admiration for her uncompromising determination to impress her line manager. However, they also noted that she struggled to control her former peer, Bery Komarudzaman, who was entrusted by Arka and Harahap with the task of managing the ministry's administrative activity in East Jakarta. Komarudzaman was left in place despite his strong connections with the 'boys club',[136] and Roostiawati was given the task of brokering a compromise with him. Komarudzaman was one of the sixty or so BNP2TKI officials who responded to the ministry's call for former Manpower officials to return to the ministry and help administer the programme. In 2009 Komarudzaman was promised a junior executive position, which he received, and would, as a result of his work under Arka and Harahap, come to expect to achieve a director level appointment before retirement.

These changes eased tension with the BNP2TKI, which enabled conversations between the minister and the agency while ministry officials adjusted to their new roles. With Harahap distracted by the challenge of managing the Directorate-General of Guidance of Labour Placement and Arka busy in an entirely different division, Iskandar held a series of closed meetings with Hidayat to talk about possible ways forward. Both parties agreed that the current focus on domestic workers posed a significant challenge to cooperation, given the recruitment industry's strong clout with the ministry. However, they acknowledged that the development of an alternative – recruitment of migrant labour for formal sector jobs – would require time. Anything but a gradual scaling down of the outward flow of domestic workers would invite aggressive lobbying, which could potentially embroil agency managers in another inter-agency conflict. It is at this point that Iskandar gave the head of the ministry's legal bureau, Sunarno, instructions to normalize the ministry's relationship with the BNP2TKI. Iskandar reportedly admitted to a confidant that he was under no illusion that the ministry had to relinquish some control but argued that he had to carefully handle staff who were directly involved.[137]

---

136 This term was used in English by my informant.

137 Interview data, Jakarta, 21 December 2010.

Iskandar had a reputation for using a cloak and dagger approach in his management of ministry staff. The minister kept details of conversations with various stakeholders secret, leading them to expect certain but sometimes conflicting outcomes, as was the case with Harahap and Sunarno. This proved to be an effective strategy for managing the politics of change. However, the fact that all top executive positions in the ministry were filled by caretakers indicates that Iskandar was reluctant to share control: caretakers have limited legal authority and so must run changes in policy direction by the minister.[138] To the surprise of mid-career bureaucrats in the BNP2TKI and the ministry, Harahap was removed from the caretaker post and sent into retirement in October 2010. Sunarno was put in Harahap's place while also maintaining his own role as head of the legal bureau. Roostiawati retained her post as Director of Overseas Placement as part of a deal in which she promised to follow the plan to normalize relations with the BNP2TKI proposed by the minister and Sunarno.[139] Komarudzaman retained his position on the condition that he would have to follow Roostiawati's lead in rolling back the ministry's involvement in administration of the overseas labour migration programme if he wanted to achieve a director level appointment before retirement.[140] This internal reshuffle replaced officials committed to maintaining the status quo with those who were more receptive to change.

Compromise on the Horizon

Events from May 2010 indicated that some sort of compromise concerning the division of labour was in the offing. At that time, Iskandar amended the insurance law but stopped short of re-incorporating the BNP2TKI, choosing instead

138 As a consequence, the ministry had limited capacity to respond to governance problems in an effective and timely way, as executive authority was concentrated in a single pair of hands. As part of this criticism, Iskandar was called on to differentiate between the strategies he used to manage a political party in his capacity as chairperson of PKB, and those he used to manage the ministry. For reports of the latter, see "Muhaimin Harus Bedakan Manajemen Parpol Dengan Pemerintahan."

139 A new ministerial regulation was signed and announced on 13 October 2010. See *Ministerial Regulation (Manpower) No. 14/MEN/X/2010 on Pelaksanaan Penempatan Dan Perlindungan Tenaga Kerja Indonesia Di Luar Negeri.*

140 A little over a year later, Roostiawati was temporarily appointed to head the Manpower and Development Centre to make space for Komarudzaman, who filled the role for one year until he retired. Having moved on, Roostiawati claimed that one of her major successes as Director for Overseas Placement was closing down the ministry's operations and pulling Komarudzaman back under the directorate's control.

to cut the central government out of the process altogether.[141] The decision surprised Hidayat, coming just one month after the presidential instruction that ordered the minister to repair their relationship.[142] After more than two years of public conflict, the BNP2TKI had gradually come around to the likelihood that the ministry would not hand the disputed administrative roles back to them. To compensate for the loss of control, the BNP2TKI turned its attention toward other policy areas in which it could build a strong pro-migrant reputation. For example, the Deputy for International Cooperation and Promotion sent delegations to destinations such as Azerbaijan, Namibia and the Seychelles to negotiate more bilateral agreements with the view to extending the existing scope of the government-to-government scheme beyond Japan and South Korea. This in turn created work for the placement and protection divisions.

Even years later Hidayat believed that the ministry's amendment to the insurance law was just another attempt to minimize the value of claims that insurers had to pay. However, four months after its promulgation, its implementation sparked a crisis that put the possibility of a favourable compromise within reach of the BNP2TKI. In September 2010, Iskandar appointed a single consortium of insurance companies to replace the insurers that his predecessor had selected.[143] This move was met by public outcry and accusations that the ministry had created an oligopoly of insurers, reducing the likelihood of competition and thus the likelihood of quality service provision to migrant workers. Harahap handled the selection process as caretaker of the Directorate-General of Guidance of Labour Placement. When he was unexpectedly removed from office, he revealed details of the process to the media. Harahap claimed that two consortia qualified but that the minister put pressure on him to recommend only one of them for appointment. Whether or not this was the case is a moot point. But, in retrospect, it shows that labour recruitment company threats to report the minister to the Corruption Eradication Commission for accepting bribes in return for the appointment may have had some bearing on the ministry's actions in the weeks that followed.[144]

---

141 As noted earlier, his predecessor had transferred the responsibility to help process claims to local government in 2008. Compare the following regulations: *Ministerial Regulation (Manpower) No. 23/MEN/V/2006 on Asuransi Tenaga Kerja Indonesia*; *Ministerial Regulation (Manpower) No. 7/MEN/X/V/2010 on Asuransi Tenaga Kerja Indonesia*.

142 "Jumhur Ngaku Heran Menakertran Cabut Kewenangan BNP2TKI."

143 "Penetapan Asuransi Dinilai Tak Transparan."

144 The Supreme Court heard the employment companies' case but accepted the ministry's argument that the consortium arrangement was not a mutual business for the one group

Anxious to find a distraction, the minister examined his options and renewed efforts to resolve the protracted conflict with the BNP2TKI. A few weeks later, the BNP2TKI and the ministry held a closed door meeting in which to resolve their differences.[145] At the meeting, ministry delegates agreed to trade administrative roles for the BNP2TKI's silence concerning the insurance controversy.[146] On 14 October Ministerial Regulation No. 14/MEN/X/2010 on the Implementation of Placement and Protection of Indonesian Workers Overseas was promulgated, which re-incorporated the BNP2TKI into the programme's administrative structures.[147] Responsibility for pre-departure training, finalization of the administrative process and the issuing of overseas identity cards was handed back to the BNP2TKI.[148] However, the regulation included provisions that allowed ministry officials online access to the BNP2TKI's data management system.[149] Mid-career bureaucrats in the ministry expressed relief that they would no longer have to defend what many of them believed had been an illegal strategy on the part of their institution.[150]

Where external mediation had failed, internal negotiation succeeded in resolving the conflict over the division of administrative labour. However, its resolution did require deep compromise. The most obvious sacrifice in the ministry camp was Harahap's ambition to gain a director-generalship. Colleagues estimate that Harahap spent in the range of Rp. 1 and 1.5 billion (USD 100–150,000) of personal funds on ministerial projects in exchange for Iskandar's continued support. To the minister, however, Harahap's commitment to maintaining the status quo made him a significant obstacle to re-incorporating the BNP2TKI into the administration of the programme. It was for this reason that Harahap was removed from his caretaker position. For the BNP2TKI's part, it acceded to the demand for access to the agency's database. It also agreed to Iskandar's condition that the head of the BNP2TKI leave the disciplining of labour recruitment companies to the ministry, a condition which, once agreed

of insurers it appointed to handle the activity although the Government had not produced a regulation to define it. See Supreme Court, "Legal Decision No. 61 P/HUM/2010."

145 "Tugas BNP2TKI"; "Dualisme Pengelolaan TKI Berakhir."

146 The Minister for Manpower, Director General for Guidance of Labour Placement, Director for Overseas Placement, head of the BNP2TKI, the BNP2TKI Secretary, Deputy for Placement and Deputy for Protection were present at this meeting.

147 "Dualisme Kemenakertrans-BNP2TKI Berakhir."

148 *Ministerial Regulation (Manpower) No. 14/MEN/X/2010 on Pelaksanaan Penempatan Dan Perlindungan Tenaga Kerja Indonesia Di Luar Negeri*, article 32. The BNP2TKI was given the option to delegate those responsibilities to provincial authorities if necessary.

149 Ibid., article 39(3).

150 Interview data, Jakarta 21 December 2010.

to, sealed the deal for return to the 2008 division of administrative labour between the agencies.

Once agreed, both sides undertook to improve coordination by instituting quarterly meetings. However, deeper structural problems that made coordination difficult were left to the legislature to solve. Law No. 39/2004 on the Placement and Protection of Indonesian Workers Overseas had already been tabled for amendment, and the BNP2TKI and the ministry had divergent ideas about how it should be revised. Iskandar wanted the legislature to revise the article that made the head of the BNP2TKI responsible to the president and put the agency firmly under the ministry. The government-recognized association of labour recruitment companies, APJATI, shared this view. It wanted the BNP2TKI to be structured more like The Philippines Overseas Employment Administration, whose head administrator is vice chairperson of the agency's governance board, chaired by the equivalent of Indonesia's Minister for Manpower.[151] Unsurprisingly, Hidayat wanted the legislature to maintain the BNP2TKI's autonomy from the ministry. He also recommended lawmakers to go one step further by extricating the ministry from all operational aspects of the programme in order to avoid the kinds of conflict of interest that had led to the establishment of the BNP2TKI. As this suggests, the October 2010 compromise was ultimately only a temporary fix to a much larger problem.

Conclusion

What emerges here is a narrative about competition for control. Under Suparno's leadership, the Ministry of Manpower expected to retain control over policymaking concerning implementation of the overseas labour migration programme. The president's appointment of a non-career bureaucrat to lead the BNP2TKI, intentionally or not, threw a spanner in the works. Hidayat quickly let it be known that he had no intention of adhering to legal process when the ministry ignored the BNP2TKI's calls for intervention. It was disagreement on this matter that drove a wedge between the two agencies, preventing any semblance of cooperation. The ministry's subsequent attempt to relegate the BNP2TKI to the insignificant government-to-government programmes was met with fierce resistance on the part of senior BNP2TKI officials, who felt aggrieved by the attack on their authority and power. They responded by undermining the ministry through the duplication of services, challenging the legality of their regulations in the court and legislature, running counter lobbies

151 Interview data, Jakarta, 13 October 2009.

in the regions and channelling their position on the matter to the mass media for wider dissemination.

Mediation in the conflict by the judicial and legislative branches of government provides insight into the internal power dynamics in Indonesia's post-authoritarian state. The fact that the ministry ignored the substance of the Supreme Court's decision to return administrative roles to the BNP2TKI and then re-issued the regulation that the court had struck down were widely seen as an abuse of legal authority. The acts highlight the unequal relationship between branches of government, pointing to executive agencies' use of legal procedure to avoid the consequences of judicial and legislative decisions pertaining to legal substance. As noted earlier, this particular use of the law is not unique to Indonesia, but it does reveal a great deal about how the law matters to those with authority to use it. Lawmakers in the national legislature's Commission IX, Tax Office officials and police officers were concerned that the ministry showed such contempt for the Supreme Court's judgement. However, none of these institutions could act on their belief that the Minister of Manpower had misused the law. This reveals an important feature of the Indonesian system, namely that government agencies operate largely autonomously from one another.

In many ways the fall-out from the conflict was felt most by street-level bureaucrats in both agencies who had little influence over the policy direction that their institutions took. As a consequence of the misalignment between policy objectives and directives, these bureaucrats had to juggle competing expectations, which put them in a very difficult position. The next chapter offers cases about how the drama played out in six administrative sites across the archipelago. Whereas this chapter focused on events at the state's centre, these case studies provide snapshots of the administrative landscape in disparate parts of the country, revealing the diverse ways in which central government agencies interact with sub-national levels of government. This focus on the peripheries draws out the influence that local institutional arrangements, local administrative cultures and other place-specific considerations have in shaping the context of reception for the transmission of policy direction from the centre.

CHAPTER 4

Accommodation and Conflict in the Periphery

The state's transit and embarkation sites for the overseas labour migration programme are mostly located in provincial capitals, where national and sub-national government agencies share the associated administrative work.[1] The way in which they share that work differs, however, because of historical and place-specific factors. These factors have a strong bearing on the capacity of national and sub-national government agencies to cooperate in the administration of the overseas labour migration programme. They were a consideration for administrators during the New Order era, but much more so under decentralization. Under the New Order, government offices in the regions were at least formally an extension of a hierarchically superior organization in Jakarta. Moreover, these agencies in the country's capital often appointed officials from within their ranks to manage their regional offices. Since decentralization, such top down structures have given way to a highly complex system in which the regional offices fall under the jurisdiction of sub-national governments. As a consequence, central government agencies are much more limited in their ability to steer the direction of public policy even when it concerns matters within Jakarta.

The conflict between the Ministry of Manpower and the BNP2TKI, described in the previous chapter, created a dilemma for national and sub-national officials involved in administering the overseas labour migration programme in different parts of the country: whose instructions were they to follow? Through a selection of cases, this chapter draws attention to the arrangements that emerged in six locations in Java, Sumatra and Kalimantan when the BNP2TKI instructed its technical implementation units to issue overseas identity cards – a task that the ministry had told provincial authorities offices was their responsibility. The first case explains why the ministry did not delegate the task to the provincial government in Jakarta where, as a result, the BNP2TKI competed directly with the ministry. The remaining cases show what happened in the regions where the BNP2TKI was set to compete against provincial government authorities. The first reveals that in Tanjung Pinang staff of the two agencies prioritized their relationships with each other in some locations, effectively

1 Provincial capital cities in Indonesia are dense administrative sites, which host national government units as well as provincial and municipal government agencies. See van Klinken, "Decolonization and the Making of Middle Indonesia."

 | DOI 10.1163/9789004325487_005

putting more weight on horizontal networks over vertical ones. The next two portray situations in Medan and Semarang where scale trumped place and the BNP2TKI unit and provincial manpower offices duplicated services. The final pair, in Nunukan and Surabaya, demonstrate that administrators were spared having to face the dilemma altogether where a tier of government had no presence.[2]

These cases reveal the complexity of administering the overseas labour migration programme. But they also demonstrate the necessity of paying serious attention to local conditions when attempting to understand governance structures in a country with over 17,000 islands, 500 autonomous regions and an ethnically and religiously diverse population of 240 million people. The decentralization programme, which was pushed through the legislature in 1999, has been described by international observers as being nothing short of 'radical'.[3] The International Crisis Group notes that the combination of decentralized administrative and budgetary authority and direct elections at the sub-national level has severely weakened the centre's ability to govern, as provincial and district/city governments do not always feel compelled to comply with their instructions.[4] This Weberian perspective of the state interprets failure to follow directions from hierarchically superior officials – a characteristic of the 'ideal-type state'[5] – to be a sign of weakness in its institutional apparatus. As this chapter demonstrates, however, this normative understanding of power relationships risks dismissing contextual factors as idiosyncratic and lacking in broader relevance, when they are often in fact salient to understanding the way in which a particular state is constituted and becomes manifest.

National or Sub-national?

In February 2009 the ministry had reclaimed authority from the BNP2TKI to issue recruitment certificates, provide pre-departure training and furnish labour migrants it processed with overseas identity cards. However, the ministry only had an institutional arrangement in place to do so in Jakarta. In all other regions, the ministry sought to delegate the responsibilities to the provincial

2 Refer to the map to see the location of these sites in Indonesia and surrounding territories.

3 See, for example, Hadiz, *Localising Power in Post-Authoritarian Indonesia: A Southeast Asia Perspective*, 22.

4 International Crisis Group, "Indonesia: Defying the State Asia Briefing No. 138," 1.

5 Migdal, *State in Society: Studying How States and Societies Transform and Constitute One Another*, 14.

manpower office. This attempt to cut the BNP2TKI out of administrative roles that brought them into contact with labour recruitment companies and insurers was not so easily implemented. First, the ministry was forced to delegate responsibility for these tasks to provincial manpower offices because it had come to lack the structures to undertake them itself following the implementation of decentralization in 2001 and establishment of the BNP2TKI in 2007. Second, the ministry and the provincial manpower offices did not have systems in place to issue overseas identity cards in line with the law, so instead furnished labour migrants with letters exempting them from the payment of *fiskal*. In December 2009, the BNP2TKI announced a country-wide crackdown on migrants who held these letters instead of overseas identity cards, calling in immigration and the police to help with enforcement.

Jakarta

Jakarta is an unusual region because its provincial government is co-located with Indonesia's central administration. Years of centralized, authoritarian rule in Indonesia blurred the boundary of authority between what had become national and sub-national units of the state.[6] Post-New Order governments have attempted to introduce a clearer division of labour by sorting out responsibilities for administrative activity along decentralized lines.[7] However, the Jakarta region will never resemble other provinces because its structure is unique. Unlike the district and city governments in other regions, Jakarta's local administrative tier is not autonomous. Although local government agencies in Jakarta perform many of the same functions as those in other regions, they are directly subordinate to the provincial governor, who appoints civil servants to manage them much in the same way that central authorities did across the nation during the New Order era (1967–1998). For this reason, the division of labour that exists between provincial and local government in the regions is not replicated in Jakarta, where provincial apparatus in fact performs some of the work of the lower tier of administration. Moreover, the provincial government in Jakarta needs to accommodate the ministry in their administrative landscape, whereas the other provincial authorities do not.

For most of the New Order, administration of the overseas labour migration programme was organized under a single government authority. The ministry

6 For an analysis of how this has complicated subsequent attempts to decentralize state activity, see Bünte, "Indonesia's Protracted Decentralization: Contested Reforms and Their Unintended Consequences."

7 For examples of the new challenges that this policy choice presents, see Firman, "In Search of a Governance Institution Model for Jakarta Metropolitan Area (JMA) under Indonesia's Decentralization Policy: Old Problems, New Challenges."

finalized the pre-departure process and the regional manpower office, which was subordinate to the ministry, registered intending labour migrants and issued the necessary documents, such as passport recommendations, to help them meet the programme's requirements. On Jalan Gatot Subroto, the ministry furnished labour recruitment companies with licences and recruitment certificates, and on Jalan Raya Puncak the manpower office provided the documents that authorized migrant workers to leave the country, such as notes that exempted them from the *fiskal*, the departure tax for Indonesian citizens and expatriates. It is to this period of administration to which bureaucrats refer nostalgically as being neat and orderly (*rapi*) because there was a single authority, which directed the administrative activity from top to bottom. However, decentralization removed the manpower office out from under the ministry's direct control and recast it as a subordinate agency to the Special Capital Region of Jakarta (Daerah Khusus Ibukota Jakarta, DKI Jakarta). As a consequence, the ministry's network of technical implementation units, which were frequently located within the building of the provincial manpower office, were put under the provincial government's control.

The introduction of separate tiers has been a source of frustration because the ensuing turf war between them effectively destroyed the state's ability to provide a seamless service to Jakarta-based labour recruitment companies. Over time, those who profited from the business started to lobby for a reorganization of administrative roles associated with the programme. This request was partly prompted by the fact that the provincial government used ministerial regulations as guidelines because provincial ones had not yet been produced, even though decentralization had out-dated them. However, their main point of contention was that the change introduced another hurdle into the system. Labour recruitment companies had formerly interacted with one authority, whereas the new arrangement forced them to deal with two. As a result, recruiters not only had to meet the formal criteria of an extra layer of government but also respond to further demands for informal payments. The ministry recentralized the units in 2002, but the decree that did so did not specify that administrative tasks had to be performed by a central authority. This opened up space for the provincial government to establish its own unit bearing the same name as that of the ministry's. In this way, the Jakarta manpower office held on to responsibility for those tasks, the income from which, along with other informal fees collected, supplemented its budget allocation from the centre.

Another development that alarmed stakeholders in the business was that the ministry could no longer rely on the manpower office to produce the 30,000 or so passport recommendations that were needed to get travel documents for the labour recruited for Saudi Arabia each month. Saudi Arabia has always been a very important destination for Indonesians departing under the overseas labour migration programme, and, for historical reasons, the majority of labour migrants transit in Jakarta. Most come from adjacent regions, such as Banten and West Java, and other areas with strong religious affiliations to the Middle East like East Java and Muslim-majority parts of the Lesser Sunda Islands.[8] Then recruits frequently arrived without the full set of documents required to register for the migration process. The provincial government has historically been more than willing to generate real but fake (*asli tapi palsi*, *aspal*) documents, such as identity and family cards to facilitate their migration, despite the fact that legally they only have the right to do so for individuals who have residency status in their jurisdiction.[9]

In exchange for the provincial government's willingness to continue these practices, the ministry brokered an informal arrangement under which the ministry handled administration of labour migrants travelling to the Gulf region and Taiwan while the Jakarta provincial authorities handled those heading to other countries in the Asia Pacific region.[10] The ministry conceded administrative control over finalization of the pre-departure process, which in 2002 entailed collecting USD 15 tax from labour recruitment companies for each labour migrant, to whom the ministry would provide a note exempting them from *fiskal*. A National Audit Agency report on the informal arrangement pointed to some serious accounting issues that this practice caused. The accounting team noted that the ministry only held incomplete records of the amount of tax and number of exemption letters that the manpower office had issued. The official reason given for this was that the manpower office did not

8 For detailed accounts of recruitment in Lombok, see Lindquist, "Labour Recruitment, Circuits of Capital and Gendered Mobility: Reconceptualizing the Indonesian Migration Industry"; Lindquist, "The Elementary School Teacher, the Thug and His Grandmother: Informal Brokers and Transnational Migration from Indonesia."

9 Despite the fact that intending migrants come from somewhere else, however, the administration is legal by this stage because the migrants are formal residents as far as the manpower office is concerned because they hold Jakarta issued documents. For a detailed study of *aspal* documents and their role in the Riau Islands, see Ford and Lyons, "Travelling the Aspal Route: 'Grey' Labour Migration through an Indonesian Border Town."

10 Badan Pemeriksa Keuangan, "Hasil Pemeriksaan Atas Pengelolaan Dana Pembinaan Dan Penyelenggaraan Penempatan Tenaga Kerja Indonesia Dan Pelaksanaan Penempatan Tenaga Kerja Indonesia Ke Luar Negeri Tahun Anggaran 2004 Dan 2005 Pada Ditjen Pembinaan Dan Penempatan Tenaga Kerja Luar Negeri, Dinas Tenaga Kerja, Balai Pelayanan Dan Penempatan Tenaga Kerja Indonesia Serta Instansi Terkait Lainnya Di Surabaya, Pekanbaru Dan Batam," 8.

have a formal reporting relationship with the ministry and so was under no legal obligation to do so.

This arrangement became problematic when the overseas migration law was passed. Law No. 39/2004 on the Placement and Protection of Indonesian Workers Overseas, which replaced earlier ministerial regulations, effectively rendered the ministry's agreement with the manpower office illegal. It required the ministry to take responsibility for administrative tasks at the beginning and end of the overseas labour migration programme. All intermediary roles, such as registering recruits and recommending that they be furnished with passports, were transferred to local authorities, which in Jakarta meant the provincial government. However, established arrangements proved difficult to change because of stakeholders, including personnel in the ministry, who preferred the *status quo*. Despite the passing of the law, the informal division of labour persisted, in part because ministry authorities were unwilling to relinquish the benefits that they gained through it in the form of access to the provincial government's special services, which enabled recruits to be processed in Jakarta. As a result, labour recruitment companies that specialized in sending labour to Saudi Arabia were able to continue their long-standing connections with ministry bureaucrats who were often indirectly involved in the industry.

This did not mean that these arrangements were allowed to continue unchecked. In 2006 the National Audit Agency asked the ministry to deal with the illegal division of labour. By this stage, the ministry's deal with provincial authorities had already entered its fourth year. The relevant director-general explained privately that the situation was not straightforward. The ministry had in fact held conversations with the provincial government about normalizing the arrangement but no agreement had been reached. When the National Audit Agency subsequently pointed to the fact that it was responsible for financial losses, the ministry pursued resolution more aggressively to avoid prosecution under the anti-corruption law. While it cannot be proved that the National Audit Agency's intervention forced its hand, the ministry then revealed long-delayed plans to make corrections to the system by firming up control over roles to finalize the process for migrants to all countries. The first implementation regulation for Law No. 39/2004, passed that year, outlined the division of labour between the ministry, its units and manpower offices across Indonesia.

Even after this – and even at the height of the conflict between the ministry and the BNP2TKI – ministry officials continued to identify the manpower office as the most powerful of the three government agencies in Jakarta. This office had assumed responsibility for services to labour recruitment companies, such as issuing permits to set up the necessary infrastructure, including boarding houses. They registered recruits, archived placement agreements (*perjanjian penempatan*) that outlined nominal rights and responsibilities of recruits and labour recruitment companies to one another, and provided other intermediary services, such as the issuing of passport recommendations. These services constitute the lion's share of administration under the programme. By contrast, the ministry's unit, which would later be transferred to the BNP2TKI, only provided pre-departure training, witnessed the signing of employment contracts and issued notes to exempt labour migrants from *fiskal*. The fact that more than half of the programme's labour migrants passed through Jakarta meant that the manpower office effectively controlled the bulk of the programme's administration. Ministry officials who had experienced the transition from shared control to this division of labour were acutely aware of the power of the Jakarta manpower office, which they were sometimes unable to persuade to follow the ministry's preferred procedures.

It was in this political context that the ministry converted dormant offices at the rear of BNP2TKI's technical implementation unit in East Jakarta into a set of counters to re-assume control over authority to issue recruitment certificates in October 2008. Two months later, Ministerial Regulation No. 22/MEN/XII/2008 on the Implementation of Placement and Protection of Indonesian Workers Overseas reclaimed authority over finalization of the pre-departure process. The ministry's Directorate of Overseas Placement was responsible for overseeing provision of the tasks involved in the East Jakarta unit. But recognizing that the BNP2TKI still provided these services from its unit, which was located on an adjacent plot of land, the Director-General for Guidance of Labour Placement, Gusti Made Arka, gave labour recruitment companies until February to cease working with the BNP2TKI.[11] It is this series of events that led to the BNP2TKI requesting a judicial review, which declared the authorizing regulation invalid.[12] A period of service duplication ensued because the ministry refused to cancel the regulation, and the BNP2TKI announced its intention to resume service provision regardless.

Tanjung Pinang

Tanjung Pinang, the capital of Riau Islands province, is located on the island of Bintan, which is adjacent to Indonesia's international sea border with Malaysia and Singapore. As a consequence, it constitutes a major gateway

---

11 "Dirjen Binapenta I Made Arka: Selama G to G Masih Ada, Dualisme Proses Pelayanan Pemberangkatan TKI."

12 See Chapter 3.

for labour migrants exiting Indonesia. The number of labour migrants officially leaving through the town has fluctuated over time, partly in response to government policy.[13] In 2002 for example, the immigration checkpoint on Batam Island was made the only exit point for domestic workers seeking to enter Singapore.[14] This restriction was lifted in 2007, but not before a sophisticated alternative system had developed in Tanjung Pinang, where largely unlicensed recruiters worked through contacts in the Immigration Offices to secure passports for labour migrants and circumvent the requirements of the official programme.[15]

The ministry had never established an office in Tanjung Pinang because Kepri was only created in 2002, one year after the ministry's manpower offices were transferred to provincial governments. The ministry's offices were in Pekanbaru, the capital city of Riau province, where the manpower office became part of the provincial government. The ministry had maintained control over the programme's implementation unit, which was transferred to the BNP2TKI, along with the other 14 regional units under its control, in 2007. Until 2009 these central government agencies had administered labour migration exiting the Riau Islands through an extension of the implementation unit. In that year, the BNP2TKI converted the post into a fully fledged unit with exclusive jurisdiction to finalize the pre-departure process for the labour migrants departing through the Riau Islands. The decision to do so was largely motivated by the need to establish a foothold closer to the new provincial capital, Tanjung Pinang, as part of an attempt to forge the kind of collegial relationships with provincial authorities there that in Pekanbaru had been useful in implementing the programme when the Riau Islands were part of Riau province. As a result, the BNP2TKI's implementation unit in Tanjung Pinang related with the provincial government on its own terms from the outset, unlike its counterparts in other regions.

The provincial government and the BNP2TKI implementation unit performed complementary tasks in the administration of the overseas labour migration programme in Tanjung Pinang. The provincial manpower office

---

13 Interview data, 3 June 2010.

14 For an overview of this system within the broader context of the overseas migration programme, see Wijayanti, "Kendali Alokasi Sebagai Bentuk Perlindungan Hukum Bagi Tenaga Kerja Indonesia."

15 Ford and Lyons, "Travelling the Aspal Route: 'Grey' Labour Migration through an Indonesian Border Town." The major reason for this policy shift was to prevent the BNP2TKI from assuming authority to enforce it. See also Lindquist and Piper, "From HIV Prevention to Counter-Trafficking: Discursive Shifts and Institutional Continuities in Sout-East Asia."

serviced labour recruitment companies licensed by the ministry, providing them, for example, with the necessary authorizations to approach local governments about setting up offices and boarding house facilities. During my fieldwork, the official responsible for administering the system in the manpower office produced relatively straightforward templates and criteria for the permission-seeking process – unlike in other regions, where labour recruitment companies claimed that the entire process is subject to rent seeking. The threat of sanction and rent seeking associated with maintaining the many illegal boarding houses found in the Riau Islands made this authorization extremely valuable.

To complement these activities, the BNP2TKI's unit finalized the predeparture process for recruited labour: for example, verifying their documents to make sure that they meet the administrative requirements. They must hold a valid passport, work permit and insurance. The unit processes around 40,000 workers each year. The most significant group by far consists of women from rural areas in East Java transiting on the way to Singapore, where they are mainly employed as domestic workers. By contrast, the unit only processes around 5,000 labour migrants who have formal sector jobs in Malaysia.[16] Of this group, only slightly more than half are men. Many of these workers come from within the Riau Islands itself rather than deeper within Indonesian territory. It is important to note that these records represent only a portion of labour migration, given the large numbers of migrants who circumvent the formal system.[17] As a consequence, Kepri is host to a large informal industry in which a wide range of government officials are involved,[18] including the BNP2TKI's own unit.

Another local factor that shapes the way things are done in the Riau Islands is the fact that Tanjung Pinang is a major point of return for Indonesian labour migrants who have been deported from neighbouring countries. In 2002 Malaysian authorities deported 356,256 people to Indonesian border towns in Sumatra and Kalimantan.[19] This figure was exceptionally large because they were cracking down on migrant labourers lacking valid work permits. At first, sub-national government authorities at designated return points set up local

16 Badan Nasional Penempatan dan Perlindungan Tenaga Kerja Indonesia, *Data Penempatan TKI Ke Luar Negeri: Tahun 1994–2007*, 25.

17 Ford, "After Nunukan: The Regulation of Indonesian Migration to Malaysia."

18 Ford and Lyons, "Travelling the Aspal Route: 'Grey' Labour Migration through an Indonesian Border Town."

19 Kementerian Koordinator Kesejahteraan Rakyat, "Kinerja Tim Koordinasi Pemulangan Tenaga Kerja Indonesia Bermasalah Dan Keluarga Dari Malaysia (TK-PTKB) Tahun 2008," 62; Ford, "After Nunukan: The Regulation of Indonesian Migration to Malaysia."

taskforces to anticipate the deportations. However, after the deaths of around 70 deportees in Nunukan were reported in the national media, these efforts were quickly expanded to include central government agencies. In 2004 the Tanjung Pinang taskforce was subsumed into an institution to coordinate a national response to the problems associated with deportations created by President Megawati Sukarnoputri. Since then, the Tanjung Pinang branch, which handles in the vicinity of 35,000 deportees year, has had to establish local mechanisms for financing this operation.[20]

The majority of deportees from West Malaysia disembark at the Port of Kijang on the southeast side of Bintan Island.[21] This prevents the Tanjung Pinang international ferry terminal from being dominated by deportation traffic, serving to keep deportees out of the public eye. Malaysian authorities pay for all expenses up until disembarkation.[22] Indonesian authorities are then responsible for organizing transportation to Tanjung Pinang, their temporary board there and eventual repatriation to their province of origin. In 2007 significant debts were incurred for these services with the state owned enterprises PT Pelni (shipping) and PT Damri (buses).[23] The cost of transportation from the point of arrival to deportees' home cities and districts in other parts of the country was the responsibility of counterpart taskforces in those areas. This undertaking also required resources from sub-national authorities in the transit zones, such as the Riau Islands government based in Tanjung Pinang. The governor of Riau Islands even issued a regulation that established a coordinating team to ensure the provision of services, such as medical check-ups, which enables authorities, such as the manpower office, to charge related expenses to the province's budget when necessary.

The provincial legislature, however, has publicly opposed the province's involvement in repatriation. As a consequence, the governor is not always able to secure a formal budget allocation for these expenses and so provincial authorities involved in the effort to handle the high volume of deportation from

20 Kementerian Koordinator Kesejahteraan Rakyat, "Petunjuk Pelaksanaan Penanganan Dan Pemulangan Tenaga Kerja Indonesia Bermasalah Dan Keluarganya (TKI-B) Dari Malaysia," 10.

21 Lindquist, "Rescue, Return, in Place: Deportees, 'Victims,' and the Regulation of Indonesian Migration."

22 Kementerian Koordinator Kesejahteraan Rakyat, "Petunjuk Pelaksanaan Penanganan Dan Pemulangan Tenaga Kerja Indonesia Bermasalah Dan Keluarganya (TKI-B) Dari Malaysia," 21.

23 Kementerian Koordinator Kesejahteraan Rakyat, "Kinerja Tim Koordinasi Pemulangan Tenaga Kerja Indonesia Bermasalah Dan Keluarga Dari Malaysia (TK-PTKB) Tahun 2007," 19.

Malaysia have come to rely heavily on the supplementary funds it receives from the centre.[24] A strict reading of the decentralization law requires provincial governments to manage the administrative work associated with deportation. But the Riau Islands successfully lobbied central authorities and secured their involvement, arguing that deportations are a national problem.[25] The central government accepted the Riau Islands' argument that the provincial budget should not be used to cover shortfalls. But financial support from central authorities is, nevertheless, insufficient. In 2007, for example, Rp. 8 billion (USD 800,000) was allocated to cover the task force's activities – sufficient only for the first six months.[26] As part of their attempt to deal with these budgetary constraints, the Kepri taskforce has brokered deals with 'colleagues', including but not limited to other government authorities to provide services.

The shortfall was in part remedied in negotiations for the 2008 budget, in which the president specifically earmarked Rp. 350,000,000 (USD 35,000) for 'strengthening' the taskforce's institutional presence in the Riau Islands.[27] The Riau Islands group used their entire allocation, but only 35 per cent of the budget for accommodating and transporting deportees was spent.[28] The annual accountability report for the taskforce cites the fact that the Ministry of Finance did not make the budget allocation available until almost the end of the year. As a result, the task force in the Riau Islands – as elsewhere along Indonesia's international borders – were forced to buy food and transport for deportees on

---

24 The Governor of Riau Islands province has also publicly refused to cooperate with central government agencies, as was the case in his handling of the Oceanic Viking issue in 2009, presumably as part of an attempt to win greater support in the provincial legislature and the Riau Islands electorate. The Oceanic Viking was an Australian custom's ship that rescued asylum seekers from a sinking vessel within Indonesia's search and rescue area. The Australian Prime Minister struck a deal with the Indonesian President that would see the asylum seekers alight in Indonesia. However, local government authorities in Indonesia resisted the instruction to implement the deal. For more details of this case, see Ford, Lyons, and Palmer, "Stopping the Hordes: A Critical Account of the Labor Government's Regional Approach to the Management of Asylum Seekers."

25 The Riau Islands government also attempted to use its connections with governors of sending provinces, but was only successful in convincing West Java to make a budget allocation to help subsidize repatriation.

26 Kementerian Koordinator Kesejahteraan Rakyat, "Kinerja Tim Koordinasi Pemulangan Tenaga Kerja Indonesia Bermasalah Dan Keluarga Dari Malaysia (TK-PTKB) Tahun 2007," 19.

27 Kementerian Koordinator Kesejahteraan Rakyat, "Kinerja Tim Koordinasi Pemulangan Tenaga Kerja Indonesia Bermasalah Dan Keluarga Dari Malaysia (TK-PTKB) Tahun 2008," 12.

28 Ibid., 13.

credit. The situation was so bad in fact that the Ministry of People's Prosperity made enquiries with the Ministry of Finance to obtain a budget top-up so as to prevent unpaid expenses from being debited to the following year's budget.[29] Largely for these reasons, the Riau Islands taskforce had still not purchased or formally leased facilities to accommodate deported citizens even years later.

Instead, the Riau Islands taskforce, which included head of the provincial manpower office as its chair and the head of BNP2TKI's implementation unit, had brokered a deal with a local businessman who agreed to provide the use of a privately owned facility formerly used to house transiting migrants. The taskforce had awarded Aseng, owner of a local business called PT Siam, an exclusive contract to organize the mass repatriation of deportees to their province of residence, mostly in Java or the Lesser Sunda Islands. The boarding facilities were an informal condition of the deal, as were the kickbacks that he channelled to the taskforce's selection committee. The funds contributed to off-budget accounts, which officials on the committee used not only to line their own pockets, but also to protect the taskforce's activities from the vagaries of the budgeting process. In his office, Aseng presented a folder of receipts for the previous week's departures, which showed that PT Siam paid Rp. 250,000 (USD 25) for the passage of each deportee, an expense that he included in his bid to win the contract. With an average of 700 repatriations each week, the activity consumed around Rp. 700,000,000 (USD 70,000) a month. This figure was grossly inflated because Aseng and taskforce officials brokered an alternative arrangement, in which the state-owned enterprises returned a portion of the sum through kickbacks.

This arrangement made it difficult for the ministry to reassign the BNP2TKI's administrative roles to the provincial manpower office. The head of this office resisted the ministry's encouragement to assume responsibility for administration of formal labour migration out of the Riau Islands partly because of the fact that no funding was made available for the role, and partly because the recommendation that the provincial government simply produce letters in lieu of overseas identity cards as a transitional measure seemed unsatisfactory.[30] Even more troubling for him was the politics of doing so, as it entailed taking control of administrative roles that had until then been performed satisfactorily by the BNP2TKI's implementation unit in Tanjung Pinang. More importantly still, the head of the BNP2TKI unit was involved in the taskforce's selection committee, which brokered the deal with Aseng. In addition to personally benefiting from this relationship, he was also therefore privy to details

29 Ibid., 14.

30 Interview data, Tanjung Pinang, 4 January, 2010.

about how it worked.[31] The head of the provincial manpower office was thus content to leave the administrative work in the hands of the BNP2TKI unit, both to avert the risk of these details reaching the public domain and to continue with the effective arrangement that allowed the provincial government to minimize the cost of handling deportees.

Medan

Like Tanjung Pinang, Medan, the capital city of North Sumatra, is an embarkation point for West Malaysia bound labour migration. Some 11,000 labour migrants are processed in the city each year for employment on the Malaysian Peninsula,[32] although it only handles one thousand or so deportees each year.[33] Government statistics maintained by the Ministry of Manpower and the BNP2TKI show the number of women leaving from Medan is seven times higher than the number of men. More than half those women take jobs in the informal sector as domestic workers. As in the Riau Islands most of this latter group of labour migrants originate from other islands, such as Java. By contrast, formal sector migrants mostly originate from Sumatra. The men are mostly employed on construction sites and plantations, and the women in this group are typically employed in factories or the hospitality industry. In all cases, labour migrants historically transited in Medan as part of their itinerary, which involved crossing the Strait of Malacca by boat for access to West Malaysia's largest cities and plantations.

Migrants participating in the overseas labour migration programme formerly only passed through the immigration checkpoint at Port Belawan, which is 25 kilometres north of the city.[34] The port closed its direct route connecting North Sumatra to the northwest of Malaysia in 2010. An indirect route via Tanjungbalai Asahan, 150 kilometres to the south of Medan, also connected Medan to Port Klang on the central coast of the Malaysian Peninsula, which is only a 30 minute car ride to Kuala Lumpur. The Tanjungbalai Asahan-Port Klang segment of the journey takes between six and eight hours. With the introduction of multiple low cost international air routes though, Medan's airport gradually became the main administrative site for international

31 Interview data, Tanjung Pinang, 4 January, 2010.

32 Badan Nasional Penempatan dan Perlindungan Tenaga Kerja Indonesia, *Data Penempatan TKI Ke Luar Negeri: Tahun 1994–2007*, 25.

33 Kementerian Hukum dan HAM, Peran Pemerintah Daerah Di Wilayah Perbatasan Dalam Melindungi Warga Negara Indonesia Yang Dideportasi (Studi Di Propinsi Kalimantan Barat, Kepulauan Riau, Sumatera Utara, Dan Kalimantan Timur), 22.

34 Interview data, Medan, 19 April 2010.

migration.[35] In 2010 Medan International Airport offered direct flights to Penang, Kuala Lumpur and Johor Bahru in Malaysia and to Singapore – all popular destinations under the overseas labour migration programme. Cheap air travel has revolutionized international migration. AirAsia, for example regularly offers Rp. 99,000 (USD 10) flights from Medan to Kuala Lumpur, a trip that only takes one hour. Predictably, these considerations soon encouraged labour recruitment companies to move their business away from sea routes, shifting the demand for programme services closer to the airport, which at the time was located in the city centre.

The administrative culture in Medan did not produce the same kind of collegial response to changes in central regulations pertaining to the overseas labour migration programme as in Tanjung Pinang. In fact, quite the opposite happened. Following promulgation of the 2008 regulation that delegated the BNP2TKI's administrative roles to the provincial government, the relationship between the provincial manpower office and the BNP2TKI unit in Medan deteriorated. Conflict became a feature of the relationship as the manpower office showed greater interest in the administrative activity over time. When the regulation was introduced in December 2008, head of the manpower office ignored the ministry's calls largely because of the absence of an adequate budget allocation for the roles. His position changed after August 2009, when the two central government agencies entered a period of service duplication in Jakarta. The head of the manpower office was largely convinced to change track by those in Medan with commercial interests in the programme who saw distinct advantages in a division of administrative labour that gave the provincial authority effective control.

The historical and spatial particularities of the city also partly explain why conflict developed in Medan. Conflict between the ministry and the BNP2TKI centred around a particular segment of the international labour migrants, namely women with jobs as domestic workers. One of BNP2TKI's objectives in Medan had been to encourage those who migrate informally to participate in the official overseas labour migration programme. But as relatively few labour migrants with employment in Malaysia came from the Medan BNP2TKI unit's jurisdiction, which only covered North Sumatra,[36] it meant that the office mainly dealt with recruits who had been transported in from other provinces

35 Interview data, Medan, 19 April 2010.

36 The jurisdiction of BNP2TKI units sometimes includes multiple provinces, such as the office in Pekanbaru, which covers Jambi, Riau and West Sumatra. Until 2009 when the Tanjung Pinang office was established, the Pekanbaru office also had jurisdiction over the Riau Islands.

by locally registered labour recruitment companies. The head of the Medan BNP2TKI unit was at first confused by the behaviour of the recruitment industry. During conversations with labour recruitment company owners in the area, he learned that it made economic sense to the recruitment industry to concentrate on female migrants from further afield. Supplying domestic workers was a profitable business, but the major source areas for migrant labour of this kind were on islands further east, namely Java, Lombok and Sumbawa. The migration infrastructure in Medan had enabled them to channel these workers cheaply and quickly (by plane) and legally (through the BNP2TKI's unit) to Malaysia.

But the nature of services had changed since the manpower office was involved, as the overseas migration law introduced pre-departure training and replaced the departure tax exemption letter with an overseas identity card. The combination of more administrative responsibilities on a larger scale raised the stakes around control. The ministry's technical implementation unit in East Jakarta charged Rp. 50,000 (USD 5) per migrant, generating a significant source of non-tax income, which could be used to fund related administrative activity.[37] In this case, the funds were used to produce overseas identity cards. The ministry encouraged the head of the Medan manpower office to introduce a similar charge using the provincial government's authority to seek compensation from those who used their services. This opportunity was even more attractive in the context of budget transfers from the centre to subnational governments, which gave the provincial government only ten per cent of the amount earmarked for North Sumatra.[38] In this particular location, where more than 10,000 labour migrants require the service each year, this fee promised to generate Rp. 500,000,000 (USD 50,000) for discretionary purposes.

In December 2009, the head of the BNP2TKI issued a circular memorandum to the heads of its units in the regions and to the heads of provincial manpower offices requiring the government agency with the necessary infrastructure to furnish labour migrants with overseas identity cards. As was the case in Jakarta, the only government unit in Medan that had the systems and machinery in place to do so was the BNP2TKI unit. The BNP2TKI unit had billboards erected

37 *Governmental Regulation No. 73/1999 on Tata Cara Penggunaan Penerimaan Negara Bukan Pajak Yang Bersumber Dari Kegiatan Tertentu*, article 4.

38 For 2010 the North Sumatra government received Rp. 813,233,489,000, while Deli Serdang District received Rp. 793,141,685,000 and Medan Municipality received Rp. 784,139,518,000. There are 27 other local governments within North Sumatra. For further details see *Presidential Regulation No. 43/2009 on Dana Alokasi Umum Daerah Provinsi, Kabupaten, Dan Kota Tahun 2010.*

around the airport reminding migrants that they need to hold overseas identity cards. However, as was also the case in Jakarta, the police unit and immigration officers at the Medan International Airport were reluctant to intervene against labour migrants who held exemption letters, which in this location had been issued by the Medan manpower office. As a result, the BNP2TKI unit and the manpower office were enabled to effectively duplicate finalization of the pre-departure process, hindering the collection of statistics on the number of migrant workers departing through the programme.

The manpower office and the BNP2TKI unit were located on the same plot of land and, from the perspective of labour recruitment companies, both government units were strategically placed to perform the necessary administrative roles. Jalan Asrama is only 20 kilometres distance from the international airport and an exit on the Trans-Sumatra highway, which runs from the northernmost tip of the island (Banda Aceh) to the southernmost (Bandar Lampung). Also, the fact that it is a residential area enabled labour recruitment companies to not only transport labour migrants in from other parts of the country without having to pass through the city centre, but also to temporarily accommodate them there. It was this fact that the manpower office exploited to leverage greater control over the contested services under the overseas labour migration programme. The head of the BNP2TKI unit had close friends in the manpower office next door, who informed him that the official with authority to authorize the establishment of boarding houses was coercing the recruitment industry into using exemption letters in place of overseas identity cards. This gradually eroded some – but not all – of the demand for services at the BNP2TKI office.

This brief description explains how the manpower office wrested control from the BNP2TKI. But, as indicated above, the motivation to become involved in the first place came from the recruitment industry itself. In order to process labour migrants from outside the province, labour recruitment companies frequently sought to have them registered as residents in North Sumatra. This enabled them to obtain the necessary passport recommendation letters that, according to the overseas migration law, only local government could issue. The head of the BNP2TKI unit, claimed that he had made it clear to labour recruitment companies that his staff were under instruction not to finalize the departure process without this letter. This was a BNP2TKI policy to prevent the recruitment industry from circumventing the local government. It was undermined by the provincial manpower office, which began processing labour recruitment companies' requests for services without prior consent from local authorities, and at times even forging their authorization. Records from this period confirm that the number of applications processed by local administrations was dwarfed by those recorded by the manpower office and the BNP2TKI.[39]

In part, the manpower office was open to becoming involved in the administration of the programme because of pressure from local legislators. Some legislators profited directly and indirectly from the migration business, making them sensitive to the commercial interests of the recruitment industry. In this case, labour recruitment companies wanted the manpower office to help circumvent local authorities who complicated matters, for example, by demanding bribes in return for services such as registering migrants and recommending that the Immigration Office furnish them with passports. These legislators then approached the Governor of North Sumatra, Syamsul Arifin, explaining that the Minister for Manpower's regulations gave the provincial government control over finalization of the pre-departure process.[40] The Governor then instructed the head of the manpower office to determine what needed to be done in order to take on that role. The provincial parliament eventually intervened formally, calling on the provincial manpower office and the BNP2TKI unit to defend the legality of their activity in a mediation session that replicated the one that had taken place in Jakarta a few months earlier. The head of the BNP2TKI unit fully expected legislators to side with the provincial government because their priorities lay with interests in North Sumatra, unlike his, which also had a national dimension.

This competition eroded the veneer of cohesion that government agencies seek to promote, revealing how different parts of the state respond differently to stimulus in their environment. The relationships between the provincial manpower office and the BNP2TKI unit were not as strong as those in Tanjung Pinang, where the different agencies already worked on more issues together. In Medan, their administrative involvement in the programme was more or less clearly differentiated at the time that the ministry's regulation was introduced. At that point, the manpower office had responsibility for authorizing the establishment of recruitment industry infrastructure, and the BNP2TKI unit took charge of finalizing the pre-departure process for labour migrants. The provincial manpower office became involved in administration of the pre-departure process in response to lobbying by a network of labour recruitment

39 Badan Nasional Penempatan dan Perlindungan Tenaga Kerja Indonesia, "Sistem Online BNP2TKI Atasi Disparitas Data TKI Di Disnaker Sumut."

40 Syamsul Arifin was formerly regent of Langkat District. The largest discrepancy between the number of labour migrants registered with a local government and whose pre-departure process was finalized concerned this district. Arifin was removed from public office in 2011 after the Supreme Court sentenced him to six years in prison for corruption.

companies and legislators who convinced the governor to have the manpower office take on the roles. This, therefore, is a case where considerations of scale trumped those of collegiality between different levels of government in a particular place.

Semarang

Another site where scalar considerations trumped the flatter, horizontal relationships in a particular place is the capital city of Central Java, Semarang. This city is a major transit site for migrant labour, mostly from within that province but also from adjacent regions, such as Yogyakarta and East Java. Migrants are mainly female domestic workers leaving for employment in the Asia Pacific region, but around one fifth are men heading to formal sector jobs in Malaysia.[41] Semarang is the third largest administrative site for the programme on Java after Jakarta and Surabaya. As a result, Semarang officials have had to deal with the kinds of demands that the recruitment industry places on the state apparatus to administer its business, such as those illustrated above in the case of Medan. In Semarang, administration of the overseas labour migration programme was formerly dominated by the provincial manpower office but, as in Medan, changes to the political system and in local conditions have challenged the status quo. In this case, the disaggregation of the BNP2TKI unit from what would later become a provincial government agency introduced a new authority into the administration of labour migrants, unsettling networks that made the programme work in Semarang much in the same way as in Jakarta, albeit on a much smaller scale.

Semarang was formerly only a transit site for intending migrants leaving through Jakarta. But with the introduction of direct flights to popular destination countries, such as Malaysia and Singapore, it has also developed as a site of embarkation. In 1989 a Silk Air route was introduced between Surakarta, the second largest city in the province, and Singapore, creating an alternative for migrants seeking to circumvent the official system.[42] But it was the introduction of low-cost flights from Surakarta to Kuala Lumpur by AirAsia in 2006 that prompted change. The Ministry of Manpower's implementation unit in Semarang, which was to be transferred to the BNP2TKI in 2007 was called on to open a counter at Surakarta International Airport. As suggested by this move,

---

41 Badan Nasional Penempatan dan Perlindungan Tenaga Kerja Indonesia, *Data Penempatan TKI Ke Luar Negeri: Tahun 1994–2007*.

42 Labour migrants heading to Singapore ought to have passed through Jakarta. An exception occurred between 2004 and 2007 when all Singapore-bound labour migration was required to transit in Batam.

the programme's scope was adjusted in response to the success of private air carriers in securing the opening of regional airports for international routes. Eight of the 21 BNP2TKI staff eventually stationed at the Surakarta airport were reassigned to Semarang International Airport to help with administration following the introduction of another AirAsia route connecting that city to Kuala Lumpur a few years later.[43]

The history of control over the implementation unit influenced the way in which the conflict between the ministry and the BNP2TKI played out in Semarang. Until 1999 the unit was subordinate to the provincial manpower office. However, this arrangement changed when the Minister for Manpower at the time, Fahmi Idris, made units directly responsible to the ministry. In 2001 the central government began to recognize the manpower office's jurisdiction over decentralized aspects of the programme, such as authorizing the establishment of recruitment industry infrastructure in the province, as required by the two year deadline stipulated in Article 132 (2) of Law No. 22/1999 on Regional Governance. In this transition period, ministry staff were on the ministry's payroll but remained in the provincial manpower office's building. As this arrangement suggests, unit staff effectively operated under a dual management system: they were structurally accountable to the centre but were expected to toe the line in the provincial manpower office.

The fact that the unit was situated in the manpower office also meant that provincial government colleagues could sometimes exert influence over the BNP2TKI's work with labour recruitment companies. This was particularly the case, for example, when labour recruitment companies sought to have the predeparture process finalized for labour migrants who were recruited in the Special Region of Yogyakarta or East Java. Around 15 of the 40 or so recruitment companies in the province maintained an office in Semarang, where they had developed mutually beneficial relationships with the relevant officials. However, the ministry encouraged its unit to scrutinize migrants' documents more carefully in order to ensure greater accuracy in records of labour migrants' origin for planning purposes and so that the next of kin could be contacted in an emergency. Tensions also grew as labour recruitment companies that had previously received preferential treatment were overlooked in favour of others. This was particularly the case when a labour recruitment company that was closely associated to a manpower office staffer was refused special treatment. The tension was settled in 2002 when the ministry replaced the unit manager with an outsider from Jakarta, partly severing informal ties to manpower office staff.[44]

43 Badan Nasional Penempatan dan Perlindungan Tenaga Kerja Indonesia, "BP3TKI Semarang Siap Layani TKI Di Bandara Ahmad Yani."

44 Interview data, Yogyakarta, 10 October 2010.

As a next step, the ministry moved the unit into another building 20 minutes south of the provincial manpower office in 2003. Located on the highway that runs into the Semarang city centre, where the manpower office remained, the new location was also strategically south of the ring road. This enabled access by those travelling from west, south and east of the province to the unit and the airport without having to enter Semarang. Moving into their own office space disrupted the relationship of dependence that had grown between the implementation unit and the provincial manpower office. It extricated the provincial government from all processes to do with migrant workers, and firmed control over finalization of the pre-departure process in the hands of the central government. This reconfiguration of power relations enabled the central government authorities to have more say in how the programme was administered. In 2005 following introduction of the overseas migration law, the unit ran mandatory pre-departure training and started setting up systems to replace the exemption letter with an overseas identity card. On average, the unit produced around 200 such cards daily, which grew over time to 400 per day after it expanded capacity by opening up an administrative post in Cilacap on the other side of the province.[45]

The longstanding practice of re-documenting residents so that they could use the Semarang services continued, but the provincial manpower office was no longer involved.[46] Recruiters acquired the necessary migration documents from local government administrations that were amenable to their demands. Part of the reason for doing so was that labour recruitment companies source migrants from a wide catchment area, and those recruits do not always arrive with all of the necessary documents, such as birth certificates and identity cards. Moreover, some migrants even fall short of age restrictions and education standards, and so labour recruitment companies want state documents that hide those facts. Some local administrations further afield also complicated matters. For example, the head of Sragen District and even the Governor of Yogyakarta had at different times imposed bans on migration for informal sector work in order to discourage the population from taking up certain kinds of employment overseas, such as domestic work, despite high demand for it. To circumvent restrictions, recruiters organized to have other local

45 Badan Nasional Penempatan dan Perlindungan Tenaga Kerja Indonesia, "BP3TKI Semarang Terbitkan 400 KTKLN per Hari."

46 The number of cards that the unit claimed to produce exceeded the number of migrant workers that it recorded as leaving the country. Moreover, unit staff developed a reputation for prioritizing service provision to some employment companies over others. See Hariani and Lestari, "Analisis Kualitas Pelayanan Di Balai Pelayanan Penempatan Dan Perlindungan Tenaga Kerja Indonesia (BP3TKI) Semarang Provinsi Jawa Tengah."

administrations provide the documents, a practice that BNP2TKI units in most places were prepared to overlook.

It was in this context that in 2008 the Minister for Manpower sought to delegate the task of finalizing the pre-departure process to provincial manpower offices. In Semarang, head of the provincial manpower office eagerly took up the responsibility, tasking staff to provide pre-departure training, verify documents and issue overseas identity cards. However, the office issued exemption letters to migrants instead of identity cards, pointing to the ministry's assurance that this arrangement was temporary. At the same time, the implementation unit – which had been transferred to the BNP2TKI the previous year – continued to issue identity cards. This duplication continued uneasily until the end of December 2009, when the BNP2TKI instructed law enforcement agencies, including the regional head of police in Semarang, to crack down on migrant workers without the card. The head of police at the Semarang International Airport was also called on to do all in his power to make life difficult for migrant labour that presented exemption letters instead of identity cards. This situation panicked Semarang based labour recruitment companies that had used the manpower office's services, and they turned to the Governor of Central Java, Mardiyanto, to help sort out the confusing situation.[47]

Mardiyanto wrote to the Minister for Manpower three days after the crackdown started, exhorting him to resolve the conflict with the BNP2TKI. In the correspondence, he claimed that competition between the provincial manpower office and the BNP2TKI's unit in Semarang had made it difficult to apply a single standard, and that public attention to this problem was damaging public perceptions of the state as a cohesive entity. The governor sent a carbon copy of the correspondence to a range of institutions in Jakarta, including the BNP2TKI. All of Indonesia's governors also received a copy, alerting them to an issue that may also have been occurring in their jurisdiction. During fieldwork, a provincial government official in Banda Aceh brandished the letter in an interview as evidence that the conflict in Jakarta was playing out in unpredictable ways in each province. Semarang was arguably one of the worst affected sites because the BNP2TKI unit and the provincial manpower office had more business over which to compete. In places such as Banda Aceh and Banjarbaru, there was no conflict, largely because there was no real business of which to speak.[48]

---

47 Mardiyanto was re-elected Governor of Central Java in 2003. He held this position until 2007 when President Susilo Bambang Yudhoyono appointed him Minister for Internal Affairs.

48 To illustrate, in 2007 Banjarbaru in South Kalimatan processed 42 migrants and Banda Aceh recorded 99. See Badan Nasional Penempatan dan Perlindungan Tenaga Kerja Indonesia, *Data Penempatan TKI Ke Luar Negeri: Tahun 1994–2007*, 25.

The correspondence itself was not acted on immediately, but it added momentum to demands from the regions to have top managers in the central government end the conflict.

Nunukan

Located on the northeast international border with Malaysia on the island of Borneo, Nunukan is another site through which labour migrants leave Indonesia and are deported. 2,000 kilometres north of Semarang, it is the major gateway between Indonesia and the East Malaysian state of Sabah. In 2007 when the BNP2TKI assumed control of the Nunukan unit, 70,000 departures were recorded, which staff revealed mostly originated from Sulawesi and Flores, to the east.[49] The unit was the only one that the ministry established in a site that was not also the capital city of the province. It was established in 1984 by the Minister for Manpower, Sudomo, in an attempt to harness some of the 3,000 labour migrants who arrived by boat each month and entered Malaysia without valid migration documents.[50] The significance of Nunukan does not stop there. In 2002 the district became a household name following the death of deported migrants due to gross negligence on the part of Indonesian authorities – an event commonly referred to as the Nunukan Tragedy. As many as 25,000 Indonesians waited in temporary camps while recruiters looked for employers and sorted out the necessary paperwork with Indonesian and Malaysian officials so that the deportees could return to Sabah. But after evidence emerged that around 70 people had died there due to unsanitary conditions, the central government intervened by offering the local administration money to help build accommodation facilities for deportees in anticipation of more large-scale deportations.[51]

Nunukan is an exceptional site because it hosts a range of central government offices but is not a provincial capital city. Until 2013 Nunukan fell under the jurisdiction of the provincial authorities of East Kalimantan, in Samarinda, which was only accessible by multiple plane trips or a combination of boat and car travel.[52] But Samarinda was primarily concerned with the administration of the oil and gas rich areas of Balikpapan and Bontang, rather than the immigration hotspot of Nunukan. Moreover, unlike Tanjung Pinang, where

49 For more on this, see Hugo, "Population Movement in Indonesia since 1971"; Idrus, "Makkunrai Passimokolo': Bugis Migrant Women Workers in Malaysia."

50 Departemen Tenaga Kerja, *Perluasan Kesempatan Kerja Melalui Antar Kerja Antar Negara Ke Malaysia Timur.*

51 For an extended discussion of the Nunukan Crisis, see Ford, "After Nunukan: The Regulation of Indonesian Migration to Malaysia."

52 In 2013 it was transferred into the province North Kalimantan.

the transit point coincided with the provincial capital, provincial authorities in East Kalimantan could afford to ignore isolated Nunukan. The provincial manpower office also stood to gain very little from becoming involved in the situation in Nunukan, as labour recruitment companies generally maintained only a coordinating office on the island, opting to keep their main operations closer to sources of migrant labour. As a consequence, the provincial government's main function – authorizing labour recruitment companies to set up infrastructure, such as offices and boarding houses – was irrelevant. A final additional factor that influenced the provincial government's decision to forestall setting up presence in the area was the large proportion of migrants leaving via Nunukan outside the formal overseas labour migration programme altogether.[53]

By contrast, there are several central government offices in Nunukan, including immigration, customs, the police and a BNP2TKI unit, reflecting its importance as a transit point for migrants and thus as a flashpoint in Indonesia's bilateral relationship with Malaysia. Their presence also meant that central authorities were more important players than the provincial government in the district. The BNP2TKI unit, for example, is routinely involved in Nunukan government organized coordination meetings in response to frequent announcements in Malaysia about plans to deport labour migrants from Indonesia who lack valid migration documents. These central government units have also developed an informal system that helps labour migrants to circumvent the system, much like the case as described in Tanjung Pinang.[54] In Nunukan, migration intermediaries known as fixers (*pengurus*) make the necessary deals with immigration officials to secure the exit of migrants without passports.[55] Local entrepreneurs also double as migration intermediaries.[56] This local phenomenon clearly subverts all sorts of laws, but it is none the less a feature of social and administrative landscape in which the BNP2TKI unit is required to engage.

---

53 Ford, "After Nunukan: The Regulation of Indonesian Migration to Malaysia."

54 For more details on this, see Ford and Lyons, "Travelling the Aspal Route: 'Grey' Labour Migration through an Indonesian Border Town."

55 For more details on this system, see Idrus, "Makkunrai Passimokolo': Bugis Migrant Women Workers in Malaysia," 156–157.

56 Locals in Nunukan have married this business with small time international trade in items, such as sugar and plastic housewares from Malaysia, which are often considered higher quality and cheaper than equivalent products in Indonesia. They exploit the fact that international ferries compete for the business of migrant workers. In exchange for putting the migrants on their boats, the transporters offer intermediaries free passage to and from Tawau for travel on the same day.

This reality of labour migration through Nunukan poses a challenge to the BNP2TKI unit, which is tasked with the job of convincing other government agencies to discipline staff who facilitate irregular international labour migration. Central authorities based in Jakarta, Kuala Lumpur, Kota Kinabalu and Tawau want Indonesian immigration officials in Nunukan to screen border crossers to ensure that they hold a valid work permit for employment in Malaysia. However, it is not always easy to convince institutions at the peripheries to implement central rules. This is certainly the case in Nunukan, where immigration officials have been amenable to turning a blind eye in exchange for a bribe. This situation is further complicated by the fact that Malaysian authorities on the other side of the border are also complicit. In Tawau, Malaysian officials were prepared to relax immigration policy. For example, intermediaries may travel with a bundle of passports for Indonesian citizens still at work in places further inland.[57] Malaysian officials provide the necessary visa stamp when the passport leaves and when it returns.

The BNP2TKI unit is not involved in this arrangement. Instead, it focuses on labour migrants passing through the official system, and especially the administration of re-entry for deported migrant workers. The ministry showed little interest in the border area after the implementation unit was established in 1984, preferring to focus its attention on labour migration leaving international airports on Java.[58] However, the central government scaled up its presence on the island in 2005 following the introduction of a national taskforce to coordinate regional responses to the deportation of Indonesian citizens the previous year.[59] Between 2006 and 2010, the BNP2TKI unit's budget allocation was increased to purchase equipment including computers, machinery for printing identity cards and a car for the use of unit staff.[60] The additional expenditure

57 Personal observation, Tawau, 2 June 2010.

58 Ford, "After Nunukan: The Regulation of Indonesian Migration to Malaysia."

59 For details of the taskforce, see *Presidential Decree No. 106/2004 on Tim Koordinasi Pemulangan Tenaga Kerja Indonesia Bermasalah Dan Keluarganya Dari Malaysia*. For reports on its implementation, see Kementerian Koordinator Kesejahteraan Rakyat, "Kinerja Tim Koordinasi Pemulangan Tenaga Kerja Indonesia Bermasalah Dan Keluarga Dari Malaysia (TK-PTKB) Tahun 2007"; Kementerian Koordinator Kesejahteraan Rakyat, "Kinerja Tim Koordinasi Pemulangan Tenaga Kerja Indonesia Bermasalah Dan Keluarga Dari Malaysia (TK-PTKB) Tahun 2008"; Kementerian Koordinator Kesejahteraan Rakyat, "Petunjuk Pelaksanaan Penanganan Dan Pemulangan Tenaga Kerja Indonesia Bermasalah Dan Keluarganya (TKI-B) Dari Malaysia."

60 While this budget allocation increased, discretionary funds decreased each year. The year after the BNP2TKI assumed control of the unit, expenditure on officials' salaries was halved. Most retired but some were reassigned to other BNP2TKI units, including Makassar.

was justified through the claim that the state could best protect migrants by ensuring that they left the country with a complete set of migration documents. However, in fact, the decision was largely motivated by a desire to profit from the opportunities that emerged from what became routine deportations of citizens who wished to re-enter Malaysia as soon as possible.[61]

The Nunukan district government provided an integrated solution to the problem of missing state documents. The Population and Civil Registration Office, an agency of the district government, provided intending migrants from other areas of the country (including those seeking to re-migrate after deportation) with *aspal* documents that made the migrants appear as though they resided in Nunukan. The term bleaching (*pemutihan*), or regularization, was already commonly used for migrants whose migration status, was legalized by Malaysian authorities in Malaysian territory.[62] But in Nunukan, the term assumed an additional meaning as authorities furnished intending migrant workers with new birth certificates, identity cards and passports that hid the fact that they were from another jurisdiction, in some cases also changing their personal details. As in Tanjung Pinang, these documents helped migrants avoid the official programme altogether. But *aspal* documents also facilitated access to the programme in Nunukan, as they did in Jakarta and Semarang, where labour migrants were required to hold local identity documents to register.

In 2010 however, the number of migrants processed in Nunukan decreased dramatically. There were three main reasons for this decline. First, the Sabah government did not require unlawful migrants to return to Indonesia for the purpose of organizing a full set of valid migration documents that year. Rather, migrants were permitted to remain in Malaysia while they sorted out the paperwork with the Indonesian consulate in Tawau and then organized a work permit with the Sabah immigration authority. Second, the BNP2TKI unit in Makassar, South Sulawesi, had started processing labour migrants there since 2008.[63] This enabled workers to leave Nunukan on the first outward bound international ferry immediately after their arrival. Third, after 2006, the passport application process was simplified, allowing citizens to apply for travel documents at any Immigration Office in the country, whereas before they could

61 For some Indonesians, the prospect of returning to their province of origin was unattractive because it offered little in the way of gainful employment. Others were born or had otherwise spent most of their life in Malaysia and so saw that country as their home, but lacked the documents they required to be able to remain.

62 For more on regularization programmes in Sabah, see Kassim, "Filipino Refugees in Sabah: State Responses, Public Stereotypes and the Dilemma over Their Future."

63 Interview data, Nunukan, 3 June 2010.

only do so at a designated office, determined by the address recorded in their national identity card. The same policy was introduced for the full suite of services associated with the finalization of permission to depart, including for services at BNP2TKI units across the country. This enabled labour recruitment companies to organize these administrative requirements en route to Nunukan in cities such as Makassar, Mataram and Surabaya.[64]

It was at this time that the ministry's decision requiring provincial manpower offices to take over responsibility for the finalization services that the BNP2TKI units had previously provided was promulgated. However, unlike all other sites described here, there was simply no provincial authority present in Nunukan to do so. The provincial government in Samarinda could have intervened, but it was clear to all by this stage that the province was going to be partitioned, and that Nunukan was to fall within the jurisdiction of another province. The fact that there was effectively no provincial authority in Nunukan made the contest with the BNP2TKI in Jakarta, over 3,000 kilometres away, feel not only distant but also lacking in relevance in ways that was not the case in Medan and Tanjung Pinang. Moreover, the drastic decline in the number of migrant workers who required those administrative services in Nunukan as a result of a combination of Indonesian and Malaysian policy changes meant that there was very little to do. It is these factors that spared administrators working in Nunukan from the political headache of working out how to best accommodate the centre's conflicting policies concerning the administration of the overseas labour migration programme.

Surabaya

Surabaya, the capital city of East Java, is the largest administrative centre for the overseas labour migration programme outside Jakarta. Located 300 kilometres to the east of Semarang, Surabaya has an international airport that boasts daily flights to popular labour migration destinations not just in Southeast Asia but also to Hong Kong, Seoul and Taipei. Some 45 per cent of those processed in Surabaya migrate for overseas domestic employment, while the rest leave Indonesia for jobs in construction, plantation agriculture, as well as manufacturing and hospitality sectors. As many as 65 per cent are women.[65] Official statistics suggest that the main source areas for these migrants are

---

64 Evidence of the rise and fall of the migration business is visible in the main town, where each street is decorated with ageing signs that show where employment companies' representatives formerly operated.

65 Badan Nasional Penempatan dan Perlindungan Tenaga Kerja Indonesia, *Data Penempatan TKI Ke Luar Negeri: Tahun 1994–2007*, 25–26.

Malang, Ponorogo, Blitar, Banyuwangi and Tulungagung in that order.[66] East Java also has the highest concentration of labour recruitment companies (over 70) outside Jakarta. As in Nunukan, however, the state's institutional arrangement for handling the administration of the recruitment industry and their business in Surabaya is unlike any other province in the country.

In Surabaya, like Nunukan, one of the tiers of government is effectively absent – in this case, the BNP2TKI unit. This unusual situation is explained by a series of events during the New Order and in the early stages of decentralization.[67] In Surabaya, the services associated with the overseas labour migration programme were provided from a small counter in the provincial manpower office from the year of its establishment in 1984 until 1992. In this year, Abdul Latief as Minister for Manpower authorized its relocation to a standalone building to accommodate the increasingly large volume of work it was required to perform as the programme expanded. The new office was located south of the city centre near the exit of the major toll road that provided those coming from the east, south and west of the province with a faster connection to the airport. In 1999 the office was removed from the control of the provincial manpower office by Latief's successor, Fahmi Idris. But in 2001, the governor of East Java seized control of the unit, transforming it into the country's first and only special unit that implemented central government laws but was structurally subordinate to officials in Surabaya.[68]

The governor used the fact that unit staff had not received their salary from the ministry for three months as a justification for his actions. Over time, however, it became clear that the governor's motivations were much more complex. Administrators in the provincial government were concerned that decentralization laws had reduced the province's role to that of coordinator in the region. In addition, there was a formal expectation that the governor served as an extension of central government authority. According to their interpretation, which turned out to be more or less accurate, the decentralization agenda effectively hollowed out the provincial level of government, making it financially dependent on central government handouts to pay for infrastructure, personnel and programmes. Moreover, it was clear that central government authorities intended to maintain a foothold in the province by embedding various specialist units into the administrative landscape. East Java, along with

66 Badan Nasional Penempatan dan Perlindungan Tenaga Kerja Indonesia, "Penempatan Berdasar Daerah Asal (kota/kabupaten) 2011–2012."

67 For background on the relative autonomy of East Java during the New Order, see Dick, Fox, and Mackie, *Balanced Development: East Java in the New Order.*

68 *Gubernatorial Regulation (East Java) No. 35/2000 on Dinas Tenaga Kerja.*

a number of other regions, pre-empted the development by claiming control first. In other cases, the ministry successfully negotiated with provincial authorities to recentralize the units within a few years. But it failed to do so in East Java, making Surabaya the exception.

As a result of this arrangement, the provincial manpower office was able to filter the directives emanating from the centre, and apply them according to its own logic. It announced that it would accept recruitment certificates that were issued by both the ministry and the BNP2TKI in Jakarta. The province already had responsibility for pre-departure training, verifying migration documents and producing overseas identity cards, which it had come to control by default. Through control of these administrative functions, the provincial manpower office effectively shielded the East Java recruitment industry from the conflict and uncertainty that first emerged in Jakarta but, as described above, also came to feature in Medan and Semarang. While the ministry was pleased with this outcome, since it was the intention of the 2008 regulation to delegate authority over these roles to provincial authorities outside Jakarta, the BNP2TKI was less so.[69] In Surabaya, then, the unit, which in other locations was accountable to the BNP2TKI, was effectively subordinated to the provincial manpower office, obviating the possibility of horizontal conflict between national and provincial authorities concerning administration of the overseas labour migration programme.

The spoils brought by the provincial government's victory were significant. In 2001 the governor instructed the unit to deposit the migrant worker levy of USD 15 per person in the provincial government's bank account. This directive diverted revenue that would have otherwise passed through the ministry's hands. Handling of tax collection in the ministry and other state agencies usually involves holding funds temporarily in an off-budget account to generate interest for institutional and private use. Ministry statistics show that a total of 380,690 migrants ought to have paid USD 5,710,350 in levies in 2004. A conservative estimate suggests that ministry officials may have collected around USD 50,000 in interest on this amount that year alone.[70] As a result of the East Java governor's directive, the provincial government collected the tax

69 The BNP2TKI allocated the budget that it would have otherwise given to its unit in Surabaya to perform those roles, and senior officials included negotiations to gain control of the unit in an order of business in 2011. As of August 2013, the BNP2TKI's negotiations with the Governor of East Java had still not concluded so the unit remained under the control of the provincial manpower office.

70 This figure was calculated using compound interest at 10%, compounded weekly, assumption that sum is transferred to the Ministry of Finance each week.

for 97,777 migrants between 2005 and 2006.[71] This amounted to nearly USD 1,500,000 in revenue for the provincial government. Significantly, it translated into a comparable loss for the Ministry of Finance, which was deprived of the revenue, and the Ministry of Manpower, which was deprived of the opportunity to harvest the interest on those taxes before they were remitted.

As this example suggests, the governor's wresting of control over the processing of labour migrants was aimed at increasing access to resources. At the same time, authority to collect the levy also augmented the provincial manpower office's power over labour recruitment companies. The provincial government gave the East Java chapter of APJATI, the major association of recruiters in the area, an office to collect the levy in the building alongside a counter for the East Java government owned Bank Jatim. In 2005 the East Java regional secretary, Soekarwo, who would himself become governor in 2008, was appointed grand commissioner on the Bank Jatim's advisory board. This institutional arrangement effectively enabled provincial authorities to grant (and cover up) exemptions concerning payment of the levy. The fact that the provincial government controlled collection of the levy gave the officials associated with it access to funds that were handled by BNP2TKI units in other sites. In 2007 when the BNP2TKI became operational, its officials collected almost USD 9.5 million. In the same year, the East Java provincial government handled almost USD 900,000, out of sight from central government authorities.

These activities did not go unnoticed. Like all other agencies and units, the provincial government is subject to account inspection by the National Audit Agency. When its accounts for 2004 and 2005 were inspected in 2006, the auditing agency found a discrepancy between the revenue that ought to have been deposited with Bank Jatim based on the number of migrants in the provincial manpower office's records and the amount that was actually collected. The agency put the discrepancy down to negligence (*kelalaian*) and recommended that the governor fix the problem.[72] In reality, money may have been siphoned off for private purposes, but it is also likely that at least some of it had been used to pay for institutional activity, as is the practice in other parts of the bureaucracy.[73]

Control of tasks associated with labour recruitment companies offered an alternative source of revenue to fiscal transfers from Jakarta, which kept

---

71 Badan Nasional Penempatan dan Perlindungan Tenaga Kerja Indonesia, *Data Penempatan TKI Ke Luar Negeri: Tahun 1994–2007*.

72 An interview with a public auditor revealed that in her experience negligence is generally a euphemism for many kinds of maladministration, of which some are deliberate.

73 Mietzner, "Party Financing in Post-Soeharto Indonesia: Between State Subsidies and Political Corruption"; Mietzner, "Funding Pilkada: Illegal Campaign Financing In Indonesia's Local Elections."

the province dependent on the central government. The Ministry of Finance carefully monitors the production of local regulations for such attempts to generate revenue, which the Ministry of Internal Affairs then cancels, citing the justification that the rules stifle investment by raising transaction costs.[74] While this may be the case, it is also a possibility that this form of gate-keeping aims to prevent leakage from central funds. To illustrate, the National Audit Agency recommended that the Ministry of Finance reverse the loss that the central government incurred as a result of the East Java government's regulation annexing the levy charged to labour migrants. In the following year's fiscal transfer, the agency suggested that the Ministry of Finance reduce the East Java government's share by the same amount earned by the province through collection of the levy.[75] This highlights an important dynamic of centre-periphery power relations whereby the sub-national tier seeks ways to reduce dependence on the centre and the centre looks for ways to maintain the upper hand.

However unaccounted funds were used, the provincial government eventually agreed to transfer 30 per cent of the levy to the Ministry of Manpower. At first glance, it appears as though the ministry and East Java authorities agreed to redistribute the revenue according to the law on fiscal decentralization, which requires the centre to transfer 70 per cent of total revenue to the regions. But an auditing report reveals that a shadow system was used to make the transaction. The East Java governor authorized a series of payments to the private bank account of Gusti Made Arka, who was then the Director-General for Placement of Guidance of Overseas Labour in the ministry. A legal transfer would have entailed depositing the funds with the Ministry of Finance, which would then make part of it available to the Ministry of Manpower. But the fact that the governor agreed to transfer state funds into the director-general's private bank account indicates that this practice constitutes part of an informal settlement between central and provincial authorities concerning access to financial resources associated with the overseas labour migration programme, such as the levy. It may have been this informal transaction that secured the ministry's acceptance of the status quo in which the provincial manpower office controlled the technical implementation unit.

74 Butt, "Regional Autonomy and Legal Disorder: The Proliferation of Local Laws in Indonesia."

75 Badan Pemeriksa Keuangan, "Hasil Pemeriksaan Atas Pengelolaan Dana Pembinaan Dan Penyelenggaraan Penempatan Tenaga Kerja Indonesia Dan Pelaksanaan Penempatan Tenaga Kerja Indonesia Ke Luar Negeri Tahun Anggaran 2004 Dan 2005 Pada Ditjen Pembinaan Dan Penempatan Tenaga Kerja Luar Negeri, Dinas Tenaga Kerja, Balai Pelayanan Dan Penempatan Tenaga Kerja Indonesia Serta Instansi Terkait Lainnya Di Surabaya, Pekanbaru Dan Batam."

In return, the Ministry of Manpower appears to have scaled back attempts to pursue control over assets and migration business connections in Surabaya. Central authorities started making formal budget allocations to the provincial manpower office for the purpose of subsidizing the unit's activity, especially after much of the service provision became nominally free of charge with the introduction of BNP2TKI in 2007. BNP2TKI administrators in Jakarta argued that officials in the Surabaya manpower office were in a good position to carry out these tasks because they had access to budget allocations from both the central and provincial governments. However, absence of a separate unit of the BNP2TKI meant that its policies were less likely to be implemented. Immigration officials at Surabaya International Airport claimed that the provincial manpower office did not issue overseas identity cards to all migrant workers. Rather, it provided the cards to formal sector migrant workers but furnished domestic workers, especially those with jobs in Malaysia, with letters that exempted them from having to pay the mandatory departure tax.

In Surabaya, unlike in any other administrative site of the overseas labour migration programme, the BNP2TKI was unable to instruct officials to compete with provincial government authorities by issuing overseas identity cards in January 2010. The concentration of control over administration of the overseas labour migration programme in the hands of one tier of government increased the risk of arbitrary decision-making, as there were fewer checks and balances. In Surabaya, however, the provincial manpower office shielded the recruitment industry in East Java from having to make a choice between central authorities (the BNP2TKI unit) and the provincial manpower office, as was the case in Medan and Semarang. This institutional arrangement did not prevent labour recruitment companies from having to make a choice between the ministry and the BNP2TKI in Jakarta, where they apply for recruitment certificates. While some labour recruitment companies avoided making the choice by using the services of both central government organizations, others sought recruitment certificates from their preferred authority. But in Surabaya, it was business as usual because at that administrative site there was simply no central government agency to consider.

Conclusion

Each of these case studies offers a narrative about the diverse and varied administrative landscapes in Indonesia. As the cases of Nunukan and Surabaya show, institutional exceptionalism, in which a tier of government is missing, prevented the transmission of what was essentially a Jakarta-based conflict.

In cases where both the ministry and the BNP2TKI were present, local staff sometimes prioritized place-related considerations over scale, as was the case in Jakarta and Tanjung Pinang. Officials in these kinds of places are less amenable to policy directions that threaten to complicate collegial relationships, especially when they could have consequences for getting other work done. By contrast, the sites where central and provincial government agencies engaged in a struggle for power were also places where contextual factors – historical and spatial – produced a clear division of labour, and relationships characterized by low-level cooperation and mutual suspicion. The administrative culture in Medan and Semarang demonstrates all too clearly that under such conditions, administrators are more likely to prioritize their vertical allegiances over local, collegial relationships.

In all locations, the confusing situation caused by conflicting policies from central government agencies meant that discretion was the main resource for finding a solution. In the case of Surabaya, this can be seen clearly in the decision by the head of the provincial manpower office to accept recruitment certificates from either the ministry or the BNP2TKI to ensure that the conflict did not bring the recruitment industry's business in East Java to a grinding halt. In Medan and Semarang, governors played a key role. The governor of North Sumatra intervened against the BNP2TKI by instructing the provincial manpower office to take on the administrative roles that the ministry sought to delegate, and the governor of Central Java spoke out, putting pressure on the Minister for Manpower to end the conflict. Ministry officials in Jakarta, meanwhile, decided to share administrative authority over aspects of the overseas labour migration programme although the law forbade it. It is this use of discretion that undermined the state's formal structures, whereas the kind exercised by the other officials described above helped to achieve institutional objectives when institutional relationships broke down.

The following chapter continues this discussion of discretion, examining the role it played in shaping administrative systems and in the handling of particular kinds of cases in embassies and consulates in Hong Kong, Kuala Lumpur and Singapore. As the chapter reveals, not only did implementation regulations not yet exist to instruct the development of consular systems for handling migrants, but the labour attachés, who handled much of the case load, were the only Ministry of Manpower official within their consular office. The environment for handling migrants was also further complicated by the fact that these officials carried out their responsibilities in an extraterritorial setting, where their authority was circumscribed by the administrative, legal and political limitations imposed by the host state.

CHAPTER 5

Limitation in Extraterritorial Settings

In the peripheral locations examined in the previous chapter, it was evident that context varies dramatically even within Indonesia's national boundaries as a consequence of local conditions and relationships that mitigate against the direct transference of centrally defined institutions. This observation is equally – if not more – true in the case of the systems established to handle Indonesian migrant workers within the state's consular offices overseas. Administration of the overseas labour migration programme was performed in each particular institutional and legal context, but also through the decisions made by individual labour attachés who had contact with, but were working largely in isolation from, their home institution – the Ministry of Manpower. As a consequence, no Indonesian consulate or embassy's arrangements are the same.

This chapter examines the role of discretion in the establishment of the systems used to handle matters pertaining to the programme in three Indonesian consular offices. The first section explains how and why systems in Hong Kong, Kuala Lumpur and Singapore differ, pointing to variations in those countries' regulatory frameworks and the impact of decisions taken by individual officials on the form and function of those systems. The next section focuses closely on the way in which labour attachés handle particular problems, revealing the degree of discretion exercised and the rationale behind their response. The chapter demonstrates that Indonesia's consular offices were largely removed from direct impact of the ongoing conflict in Indonesia between the ministry and the BNP2TKI. However, the uncertainty at home translated into something of a vacuum abroad, which expanded the discretionary space available to labour attachés. At the same time, the attachés relationships with representatives of other ministries were far more important than they were at home, as they were located in the Ministry of Foreign Affairs' extraterritorial infrastructure.

Systemic Variation

Since the end of the New Order, the Ministry of Foreign Affairs has increasingly pressured consular offices to provide better service to Indonesian citizens overseas. Indonesian expatriates, students and those on vacation have traditionally had much better access to consular services than those employed as domestic workers or earning a living on construction sites or plantations. In some countries, however, steps have been taken to better deal with Indonesia's

 | DOI 10.1163/9789004325487_006

migrant workers. The Indonesian embassies in Jeddah and Kuala Lumpur have had labour attachés since the 1980s.[1] Elsewhere, the Indonesian government began embedding an official from the Ministry of Manpower to assist with the challenging task of handling migrant workers and dealing with labour recruitment companies in 2005, following the introduction of Law No. 39/2004 on the Placement and Protection of Indonesian Workers Overseas. The Minister for Manpower, Fahmi Idris, reported to the legislature that he wanted to position a manpower official in Hong Kong, Kuwait, Singapore, South Korea, the United Arab Emirates and Taiwan.[2] The Ministry of Administrative and Bureaucratic Reform and the Minister for Finance approved three of those posts, agreeing to send labour attachés to Hong Kong, Kuwait and the United Arab Emirates.

In these locations, the systems that developed as a consequence of this push have done so organically. As of 2010, no governmental regulations had been issued that provided instructions on how systems for handling migrant workers in destination countries ought to be set up. Furthermore, the Minister for Manpower was yet to promulgate ministerial regulations that specified the role of labour attachés. Under Law No. 39/2004, authority was delegated to the president, his cabinet and the Minister for Manpower to flesh out the content of 31 articles, which could not be done immediately.[3] In the absence of such regulations, officials in Indonesian consular offices were left to design systems for administering the overseas labour migration programme themselves. The task of doing so was in the hands of various layers of managers, with the ambassador or consul-general at the top, foreign affairs officials in the middle and the labour attaché close to the bottom. As this suggests, the absence of regulations also meant that these bureaucrats were left to negotiate their own roles and scope of authority, as demonstrated by the cases of Hong Kong, Kuala Lumpur and Singapore described here.

Hong Kong

Hong Kong's regulatory framework is designed to delegate as much responsibility for migrant workers as possible from the state to local labour recruitment companies.[4] It also outsources the responsibility to vet visa applications to the home governments of labour migrants. This policy was introduced

1 Unless otherwise stated, the information in this chapter was provided by labour attachés or other embassy and consulate staff between 2009 and 2010.

2 "Pemerintah Akan Buka Atase Tenaga Kerja Di Enam Negara."

3 Krisnawaty, "Reformasi Dibelenggu Birokrasi," 48–49.

4 See Constable, *Maid to Order in Hong Kong: Stories of Migrant Workers*; Constable, *Born out of Place: Migrant Workers and the Politics of International Labor* for detailed discussions of how foreign domestic workers in particular fit into Hong Kong society.

following bilateral negotiations between the British colonial administration in Hong Kong and the Government of The Philippines in the mid-1970s. For The Philippines, the key motivation in this negotiation probably centred on securing more overseas employment opportunities for Filipinos; however, it also wanted to exercise greater control over the conditions under which they took up employment in Hong Kong.[5]

As a result of these dealings, the Hong Kong Immigration Department requires all consular offices to sign off on their citizens' employment as domestic workers by endorsing employment contracts before visa applications may be submitted.[6] In the Indonesian case, the consul-general delegates the function to the foreign affairs official who heads consular services, based on the rationale that endorsing contracts is first and foremost a form of service provision to citizens. This system enables the consulate to exercise power over Hong Kong labour recruitment companies more effectively than would otherwise be possible. As the consulate was almost entirely staffed with foreign affairs officials until 2005, the endorsement of employment contracts was largely managed through systems designed for long-established consular roles, such as renewing passports, with little regard for how it could be harnessed to support the Ministry of Manpower's policies and regulations concerning the extraterritorial dimension of the overseas labour migration programme. This legacy provided fertile ground for conflict after the labour attaché arrived.

The Ministry of Manpower has required that Indonesian consular offices endorse the recruitment industry's plans to source migrant labour in Indonesia for overseas employment since the 1970s. The task of organizing this endorsement is given to labour recruitment companies registered in Indonesia. It requires them to provide details about the type of employment, conditions and employers in what is referred to as a demand letter or job order (*surat permintaan*). In Hong Kong, the consul-general delegates responsibility to endorse this document to the next most senior foreign affairs official, the first secretary.

---

5 Indonesia pursued an identical objective in its diplomatic relationships with governments in the Middle East only a few years later. Confidential correspondence between Indonesia's Ministry of Manpower and consular offices overseas indicates that Indonesia has encouraged its consuls to approach host governments in an attempt to design these kinds of mechanisms since the early 1980s. See Direktur Jenderal Pembinaan dan Penggunaan Tenaga Kerja, "Garis-Garis Besar Antar Kerja Antar Negara," 4.

6 It is through this administrative role that senior officials have been able to impose criteria on employment companies that want to supply Indonesian migrant labour to Hong Kong employers, such as serving as the first port of call for questions about the terms of their employment. See Palmer, "Public-Private Partnerships in the Administration and Control of Indonesian Migrant Labour in Hong Kong."

Every day, hundreds of requests for migrant labour are signed, which mostly contain details of employment for domestic work that promises to meet Hong Kong minimum conditions concerning wages and rest days. But blank forms with the official's signature also circulate in migrant source areas, such as East Java,[7] which both indicate that the process is little more than a formality and reveals that the consular staff (or the consulate as an institution) may perform the function in return for informal fees. This is perhaps not surprising since endorsement is a requirement to obtain recruitment permission from the Ministry of Manpower in Indonesia, but offers little to the consulate as a means for managing the supply of Indonesian migrant labour to Hong Kong.

What this requirement has allowed the consulate to do, however, is gain a degree of control over Hong Kong labour recruitment companies. In 1995 the Hong Kong Association of Indonesian Labor Recruitment Companies (Asosiasi Perusahaan Pengerah Tenaga Kerja Indonesia Hong Kong, APPIH) was established with the consul-general as its head.[8] Since that time, only members of the association have been entitled to submit applications for endorsements on behalf of Indonesian migrant workers.[9] The arrangement mirrors the approach to service provision in Indonesia, where labour recruitment companies must first obtain a recommendation letter from the government recognized professional association to confirm that their documents are in order.[10] In Hong Kong, the association's records of members' contact details enable consular officials to effectively convey information about changes in policy without having to maintain their own database. Reflecting the institutional arrangement that positions the consul-general, always a career bureaucrat from the Ministry of Foreign Affairs, at its helm, foreign affairs officials dominated the Indonesian government's relationship with the association for at least the first ten years of its establishment.

This arrangement changed in 2005 with the arrival of the consulate's first labour attaché. The consul-general retained his position as head of APPIH but the labour attaché was appointed to represent the consulate on the

7 Interview data, Blitar, 17 March 2010.

8 For the association's written constitution, see Asosiasi Perusahaan Jasa Tenaga Kerja Indonesia, "Anggaran Dasar: Asosiasi Perusahaan Penempatan Tenaga Kerja Indonesia Di Hong Kong."

9 As was observed in a Hong Kong High Court judgement, the fact that the consulate generally only notarizes domestic helper employment contracts obtained through the association, is entirely acceptable to the Hong Kong authorities. See Palmer, "Public-Private Partnerships in the Administration and Control of Indonesian Migrant Labour in Hong Kong."

10 See, for example, Asosiasi Jasa Penempatan Asia Pasifik, "Pengantar Rekrut SIP Agensi Al Ahliya (EST) Labour Suplay."

association's advisory board. She served two consecutive terms until 2010, when her posting ended and she was replaced by another colleague from the Ministry of Manpower. Formally, her inclusion on the advisory board was intended to provide a channel through which Hong Kong labour recruitment companies could raise issues with the Indonesian consulate. In practice, however, her involvement was merely for show, as senior foreign affairs officers continued to dominate the consulate's relationship with Hong Kong labour recruitment companies through their control of the two above-mentioned endorsement roles. To illustrate, the association's 'protection division' was encouraged and indeed preferred to handle cases involving migrant workers and the labour recruitment companies without involving the labour attaché. In addition to the requirement that APPIH prevent problems from ending at the consulate, the labour attaché could not threaten the association's members' chances of endorsement of future recruits' employment contracts if her advice went unheeded.

The consulate imposes additional conditions on Hong Kong labour recruitment companies to expand their role in dealing with migrant labour cases. Before 2009 local labour recruitment companies only had to meet the basic requirements of having a permanent office, a boarding house, and Indonesian-speaking staff to be eligible for accreditation. However, in 2009 the consulate introduced a Business Accreditation Certificate (BAC) that permits Hong Kong businesses to 'operate an Indonesian agency'.[11] Staff decided against calling the document a licence because of uncertainty about how the Hong Kong administration would respond to the representative of another state licensing labour recruitment companies it has already authorized. Nevertheless, the document is in effect an Indonesian government licence that gives Hong Kong recruiters permission to broker employment for Indonesian citizens in the territory.[12] The consul-general and first secretary exercise greater power within the committee, serving to relegate the labour attaché to a supporting administrative role. This reflected the scope of her authority more generally. In the labour section, she managed the locally hired staff, who accepted applications for licences, and then channelled them to the first secretary's office to be checked for compliance.

Under the consulate's system, Hong Kong recruiters are evaluated each year. Labour recruitment companies that fail the assessment risk losing their

11 Indonesian consulate (Hong Kong), "Renewal: Business Accreditation Certificate (BAC) to Operate an Indonesian Employment Agency."

12 This section draws heavily on Palmer, "Public-Private Partnerships in the Administration and Control of Indonesian Migrant Labour in Hong Kong."

accreditation. The labour attaché role in the evaluation committee is an administrative one, in which she sends out formal invitations for labour recruitment companies to attend an interview at the consulate.[13] In the course of the interview, committee members ask labour recruitment companies for information on the number of migrant workers they have sourced from Indonesia. These companies are also interrogated about how they have complied with consulate policy, such as the contemporary position on the rights and responsibilities of the consulate and labour migrants in relation to the recruitment industry. The encounter also gives the consulate an opportunity to gather information about the recruiters' experience operating as partners of Indonesian companies. The first secretary might bring this information up in the course of assessing Indonesian recruiters' requests for endorsement of their job orders if necessary. But Hong Kong labour recruitment companies that fail the licensing committee's assessment may have their licence cancelled. A negative result includes notification that future applications for endorsements should be rejected by the head of consular services, and the success or failure is communicated through the first secretary.

The consulate also uses the threat of blacklisting to guide (*membina*) the behaviour of labour recruitment companies in Hong Kong. Known as *skorsing* in Indonesian, this process involves the temporary or complete cessation of recruiters' business activities.[14] This alternative to fines puts licensed companies on a watch list that ought to prevent them from applying for consular services, such as endorsement of job orders.[15] In Hong Kong, labour recruitment companies are given three warnings in response to illegal or otherwise unacceptable conduct before being blacklisted. Once *skorsing* is applied, the consulate refuses requests for endorsement of employment contracts, which means that companies are unable to recruit workers from Indonesia or secure work permits for Indonesians already in Hong Kong. This two-pronged approach has the effect of cutting off access to Indonesian labour migrants, who have historically been very profitable for agents. As a consequence, Hong Kong recruiters are eager to cooperate with the Indonesian consulate. The consul-general is aware of the power that the consulate gains through this system and claims to exercise it carefully so as to avoid accusations that they abuse it.

13 Their facilities are sometimes reassessed as part of the evaluation process.

14 *Ministerial Regulation (Manpower) No. 5/MEN/III/2005 on Ketentuan Sanksi Administratif Dan Tata Cara Penjatuhan Sanksi Dalam Pelaksanaan Penempatan Dan Perlindungan Tenaga Kerja Indonesia Di Luar Negeri*, article 3b.

15 *Ministerial Regulation No. 38/MEN/XII/2006 on Tata Cara Pemberian, Perpanjangan Dan Pencabutan Surat Izin Pelaksana Penempatan Tenaga Kerja Indonesia*, article 8(2).

The consulate uses this power to coerce Hong Kong labour recruitment companies into complying with requirements that effectively contract out its responsibility to assist and support Indonesian citizens to the private sector.[16] The consulate requires labour recruitment companies to mediate conflicts that arise between Indonesian workers and their employers. The consulate facilitates settlement of some disputes through its labour section, but the vast majority of cases are resolved by Hong Kong recruiters without involving the consulate. In addition, labour recruitment companies are expected to help migrant workers report employers for alleged criminal behaviour. Non-government organizations and other migrant support groups perform that function when workers have left their employers' household.[17] But while migrant workers are still there, Hong Kong labour recruitment companies continue to serve as Indonesians' first port of call. It is for this reason that the consulate also requires them to employ Indonesian-speaking staff. By forcing Hong Kong labour recruitment companies to act as a front office for such matters, the consulate has freed itself up to focus on providing conventional consular services (i.e. services not related to employment). This system also simplifies the labour attaché's job, as the bulk of employment related problems never reach her desk.

Ultimately, labour recruitment companies comply because cooperation with the consulate has made them fabulously wealthy. The system may require companies to service workers, but it also helps those involved in the migration business extract recruitment fees well in excess of the amount set by the Indonesian Ministry of Manpower. The wealth of Hong Kong labour recruitment companies is legendary in both industry and government circles. In part, involvement of consular and Ministry of Manpower officials is responsible for the profitability of labour recruitment companies, as it has enabled them to collect a 'management fee' in contravention of Hong Kong law.[18] Although the ministry has unsuccessfully attempted to eliminate the fee for the best part of a decade, Hong Kong labour recruitment companies continue to collect it in return for the access they provide to the Hong Kong labour market and the

---

16 In response to campaigns against the way in which the commercial interests of employment companies have come to dominate service provision to migrant workers, the consulate has instituted alternative mechanisms to enable more direct access, such as an online portal to apply for passport renewal and Sunday opening hours. Nevertheless, employment companies continue to provide the majority of services.

17 Sim, "Organising Discontent: NGOs for Southeast Asian Migrant Workers in Hong Kong."

18 Palmer, "Public-Private Partnerships in the Administration and Control of Indonesian Migrant Labour in Hong Kong," 6.

role they play in coordinating financing and the post-deployment payment of recruitment fees. The division of the overall fee is referred to as '7–11' within the consulate, a reference to the chain of 24 hour convenience stores used here to describe an arrangement whereby Hong Kong labour recruitment companies collect HKD 7,000 (USD 900) and their Indonesian partner, HKD 11,000 (USD 1400) from each migrant worker.[19] This level of profitability and the ability of consular officials to rent-seek in support of it predictably complicate the consulate's relationship with migrant workers, as the commercial interests of those in the consulate are often closely aligned with the labour recruitment companies.

Kuala Lumpur

In Malaysia, the system for handling migrants is set up to help the embassy respond to the high number of labour migrants who enter the country illegally or who have left their employment and lost legal migration status. There are roughly 1,200,000 Indonesian migrant workers lawfully employed in Malaysia,[20] but estimates suggest that the Indonesian migrant population is closer to two million, including those who do not hold valid migration documents.[21] Both groups require assistance with employment and immigration matters. The Malaysian government regularly cracks down on undocumented migrant workers, forcing them to return to Indonesia, while the Indonesian government periodically imposes moratoria on the placement of foreign domestic workers in Malaysia in response to public outcry about high profile cases involving Malaysian employers who physically abuse Indonesian domestic workers.[22] The embassy receives requests for tens and sometimes hundreds of thousands of international travel documents each year for Indonesian citizens who have somehow invalidated their conditions of stay. On an everyday basis, the embassy is also forced to deal with migrant workers who report not having received wages or who want to return to Indonesia but are unable to do so because their passports remain in their employers' hands.

19 A conservative estimate suggests that Hong Kong employment companies have collected HKD 980 million (USD 13.25 million) from the 140,000 Indonesians working there as of 2013. The value is of course much higher, as it does not include migrant workers who have come and gone.

20 For an estimate of the number of lawfully employed Indonesian migrant workers in 2014, see Shymala and Meng, "Policies and Laws Regulating Migrant Workers in Malaysia: A Critical Appraisal," 19.

21 Interview data, Kuala Lumpur, 21 June 2010.

22 See Ford, "Constructing Legality: The Management of Irregular Migration in Thailand and Malaysia."

Before 2006 the embassy provided few services to the large population of Indonesian migrant workers in the country. There was no information desk to direct migrant workers to the relevant attaché for their problems. The service in highest demand – passport renewal – was performed in an area that was full of rubbish and, even where migrant workers used the services of informal intermediaries (*calo*) to lodge their applications, they often had to wait weeks before the document was ready for collection. Service provision in the labour section was equally appalling. The labour attaché, in place from the 1980s in this case, focussed on services for Indonesian labour recruitment companies rather than on assisting migrant workers with their problems. Local staff were hired for the purpose of accepting requests for endorsement of mandatory job orders and cooperation agreements between Indonesian recruiters and their business partners in Malaysia. Requirements for the latter document were not enforced by the consulate in Hong Kong, where consular officers had restricted the ability to participate in the industry to only those companies it approved. This was not the case in Malaysia, as the host government provided no such mechanism to enable Indonesian officials to license local agents. As a result, the embassy was particularly interested in adding layers of administration that would at least bring Malaysian recruiters involved in the business to its attention.

This system began to change following the intense politicization in the Indonesian mass media of a particularly gruesome case of abuse involving a young Indonesian domestic worker.[23] The embassy established an emergency women's shelter to accommodate 70 migrants in response to Megawati's decision to make better service to migrant workers part of her campaign to be re-elected as president in 2004. By the end of that year, the shelter regularly exceeded its capacity by almost 300 per cent each month. The system changed further in 2006, when a 'pro-migrant'[24] orientation to administration was announced by the ambassador following a visit by the new president, Susilo Bambang Yudhoyono, during which he promised migrant workers that the government would improve service provision. Consular resources were

23 See Chapter 2 for details about how this event also expedited the process to produce the country's first overseas migration law. Nirmala Bonat was hospitalized in 2004 after being severely beaten by her employer who broke her nose with a metal jug and burnt the girl's chest with a hot iron. The abuse occurred in May as President Megawati and her competition were already vying against each to win public support for their candidacy in the first round of Indonesia's first direct presidential election, which was scheduled for June.

24 Migrant worker support groups use 'pro-migrant' to describe government policies that are sensitive to the needs of migrant workers.

reorganized to ensure, for example, that migrant workers left the embassy with their renewed passport on the same day, cutting out the need for intermediaries. The embassy also organized a roster system for consuls to monitor locations where Indonesian migrant workers were employed without a valid visa to anticipate cases where Malaysian businesses called in immigration officials to avoid paying their wages. In addition, an information desk was set up to direct migrants to the attaché with expertise concerning their problem in line with the division of labour as outlined in the ambassador's establishment of a task force to improve service to citizens in 2007.[25]

The labour section also became more involved in employment related matters. On the labour attaché's initiative, the embassy introduced a mandatory employment contract for Indonesian domestic workers, which included a minimum wage, regular rest day and other conditions of employment. Use of this contract was made a mandatory requirement of the passport renewal process. The labour attaché was prompted to impose this condition by cases in which migrant workers claimed that their employer had verbally agreed to certain conditions but were unable to substantiate their claims.[26] The labour attaché first approached the immigration attaché about the possibility of requiring migrant workers to include a signed employment contract in the passport renewal process. When that officer resisted, arguing that immigration and labour policy should be kept separate, the labour attaché escalated the matter to the ambassador, who saw the potential of the requirement to make it easier for the embassy to intervene on behalf of migrant workers.

This pro-migrant shift in orientation, then, was driven by the embassy's desire to simplify the resolution of migrant labour problems through strengthening of workers' position vis-a-vis employers. A central problem for the embassy was that responsibility for the accommodation and repatriation of migrant workers often fell on their shoulders, as the migrant worker population generally lacks the economic resources to pay for such services themselves. The routine expenses of dealing with situations in which the labour migration experience has gone wrong, leaving migrant workers without stable income or a permanent address in a foreign country, prompted the labour

25 Palmer, "Discretion and the Trafficking-like Practices of the Indonesian State."

26 Malaysia introduced a standard employment contract for Indonesian domestic workers in 2006, following the signing of a bilateral agreement with Indonesia. The contract did not include entitlement to a minimum wage or regular rest day. See Government of Indonesia and Government of Malaysia, "Memorandum of Understanding between the Government of the Republic of Indonesia and the Government of Malaysia on the Recruitment and Placement of Indonesian Migrant Workers."

attaché to turn his sights towards the recruitment industry as an alternative source of financing. Through the embassy's administrative functions, including the endorsement of cooperation agreements and frequent requests to source migrant labour from Indonesia, the labour attaché can extract support from Indonesian labour recruitment companies. In return for business, companies are amenable to the labour attaché's frequent demands that they cover the expenses involved in handling migrant workers whom they recruited for employment in Malaysia.

By contrast to its counterpart in Hong Kong, the Indonesian embassy in Kuala Lumpur has no means of imposing similar demands on Malaysian labour recruitment companies. The labour section does not operate a formal accreditation system for Malaysian labour recruitment companies, partly because the labour attaché understood that his function was to evaluate rather than accredit but also because he anticipated resistance from the wealthy and politically well-connected Malaysian Association of Foreign Maid Agencies (Persatuan Agensi Pembantu Rumah Asing, PAPA). As in Indonesia, labour recruitment companies in Malaysia play a role in the development of public policy. They also have the power to create bilateral conflict around Indonesian interventions by encouraging Malaysian authorities to take the issue up with the embassy. In the absence of the ability to licence them, the embassy exerts pressure on PAPA and its members through its ability to determine which Indonesian labour recruitment companies can channel workers to Malaysia. Through providing the endorsement Indonesian companies require them to seek authorization from the Indonesian Ministry of Manpower to recruit migrant labour, the embassy effectively compels labour recruitment companies to put pressure on their Malaysian partners to cooperate.

The form and function of these kinds of systems depend heavily on who occupies the labour attaché position, as they are not fully recorded with the Ministry of Foreign Affairs' Director for Protocol in Indonesia. The labour attaché posted to Kuala Lumpur between 2005 and 2010 was frustrated that the Indonesian labour recruitment companies did not always report the particulars of labour migrants and employers at the end of each month as required by the Ministry of Manpower. Further, he found that Indonesian recruiters do not always hold accurate data concerning employers or places of employment in Malaysia. As a work-around, he kept a tally of job orders that they submitted for endorsement and maintained a list of Malaysian recruiters through which Indonesian labour recruitment companies placed labour migrants in the country. The labour attaché then required that Indonesian labour recruitment companies only cooperate with Malaysian recruiters that sent him a list of migrant workers' particulars within a week of arrival. The recruitment industry can circumvent the system by exploiting the loophole in which Malaysian law allows the issuance of work permits regardless of how labour migrants arrive, but licensed recruiters in Indonesia conduct the largest part of their business under the formal system. Recognizing this, evidence of non-compliance by Malaysian recruiters was used as grounds for refusing to endorse future requests by Indonesian labour recruitment companies to supply their Malaysian counterparts with labour migrants.

Singapore

The primary driver of the system in Singapore is the desire to handle migrants according to the conditions set by the Indonesian Ministry of Manpower. Foreign labour makes up about 35 per cent of Singapore's workforce. Some 190,000 of this total are domestic workers from just a few approved countries, including Indonesia.[27] Singapore is located on Indonesia's sea border, close to the Riau Islands. Indonesians living close to the border can get access to employment in-country more easily without assistance from labour recruitment companies. The majority of domestic workers come from elsewhere in Indonesia. This group can also circumvent the Indonesian system courtesy of the fact that the Singaporean immigration authority enables foreign citizens to enter the island state on a tourist visa and then convert it to a work permit. As a consequence, it is more difficult to impose Indonesia's administrative requirements regarding ceilings on fees payable to recruiters and the use of contracts that impose conditions of employment, such as a minimum wage.

Indonesian labour recruitment companies register the departure of around 40,000 labour migrants to Singapore through the overseas labour migration programme each year.[28] Having grown weary of instances where Ministry of Manpower officials refused to accept recruitment paperwork because of errors that foreign affairs officials in Singapore had missed, APJATI lobbied the Minister for Manpower to prioritize the appointment of a labour attaché to the embassy for the purpose of aligning its systems with the ministry's regulations. When the first labour attaché was appointed to the embassy in 2008, she was given two major tasks. First, she was expected to address problems arising from the fact that the foreign affairs officials who handled administration of the overseas labour migration programme were ignorant of the Ministry of Manpower's regulations. She was also asked to make it more difficult for officials to collect rents in exchange for endorsement, a practice brought to the

---

27 For government statistics, see "Foreign Workforce in Numbers"; "Labour Force."

28 Badan Nasional Penempatan dan Perlindungan Tenaga Kerja Indonesia, "Realisasi Penempatan TKI – LN TA 2008."

ministry's attention by Indonesian labour recruitment companies. Second, the Director-General for the Guidance of Labour Placement and the Director for Overseas Placement encouraged her to find a way to get Indonesian migrant workers who remain in Singapore to negotiate new employment contracts, something that host country laws did not require.

In attempting to deal with these issues, the labour attaché found herself in a hostile institutional context. Upon arrival, she was told that her assistance was not necessary, and that her expertise would be of greater benefit to Indonesia at home. Following telephone calls to the Ministry of Manpower's Human Resources Bureau, the ambassador instructed the foreign affairs official in the citizen service section to involve the labour attaché in the system he had set up to handle migrant workers' problems. At the time, the consular division focussed on general services such as providing birth certificates and accepting applications to relinquish Indonesian citizenship.[29] However, Indonesian migrant workers were also using this service to report labour issues, such as employers reneging on promises to raise the workers' wage and give them rest days. Another common problem was that employers would also unilaterally change the terms of employment, for example, by requiring labour migrants to work in more than one household. The foreign affairs officer ultimately agreed to delegate responsibility for handling these kinds of cases to the labour attaché.

Having inserted herself into the system, the labour attaché then lobbied the ambassador to authorize inclusion of an employment contract as a condition for migrant workers to renew their passports. The fact that the labour attaché in Kuala Lumpur succeeded in doing so at the same time suggests that this was more of a ministry initiative than her own. Nevertheless, she took responsibility for drafting the contract, and re-trained four local staff to help check that it was attached to migrant workers' passport renewal applications. In addition, she required that employers accompany applicants to an interview with her staff so that they could explain the contract and consequences for not complying with it. The labour attaché showed significant initiative in ensuring that this process was followed. She asked that the security staff who guarded the embassy's entrance check that migrant workers were in fact accompanied by their employers and not a labour recruitment company. Her staff would then require the employer to produce their Singaporean identification card to verify that they were the individual recorded in the migrants' work permit to ensure that only employers could attend. This had the effect of shifting the bulk of

29 Indonesian law requires those who acquiring citizenship in another country to relinquish their Indonesian citizenship.

this section of the embassy's workload towards migrant workers, who came to outnumber other groups of Indonesians who sought consular services.

Turning her attention to the demand side, the labour attaché convinced the foreign affairs official responsible for relationships with labour recruitment companies to let her help him refine his system for administering the recruitment industry. First, she overhauled the accreditation system for labour recruitment companies in Singapore. In addition to simplifying the registration process, this allowed her to impose a new set of criteria on companies seeking accreditation. In recognition of the fact that Singaporean companies were not legally obliged to apply for Indonesian accreditation, she made it easier for them to do so by registering them at any time of the year (the embassy formerly only held registration between certain dates). In order to qualify for accreditation under the new system, labour recruitment companies had to produce a business licence from Singapore's Ministry of Manpower. As the ministry required labour recruitment companies that supply foreign domestic workers to hold active membership in one of the two government recognized professional associations, applicants had to submit those details to the labour attaché as well. She would then check that recruiters had no demerit points recorded against them by the Singaporean Ministry of Manpower. Finally, the labour attaché required that labour recruitment companies had no outstanding issues with the embassy, such as a client staying in the emergency shelter or instances where they did not respond to her calls, which she recorded on post-it notes on her desk.

The labour attaché claimed that her new system has raised awareness among Singaporean labour recruitment companies about the standards that are acceptable to the embassy. However, investigation of 60 accredited companies revealed that only half promoted Indonesian labour migrants in line with the embassy's standards concerning wage level and rest days. It was explained that the higher wages and provision of rest days were only applicable after the workers' passports were renewed. One accredited recruiter even promoted the fact that his workers always held the standard five year passport instead of the two year passport that labour migrants should hold. Promotion strategies aside, this investigation uncovered that some accredited recruiters did not even hold a business licence from the Singaporean Ministry of Manpower. When questioned about how this could be the case, the labour attaché lamented that she was the only official with responsibility to make the assessment and did not have time to carry out physical inspections for each application to verify that submitted documents were all valid. It was normally sufficient to check the Singaporean Ministry of Manpower's website and contact the relevant professional association to resolve inconsistencies.

A more serious issue identified by the labour attaché was the fact that the embassy had never imposed a cap on the level of recruitment fees that accredited companies could charge Indonesian migrant workers. Indonesia's Ministry of Manpower requires that labour recruitment companies submit a cooperation agreement (*perjanjian kerjasama*) as part of their application for a recruitment certificate, as it details arrangements with overseas recruiters concerning such matters. In practice, before the labour attaché arrived, Indonesian labour recruitment companies rarely signed them with their business partners in Singapore. Attempting to make the agreements compulsory, she informed her line manager, a foreign affairs official, about the relevant ministerial regulation. She then convinced him not only that the agreement was necessary for administrative purposes in Indonesia, but also that the embassy could use it to steer the recruitment industry away from excessively exploitative arrangements which frequently resulted in migrant workers seeking the embassy's assistance. For this reason, she was authorized to inform labour recruitment companies in Indonesia that a copy of their cooperation agreement was necessary as part of the application for endorsement. The foreign affairs official also agreed that she would oversee the implementation.[30]

The labour attaché then lobbied the foreign affairs official to let her help him with the administration associated with endorsing requests for migrant workers, offering to ensure that they complied with relevant regulations and policies once they arrived on his desk. The foreign affairs official resisted at first but conceded after the labour attaché agreed to the condition that her signature would only be a pre-endorsement, and that the official would retain the right to grant or deny the embassy endorsement required by the Ministry of Manpower. Every day, she checked requests for migrant labour from Indonesia to ensure that they included details of the type of job proposed, conditions of employment as well as the name and address of the future employer. She returned applications that included details that did not comply with her system, and would have liked to have also vetted the applications based on a blacklist of employers who were reported for abusing migrant workers or not paying wages. Nevertheless, the measures the attaché did put in place helped her insist that the recruitment industry settle outstanding matters, such as

30 Following this incident, Indonesian companies became increasingly aggrieved, as the labour attaché required that she witness them sign the agreement with their accredited partner in her office at the embassy. The labour attaché reasoned that employment company owners frequently travel to Singapore so could do it on one of their trips, but they deemed it to be a burdensome requirement, to which their business partners in Singapore would not be easily amenable.

repatriating migrant workers in the embassy's shelter, by turning down Indonesian recruiters' requests to supply labour migrants to labour recruitment companies in Singapore that fell foul of her system.

The labour attaché was aware that the foreign affairs official endorsed requests she had turned down, or which had never crossed her desk. In response, she set up an informal system for ensuring that such applications were flagged. She made a deal with staff at the reception desk, which resulted in their reporting the number of applications for endorsement they received each day. They also agreed to inform her if the foreign affairs official requested a deviation from the standard operating procedure, according to which requests were first passed to her. However, after confronting the official with evidence that he had broken their agreement, the labour attaché was told to mind her own business. Taking a different tack, the labour attaché contacted the Ministry of Manpower's Director for Overseas Placement and explained that all endorsements that complied with procedure had both her signature and her line manager's endorsement. She recommended that the ministry not only re-inspect documents that had her manager's signature only, but also ask recruiters why the document had not been pre-endorsed by the labour attaché. The ministry also passed on names of labour recruitment companies that circumvented the labour attaché's system, allowing her to raise the issue with them in future interactions. Predictably, rumours of this arrangement reached the foreign affairs official, who – angered by the way in which the labour attaché subverted his authority – cut her out of the process altogether.

The Handling of Particular Cases

Attention to the way in which particular cases are handled by consular officials also brings into stark relief the extent to which discretion shapes administrative roles. This is more evident in consular offices than at home. Staff in consulates and embassies often have sole responsibility for particular administrative tasks. They also lack access to the full suite of mechanisms and resources that would otherwise be available to them in Indonesia. To further complicate matters, they perform their roles in an extraterritorial setting, where they must be mindful of how their administrative work is supported or undermined by host laws. These factors coalesce to extend opportunities for the exercise of discretion, which accounts for the development of particularistic approaches to case management within Indonesia's system of consular offices. In part, this differentiation is due to the particular set of opportunities and limitations that the host context presents. However, the fact that a single person may often be charged with the responsibility to carry out a function also means that the performance of administrative roles has an individualized dimension, which is the product of choices that they make about how and why to take a particular course of action.

The ways in which discretion is operationalized in the handling of problems related to international labour migration are revealed by close scrutiny of labour attachés' decision-making. The Hong Kong case study presented below examines the conditions under which the labour attaché assists migrants wanting to reclaim their passports from a local labour recruitment company. In Kuala Lumpur, the labour attaché is under pressure to ensure that the recruitment industry shares responsibility for costs incurred when migrants seek the embassy's assistance to return home. In Singapore, the labour attaché's approach to instances where migrant workers hold authentic passports with fake names and dates of birth is related not only to her experience of dealing with other Indonesian authorities but also to personal knowledge of what she sees as systemic problems. These cases are not directly comparable. When combined, however, they demonstrate the impact of contextual factors, such as the labour attachés' relationships with the recruitment industry, the degree of influence those officials have in their home institution, the depth of their connections with other authorities in Indonesia and the quality of their personal relationships with others working in their embassy or consulate on the level of discretion available to them and how they choose to exercise it.

Hong Kong

The Indonesian consulate in Hong Kong contributes to the recruitment industry's strategy for financing Indonesian labour migration to the special administrative region, which entails migrant workers handing over their passport as security for a loan to pay for recruiters' fees. Before leaving Indonesia, migrant workers enter a formal financing arrangement with their labour recruitment company, responsibility for which is then transferred to Hong Kong-based financiers. Migrant workers bring copies of the loan documents with them to Hong Kong and then hand them, along with their passport, over to the local labour recruitment company that picks migrants up at the airport. Although the Indonesian Director-General for Immigration forbids the use of travel documents as security for debt, it is accepted practice in most, if not all, countries that receive Indonesian domestic workers through the overseas labour migration programme. In Kuala Lumpur and Singapore, employers retain migrants' passports. In Hong Kong, consulate accredited labour recruitment companies do so. This practice is tolerated by Indonesian officials. However, it is also a source of irritation, as migrant support groups and non-governmental organizations, wage campaigns against the consulate and lobby the Hong Kong police to act against those involved.

The labour attaché's position on passport confiscation was evident in the Welcoming Program, where the consulate inducts newly arrived migrant workers into life and work in Hong Kong. Her main role in the program was to explain the content of the employment ordinance, especially procedural requirements, such as that workers give employers one month's notice of resignation. However, neither she nor any other consular officer mentioned that it is illegal for labour recruitment companies to confiscate migrants' passports. Her position became clear following an excursion to evaluate the services that the consulate offered to Indonesian migrant labour in Macau, during which the labour attaché was temporarily replaced by one of her subordinates. Addressing migrant workers' concerns about their passports, this junior official told them that labour recruitment companies had not 'confiscated' their passports, but were holding the documents as security for the loan covering the recruitment fees. In a meeting the following week, the labour attaché explained that such a public announcement was not necessary, as everyone – including migrant workers – knew the drill. Privately, she also admitted that it was consulate policy to tolerate the practice.

Despite the ubiquity of passport confiscation and the consulate's tolerance of it, the labour attaché frequently received requests for help from Indonesian migrant workers seeking to reclaim their travel documents from Hong Kong labour recruitment companies, in the form of personally addressed letters. These letters are typically authored by non-governmental organizations, migrant worker support groups or non-Indonesian friends who understand that the labour attaché is more likely to act in response to formal requests. In most cases, on receipt of such a letter the labour attaché called the labour recruitment company or even the personal mobile of company staff to inquire about the situation and determine if the recruiter would be amenable to returning the migrant's passport. This was never a problem in cases where migrant workers had already settled their debts with Hong Kong financiers, as labour recruitment companies no longer needed a passport as security. In cases where debts were still outstanding, the labour attaché was reluctant to push labour recruitment companies to return migrants' passports, instead reporting that they claimed not to be in possession of the document. The labour attaché knew from her contacts in those companies that migrant workers escalate their request to the Hong Kong police.

In all cases where the company refused to return migrants' passports, the labour attaché would report the response to the committee that evaluates the consulate's accreditation of labour recruitment companies. Although the labour attaché has some input into the evaluation process, her role is largely to inform accredited companies of a date and time for an annual interview with the committee. The decision-making process is dominated by senior foreign affairs officials, as described above. Early in her posting, the labour attaché learned that those officials expected her to leave managing the recruitment industry up to them and to focus instead on providing employment related services to migrant workers. To her mind, these areas of responsibility could not be so neatly divided. Arrangements for recruitment and financing strategies in the international migration industry, including the use of state travel documents as a security for loans, had clear implications for the experiences of migrant workers. Forced to accept the division of labour, the attaché left the difficult task to broker new arrangements to her superiors, who she acknowledged have much better connections with other potential industry players, such as bank owners in Indonesia.

The labour attaché's response to less formal requests by migrant workers for assistance was slightly different. She often received short message service (SMS) texts from migrant workers about how they should go about reclaiming their passports from labour recruitment companies. Generally, the labour attaché responded that they could do so if there were no monies outstanding on loans. Less frequently, migrant workers seeking to break their contracts early to change employers or return to Indonesia would approach her in person about getting their passports back. In these cases, she would explain that the consulate would only intervene if migrant workers could demonstrate that they had settled their debt. However, senior foreign affairs officials were sometimes forced to act, as demonstrated in a 2009 case where the consulate instructed a labour recruitment company to return passports regardless of whether debts were settled following media coverage of demonstrations outside the recruiter's office in which migrant workers demanded their documents back. The negative publicity put the consulate in a very difficult situation: while it tolerated the use of passports as a form of security for loans, it was legally bound to suppress the practice. The consul-general, who recalls that the situation was difficult, decided the best option for the consulate's image was to order the company to return the passports regardless of any prior arrangement.

The labour attaché felt partly responsible for the situation, as the migrant workers concerned had asked her informally for assistance to obtain their passports before mounting the demonstration. At the same time, she took some pleasure in the fact that her foreign affairs colleagues were compelled to intervene against a practice that the consulate sanctioned. This response reflects frustration with her subordinate position in the consulate and tensions in her personal relationships with other consular officials. It also hints at the complexity of the passport issue. On the one hand, the Ministry of Manpower's position on the retention of passports was clear. On the other, the labour attaché believed that migrant workers understood the financing arrangement before leaving Indonesia. In her experience, the large majority of Indonesian labour migrants in Hong Kong accepted the arrangement in place of paying recruitment fees upfront in Indonesia. Moreover, she had learned from labour recruitment company staff in Hong Kong that migrant workers in possession of their passports often disappeared, leaving labour recruitment companies in Hong Kong and Indonesia as well as Hong Kong financiers with the cumbersome task of working out who owes what.[31]

For the labour attaché, these considerations posed a perplexing problem: did the fact that the loan arrangement gave poor Indonesians access to overseas employment without requiring them to pay upfront compensate for its excesses? She acknowledged that the recruitment industry reaped excessive commercial benefits because poverty at home, and that uncertainty about how the employment would work out, motivated migrants to accept the arrangement. As a solution, the labour attaché believed the Indonesian government should provide a greater mix of subsidies and credit to intending labour migrants. From her perspective, however, this would only work if the Hong Kong administration lowered the fee labour migrants pay by forcing labour recruitment companies to charge employers more. At the same time, the labour attaché recognized that the supply of labour migrants is much greater than demand by employers, and that the process entails organizing the migration documents from two states. In her view, this combination of factors stacked the odds in favour of the status quo. On balance, however, she believed that moving closer to this division of fees would significantly reduce the problem of indebtedness in the system, and perhaps remove the need to use passports as collateral in the host country.

Kuala Lumpur

The Indonesian embassy in Kuala Lumpur runs a women's shelter for migrant workers who are waiting for their problems to be addressed. Construction of the shelter, which was funded by Indonesia's Coordinating Ministry of People's Prosperity and a Malaysian bank, was finalized in March 2004. The shelter had

31 For obvious reasons, most migrant workers do not admit that they want to cut their contracts short when asking for help in recovering their passports. In a small number of cases, they would explain that they were unhappy with their current employer and needed their passport to register change of employment with the Hong Kong Immigration Department.

the capacity to appropriately accommodate 70 people. However, by November, it was accommodating numbers of migrant workers that rarely fell below 260. While victims of trafficking constituted a small proportion of the occupants, most were Indonesian domestic workers who entered the country with valid migration documents but then ran away from their employers. Consular officers, including the immigration, labour and police attachés, were expected to deal with occupants' cases as quickly as possible to help manage the problem of over-capacity occupation in the shelter. As the majority had employment related issues, this task fell primarily to the labour attaché, who lamented that almost as soon as he finalized one case another migrant worker in need of emergency accommodation would arrive at the embassy.

The labour attaché's handling of these cases revealed the extent to which his thinking determines the embassy's orientation towards Indonesian migrant labour. He was frequently surprised at the speed with which news travels when a bed became vacant in the embassy shelter, and initially suspected that a network of consular officers and external actors, such as non-governmental organizations, collaborated to ensure that some migrant workers had better access to updates concerning the shelter than others. In interviews with occupants, he quickly learned, however, that information about vacancies was disseminated by occupants themselves to relatives and friends. Some of those who arrived with the expectation of being admitted to the shelter had already run away from their employer and were working illegally to support themselves in the meantime. Others had been more cautious, waiting until they received news about a vacancy in the shelter before leaving their employers. The labour attaché would immediately admit those whose migration status had become unlawful but carefully interviewed those who had just left their employers to find out whether their case could be handled without them staying in the shelter.

Those admitted to the shelter were presented with two options: remain there until their problems were resolved or leave as soon as it was administratively and logistically possible to do so. Those who stayed were screened by locally hired staff in the labour section to determine a course of action with regard to their complaint. Immigration matters, such as a missing passport, were directed to the immigration attaché, while cases involving criminal acts, such as physical abuse, were passed to the police section. The labour attaché's mandate was to assist migrant workers address employment related problems, such as the non-payment of wages. His local staff ascertained whether the worker entered Malaysia under the overseas labour migration programme, in which case the labour migrant ought to have an employment contract. Migrant workers who arrived through the official programme were also required to hold insurance policies that offer compensation for such situations – although the labour attaché found that this is frequently not the case in practice. In the case of migrant workers who travelled to Malaysia through informal channels, the labour attaché would seek details of migration intermediaries to identify an alternative source of funds to cover the costs of repatriation or accommodation in the shelter.

Reliance on the limited budget allocated by the embassy for repatriation meant that it was not always able to send migrant workers home immediately. In order to get around this problem, the labour attaché would work with his counterparts in the embassy to find a 'creative' solution. In one example, he and his colleagues in the police section worked out an agreement under which certain categories of migrant workers, such as those who held passports that overstated their true age, were classified as victims of trafficking in order to gain access to the repatriation component of the International Organization for Migration's (IOM) anti-trafficking programme. In most cases, however, the labour attaché succeeded in identifying the labour recruitment company or private individual who helped place the migrant worker in question in overseas employment. This actor could then be convinced to cover expenses such as hospitalization and repatriation. However, in order to do so, the labour attaché would present the intermediary with evidence that the law had been broken. Through demonstrating failure to organize insurance policies and pointing to the mix of legal punishments, which includes fines and prison sentences, for example, the labour attaché could coerce them into footing the bill.

The labour attaché used similar tactics when evaluating labour recruitment companies. Those that complied with his demands benefited from faster endorsement of cooperation agreements and more efficient processing of recruitment requests. Those who resisted or refused were added to an informal blacklist, to which the labour attaché referred before providing endorsement. The labour section would then scrutinize their applications for endorsement much more closely with the view to complicating the process. Labour recruitment companies typically expected endorsements on the same day, but labour section staff would take the maximum time allowable to inspect documents, and if they turned up deficiencies or inconsistencies, would then return them to the applicant and ask that the application be re-submitted once it was in order. Where applications were complete, staff would justify a delay in processing on the basis that they wanted to check the veracity of items, such as details of cooperation and proposed employers. Non-compliance with the labour attaché's demands thus threatened to complicate labour recruitment companies' administrative relationships with government agencies in Indonesia, as the endorsement was necessary to legally recruit migrant labour there. For this reason, Indonesian labour recruitment companies most frequently agreed to these special requests.

The labour attaché also extracted informal fees from Indonesian labour recruitment companies. In August 2008 the ambassador decreed that the labour section could charge labour recruitment companies MYR 70 (USD 22) for inspecting applications for endorsements. According to a labour recruitment company in Indonesia and its business partner in Kuala Lumpur, labour recruitment companies were expected to pay an additional fee, which in 2010 was calculated at MYR 2 for each migrant worker to be recruited. The labour attaché explained that this fee served to ensure that labour recruitment companies only requested the number of workers for which they could find work, as grossly inflated requests also translated to high informal fees. Further investigation revealed that the purpose of the charge was first and foremost to generate a steady flow of income for the labour section's off-budget account, which was used to subsidize migrant worker expenses, but also to cover items that could not easily be debited to the embassy's account, such as accommodation and entertainment expenses for visiting Ministry of Manpower officials, including the Director for Overseas Placement, Director-General for Guidance of Labour Placement and the minister himself.

In addition, the labour attaché had a reputation for dealing harshly with instances where Indonesian migrant workers were found stranded at the Kuala Lumpur international airports. The conflict between the ministry and the BNP2TKI had exacerbated the situation, as it meant that labour recruitment companies could easily circumvent the requirement that full travel itineraries for migrant workers be submitted as part of the finalization process. In response to notification from airport authorities that Indonesian labour migrants en route to another country lacked onward tickets, for example, he would contact the sending labour recruitment company in Indonesia and order them to fix the situation by either repatriating migrant workers or organizing the necessary onward travel immediately. As a consequence of the labour attaché's punitive approach, the recruitment industry started to redirect candidates that did not conform fully to the programme's requirements through Singapore. He became aware of this practice following conversations with his counterpart there, in which she complained that the embassy had started to encounter greater numbers of stranded migrant workers at Singapore International Airport. The labour attaché in Kuala Lumpur explained his zero-tolerance policy in Kuala Lumpur would not be possible in Singapore where the labour attaché lacked control over the necessary administrative functions, such as endorsement of job orders.

Singapore

As noted in the first section of this chapter, Indonesian domestic workers in Singapore must report to the embassy's labour section as part of the process of renewing or replacing their passports. In an interview with one of four locally hired staff, the applicant and her employer are required to sign a standard employment contract provided by the embassy. This step must occur before they can collect new passports from the immigration section. Technical staff are required to ensure that the interview is attended by employers so that both parties agree to the Indonesian government's minimum wage in the presence of an embassy official. Domestic workers are also asked to confirm their name and date of birth during the interview. During the period examined in this study, routine cases were handled by these technical staff, who passed the signed contract to the labour attaché for counter-signing. When irregularities arose, the migrant worker was referred to the labour attaché, who then decided on the best way to deal with the case.

The labour attaché claims that the interview process turned up at least two clear cases of human trafficking each month. The cases mostly involved girls aged between 14 and 16 who had been placed in domestic employment using passports that overstated their ages. Identification of such cases is not always straightforward because under-age migrants, who may look older than they really are, work hard to conceal their true age. During an interview, the labour attaché presented me with a binder full of such cases, pointing to the most recent one, which involved a girl holding a passport stating she was 23 but who was later found to be only 14 years and 9 months old. The discrepancy was uncovered when the labour attaché probed into the girl's education history, asking when she started and finished primary school. Employers typically claim that they had no idea that their workers were children, arguing that in any case they are not responsible for recruitment and documentation processes in Indonesia. Meanwhile, many migrants acknowledge that they consented to falsification of their documents because they wanted the work to help support their families. The labour attaché generally reported such cases to authorities in Indonesia, recognizing that it is usually parents and not the children themselves who give consent.

The labour attaché corresponded with the Ministry of Foreign Affairs, the Criminal Investigation Agency of the National Police, the BNP2TKI, the Ministry of Women's Empowerment and the Ministry of Manpower in Jakarta about such cases. In that correspondence, she provided information about the worker's identity, a brief description of the case background, the name of the labour recruitment company in Indonesia that organized the documents, and details of the articles of the national migrant worker law that may have been contravened. She claimed that the Ministry of Manpower was the only agency that responded with any regularity. Unlike many of the other institutions, the ministry had the power to discipline labour recruitment companies; moreover, it was party to arrangements whereby the police defer authority to the ministry's civil servant investigators when relevant crime is detected. These bureaucrats were tasked with establishing whether there is sufficient evidence to pursue criminal punishment or if administrative sanctions should be applied instead. The immediate effect of these sanctions on the ability of labour recruitment companies to operate legally motivated the recruiters to comply with the ministry in Indonesia and its labour attachés overseas. For this reason, the labour attaché chose to address all correspondence on illegality involving labour recruitment companies to the Ministry of Manpower, notifying other state institutions with a carbon copy only.

But the labour attaché did not always report labour recruitment companies through official channels. In some cases, she instructed company owners to report directly to the Ministry of Manpower. In such instances, the labour attaché corresponded privately with colleagues in Indonesia to brief them on the case thereby ensuring that it was handled within the ministry, and without notifying the police. This strategy reflected her understanding that police officers often accepted bribes from company owners in exchange for dropping charges. Labour recruitment companies also complained to her that police officers targeted them for extortion by threatening to push for formal investigations into evidence of illegal behaviour. Such investigations could lead to more extortion and possibly even fines and imprisonment. So mistrusting one of the country's prime law enforcement agencies, she personally conducted preliminary investigations, taking note of the labour recruitment companies' version of events, and then deciding how best to report the case.

On some occasions, the labour attaché chose not to respond to the inclusion of false data in migrant workers' travel documents at all. In instances where migrant workers were found using forged or misappropriated passports, she mostly chose not to file reports with law enforcement. Rather, she coordinated with the immigration attaché, who issued the migrant worker in question with a limited validity travel document so that they could legally return to Indonesia. Her reasoning for this course of action was twofold. After President Yudhoyono's visit to the embassy in Kuala Lumpur, where he announced that the Ministry of Foreign Affairs would improve service provision to labour migrants, consular offices had progressively sensitized their policies to minimize negative consequences for migrants. In this case, reporting misappropriated passports would not only cause complications with Indonesian authorities, but could also land migrants in a Singaporean prison for ten years or result in a fine of up to SGD 10,000 (USD 7,900). On a practical level, it was also motivated by the fact that there was no police officer in the embassy at the time, which limited their capacity to fully investigate matters.

Similarly, while she was reasonably consistent in reporting labour recruitment companies that transgressed the minimum age requirement for recruitment when first posted, she later started to make exceptions. Labour recruitment companies frequently complained that it was difficult to find suitable recruits who met the Singaporean requirement that candidates be at least 23 years of age. Some migrants even admitted to having approached labour recruitment companies with full sets of modified papers, arguing that use of false documents was necessary because barriers to overseas employment were too high. For the labour attaché, stories about the lack of employment opportunities at home eventually tipped the scale in favour of ignoring some such transgressions. On the basis of these encounters, she began to turn a blind eye to the overstating of migrants' ages when the passport bearer was over the age of 18 and appeared to have the level of maturity required to deal with the challenges of working in Singapore. She also instituted a 'two-strikes-and-you're-out' system for cases that involved women below the age of 18, giving labour recruitment companies a verbal warning for the first transgression and reporting them through formal channels for any subsequent violation.

The labour attaché also chose to ignore evidence that passports did not contain true names. Migrant workers who have formerly worked in Saudi Arabia frequently hold such documents because labour recruitment companies change the names of recruits in order to comply with that country's immigration law, which requires visa applicants to have more than one name. Those with only one name tend to add their father's given name using the Arabic patronymic system with *bin* (son of) or *binti* (daughter of). But labour recruitment companies also change recruits' identities to avoid detection by authorities. In pursuing this issue, she learned about the difficulties of guaranteeing the integrity of migrant workers' passports in informal discussions with colleagues affiliated with the Directorate-General of Immigration. The police attaché in another consular office told her that the Indonesian National Police's (Kepolisian Republik Indonesia, INP) Criminal Investigation Agency prioritized investigations into other more serious illegal practices. Having reported a few cases, she decided that efforts to identify and report false names in passports were an unwise use of her time.

Another consideration for the labour attaché was the reality that a formalistic response to doctored identities – which she believed were a symptom of systemic failure rather than individual deviance – disproportionately penalized Indonesian migrant workers themselves. Once in a destination country, migrant workers hold work permits and identity cards based on the data recorded in their travel documents. If the embassy were to issue passports containing new data, migrants would have to undergo a number of complicated processes to change their identity or might even lose the right to work. For the labour attaché, confiscating passports and forcing migrants to return home posed an ethical dilemma because of the costly nature of the migration process and the fact that such acts deprive poor Indonesians of much needed gainful employment. She also observed with a sense of irony that destination countries set high minimum age requirements but turn a blind eye themselves, as she had discovered in her dealings with Singapore's Immigration Checkpoint Authority. In her view, it was clear to all that higher age limits simply resulted in greater demand for *aspal* documents in Indonesia because the policy did not address supply and demand issues in the labour market.

The labour attaché took a very different stance on cases where migrant workers claimed to have experienced coercion in the course of migrating. Occasionally a migrant would confide to the labour attaché that she was pressured into registering for international labour migration by her father or husband. More frequently, women would explain that labour recruitment company personnel had imprisoned them in a training centre dormitory, ignoring their requests to leave even temporarily. This practice was well known to officials in the Ministry of Manpower, and the labour attaché believed that it was only a matter of time until labour recruitment companies would be forced to overhaul their business model. As another example, she pointed to the practice whereby labour recruitment companies and the commission seeking fieldworkers gave women financial inducements, referred to as pocket money (*uang saku*), in order to convince them to sign up. The labour attaché would frequently ask migrant workers how much they received, motivated by the belief that financial inducement was a much more serious issue than the use of false identities because it induced rather than facilitated international labour migration. The payment of pocket money is in itself not illegal. But forcing people to migrate is. In handling these cases, the labour attaché gave those migrants the option to either report the matter or just return home.

Conclusion

This chapter shows how discretion on the part of individual officials not only shapes the development of administrative systems but individualizes the handling of particular problems. A central theme in the Hong Kong case studies is the idea of institutional hierarchy. As a junior official in the consulate, the labour attaché had much less say in the development of administrative systems to handle administration of labour recruitment companies and labour migrants than her more senior colleagues from the Ministry of Foreign Affairs. As a result of their affiliation, foreign affairs officials cared very little for the enforcement of regulations from the Ministry of Manpower, which they saw as further complicating their relationships with the local recruitment industry. This also holds true for the insistence of the Ministry of Justice and Human Right's Directorate-General of Immigration that passports must not be used as collateral for debt, as they are in Hong Kong. Yet, despite the labour attaché's much circumscribed role, formal and informal requests to assist with reclaiming passports still land on her desk. Moreover, it is in her handling of these cases that the limits of her authority are clearly visible, and through the logic of the actions she takes that the individualized dimension of administration becomes much more apparent.

The Kuala Lumpur and Singapore examples reveal other influential factors related to the exercise of authority. The labour attaché in Kuala Lumpur could play a determining role in refining administrative systems in the embassy largely because of his exclusive authority to handle matters to do with administration of Indonesian and Malaysian labour recruitment companies. This, in turn, enabled him to harness the recruitment industry as an alternative resource to subsidize the embassy's growing responsibilities with regard to the provision of emergency accommodation and repatriation of migrants. Both this labour attaché and his counterpart in Singapore were able to secure the introduction of a mandatory employment contract for Indonesian domestic workers seeking to renew their passports. They did so by going over the immigration attaché's head and working directly through the ambassador, risking a turf war in doing so. This aspect of life and work in these Indonesian consular offices hints at a central problem in all settings: what happens when control of administrative roles becomes the object of competition? Institutions can break down or become erratic, thus prompting even more personalized strategies than would otherwise be the case.

This observation brings the case studies in this and the preceding two chapters to full circle by showing how the individuals and agencies that comprise the state's institutional architecture operationalize discretion in performance of their public functions. In Hong Kong, Kuala Lumpur and Singapore, the Indonesia-wide conflict between the Ministry of Manpower and the

BNP2TKI was largely irrelevant largely because the administration performed there either preceded a contested role (such as signing job orders as part of applications for recruitment certificates) or because it entailed handling situations that arise once labour migrants are already overseas. The following chapter, which concludes this study, situates a discussion of these phenomena within the broader context of what is currently known about the Indonesian state.

CHAPTER 6

Conclusion

This book has provided a sustained analysis of interactions between the principal government agencies, units and individuals that comprised Indonesia's migration bureaucracy between 2007 and 2010. The objective was not to measure the degree to which these interactions affected the state's capacity to achieve particular objectives, influenced the profitability of the migration business or altered the experience of labour migrants. Rather, it examined the discretion exercised by those individuals who constitute the state in the development and implementation of the overseas labour migration programme, paying particular attention to historical and geographical context. The book systematically examined the role that discretionary acts played in administration at the centre, six sites in the periphery and three extraterritorial locations. This geographical approach enabled the identification of three themes that characterized the context in which discretion was used at the time. Focus on contestation at the centre revealed the role that discretion plays in producing, sustaining and resolving inter-agency conflict. Attention to accommodation in the periphery demonstrated that discretion is a resource that allows the state to function when institutional relationships have broken down. Extraterritorial locations exposed the extent to which discretion shapes administrative systems and determines implementation when institutional capacity and bureaucratic authority are limited.

Democratization, Decentralization, Patron-client Relations and Government Programmes

The fall of Suharto did not result in immediate changes to service provision within the overseas labour migration programme. In large part, the reason for this was that most interaction with intending migrants involves privately-owned labour recruitment companies rather than government officials. This meant that agents of the state had to influence practice within the recruitment industry to improve service provision. It was not until 2004 that the state criminalized the worst behaviour of labour recruitment companies towards intending migrants, including treating those who stayed in company boarding houses 'inhumanely' (*tidak manusiawi*).[1] As a further measure of redress and

1 *Law No. 39 on Placement and Protection of Indonesian Workers Overseas*, article 103(h).

 | DOI 10.1163/9789004325487_007

in recognition of systemic failure of the Ministry of Manpower to address these problems, the legislature transferred administration of labour migrants to a purpose-established government agency – the BNP2TKI. Not surprisingly, this sparked conflict between the Ministry of Manpower and the BNP2TKI over control of the programme. These changes to the institutional and legal context of the programme certainly impacted the recruitment industry and shaped its relationships with the state. They also influenced the ways in which the state then operated to achieve its own objectives.

Democratizing effects of the 1998 regime change are largely responsible for the timing of the overseas migration law. It was the career aspirations of presidential candidates, including Megawati Sukarnoputri, the incumbent in the 2004 election, which brought the state to enact Indonesia's first statute regulating the programme. Megawati ultimately lost the election but her efforts to seek re-election provided the necessary impetus for the law to be tabled and passed. It is outside the scope of this study to evaluate if, how and when the law improved the lot of Indonesian migrant workers. However, it has shown that the resulting dispersed control of administration precipitated a breakdown in coordination around the state's dealings with migrant labour recruiters and appointed insurers. In addition, the intra-agency competition between the newly-formed BNP2TKI and the Ministry of Manpower attracted a great deal of negative media about implementation, prompting senior government officials to openly criticize and defend policy choices, something not seen at any other time in the overseas labour migration programme's 40 year history.

Democratization was not the only form of regime change at play in the years between the New Order's end and passage of the law. After implementation of decentralization in 2001, government officials experienced a rise in what they describe as 'vertical institutional egotism' (*ego vertikal instansi*), in which government agencies operate much like silos with bureaucrats pursuing their institutional objectives at the expense of others' objectives. This added to the existing problem of 'sectoral institutional egotism' (*ego sektoral instansi*), in which agencies prioritize their own policy area. Successive New Order governments sought to contain this tendency by hand-picking managers loyal to the president and his inner circle. But the transfer of bureaucratic loyalty from the president to political parties disrupted this locus of control, as senior party cadres came to act as the primary sponsor of top-level officials. Further, policy-making and implementation became much more complicated processes after the state was restructured into three distinct tiers with varying degrees of interdependence and autonomy. In the context of the overseas labour migration programme, this meant that the Ministry of Manpower and later the

BNP2TKI could not as easily count on other government agencies or units to help achieve their policy objectives.

Decentralization of control forced the central government to negotiate closely with lower levels of government around implementation. These negotiations frequently involve the lowest tier of government, which came to perform the bulk of direct service provision. In the main, central government agencies believe that the lowest tier of government lacks the administrative and technical capacity to do so. But it is negotiations with the provincial tier – which has the difficult task of acting as an administrative extension of the central government while coordinating the administrative activity of autonomous local governments the leadership of a directly elected governor – that have most influenced implementation of the overseas labour migration programme. Provincial governments promised to be a much better alternative in most areas because their capital cities tend to double as embarkation points, where labour migrants could have their documents processed in a single place. This, however, proved to be little more than an exercise in justification for the Ministry of Manpower to cut the BNP2TKI out of the programme, which it clearly demonstrated in the case of Jakarta. Here the central government did not involve the provincial authorities at all, choosing instead to take care of matters itself because of the egregious turf war that followed a previous attempt to decentralize the overseas labour migration programme there.

But decentralization has also diluted the ministry's reach in the regions. In the past, the Ministry of Manpower circulated personnel from within its own ranks to manage its offices outside Jakarta. But since decentralization, office managers have been mostly drawn from the regions themselves. Loss of control over these positions has removed an opportunity for the ministry to forge the informal relationships often essential for achieving policy implementation. Abdul Malik Harahap and his 'boys' club' experienced this first hand when they attempted to enlist the provincial governments in their plan to isolate the BNP2TKI. By contrast, the BNP2TKI retained a string of units in the regions, which embedded it in the administrative landscape of those places. In each place, the BNP2TKI sought to foster collaborative relationships with government officials working in different tiers and sectors of the government to enhance its capacity to achieve institutional objectives such as bringing more recruitment of labour migrants under the programme. The Ministry of Manpower – and most other national government agencies – lacked the legal mandate to do the same.

This combination of democratization and decentralization has changed patterns of patron-client relationships in the context of government programmes. Since the state criminalized failure to meet administrative procedures concerning recruitment of migrant labour in 2004, police officers have emerged as useful patrons for recruiters seeking to avoid investigation, prosecution and punishment. Furthermore, Ministry of Manpower officials also claim that the police use their expanded role to extort recruiters for money in exchange for silence about alleged crimes. At the national level, insertion of the BNP2TKI into the administrative landscape has further diversified the patronage network, with the effect that it has further disrupted the historical monopoly that the Ministry of Manpower had to support those who profit from the recruitment industry. Decentralization has also empowered sub-national governments to provide patronage to local clients as is clearly demonstrated in the case of the businessperson in Tanjung Pinang, who provides repatriation services to deported migrant workers.

Discretion, Place and Scale

The transfer of administrative authority and budget control to sub-national governments since decentralization has sparked great interest in the study of political relations between different tiers of government. Historically, the centre-periphery model most accurately reflected the arrangement of state institutions in Indonesia. It continues to provide a primary frame of reference for discussing decentralization, where the national tier of government is described as the centre (*pusat*) and intermediate and local tiers as regions (*daerah*). The model also illustrates relations between tiers of government in particular sites within the periphery, which was useful to identify different ways in which relationships between national, intermediate and local tiers of government have evolved across the archipelago. In Jakarta, unresolved tension between national and sub-national authorities meant that the Ministry of Manpower ultimately chose not to collaborate as part of their effort to isolate the BNP2TKI. But in other provinces, it attempted to do just that, putting pressure on authorities to lend support to the ministry's effort. The administrative landscape of each location – each the product of history and place – influenced the outcome in different ways.

The enormous impact of place-based considerations within government agencies became evident following examination of the way that administrative landscapes actually are rather than how they are meant to be. Greater distance from an agency's head office in many cases enables local social and economic structures to influence more how bureaucratic units function. The case studies presented here demonstrate the ease with which regional units of national agencies came to prioritize the aims of sub-national government over the objectives of their own agency. Indeed, a key finding of this book is the extent to which institutional breakdown results in the abandonment of vertical hierarchy as an ordering principle in a range of administrative sites. This illustrates just how tenuous the internal relationships within a particular tier of government can be. It reveals the myriad ways in which discretion is operationalized within different sets of geographic, legal-administrative and political constraints, as national level bureaucrats especially struggle to achieve institutional objectives. The finding confirms that discretion is a key concept to make sense of Indonesia's culture of administration, which makes the state work.

Scale, then, emerges as a social construct, which is open to negotiation, and thus dynamic. This is not to say that scale as structure does not matter. It certainly does, as demonstrated in each of the case studies. However, it is not always the primary factor that defines the complex system of affiliations and purposes of government officials in a given context. As distance in centre-periphery relations should also be measured in economic, political and other terms, so too must it be when examining scalar relations. This study explored this by focusing on interactions of government officials around administration of the overseas labour migration programme in a range of places. In the performance of their roles, officials negotiated the importance of scalar considerations in their respective locations. Actor-network theory positions scale as structure as only one factor that influences relations between individuals, units, agencies and tiers within government. In this case study, place-based considerations and related negotiations determined implementation, showing too that salience of the concept can and does change over time in the minds of those tasked with running government programmes.

The Discretion-illegality Nexus

Discretion plays a vital role in lubricating the machinery of the modern state. Discretion is indeed exercised for personal gain. But personal and institutional interests are rarely discrete. The cases presented here demonstrate that the pursuit of a promotion or the lining of one's own pockets does not necessarily preclude interest in the welfare of the institution or a genuine desire to pursue its goals. Similarly, involvement in illegal activity does not necessarily frustrate institutional objectives. In fact, acting illegally might achieve just the opposite. Law is then little more than a tool that helps achieve institutional aims, especially when its statements about how things should be done align with those objectives. But the usefulness of law diminishes in difficult situations, including where it and institutional objectives do not align. In these situations, the law does not facilitate implementation and so implementers look to other means for achieving that objective. It is here that discretion becomes a particularly important resource, especially when exercised in conjunction with legal authority, which empowers officials to make choices about how to do things.

Discretion was the primary resource available to bureaucrats seeking to perform their roles after institutions had broken down in relation to the overseas labour migration programme between 2008 and 2010. Street-level bureaucrats were faced with a dilemma: whose instructions to follow? In Jakarta, the Ministry of Manpower duplicated services already provided by the BNP2TKI. Officials in both government agencies followed their managers' directives. By contrast, immigration, police and tax authorities were forced to choose an agency to follow and were not always comfortable with doing so. Outside Jakarta, the ministry wanted provincial governments to follow suit. In Surabaya, this was no problem at all because the provincial government already performed the BNP2TKI's administrative roles. In Nunukan, there was no provincial government authority to speak of. As a result, there was no choice to make in either place. But in other locations, such as Medan, Semarang and Tanjung Pinang, provincial government authorities had to choose. In these cases, conflicting institutional objectives added an extra layer of complexity to the context for accomplishing bureaucratic tasks. It was discretion that enabled them to continue with their work despite institutional breakdown and the added complexity.

Discretion can generate informal institutions that serve as a kind of 'institutional fix' in the absence of effective formal structures and processes. The various arrangements examined here explain in detail how government officials implemented the programme in the face of uncertainty about which central government agency would prevail. Together they constitute a set of decisions that aim to free up space for the institutionalization of a way of doing things preferred by those tasked with implementation.[2] These informal institutions may serve to delay the implementation of much needed reforms, and such strategic use of legal authority might enable bribery and other forms of corruption. But given that personal gain and furthering sectional interests are not always detrimental to the government agency concerned, it is necessary to study these institutions and the discretion that enables implementation as alternative resources for government officials to achieve institutional objectives. The purpose here is not to advocate for more use of them instead of addressing

2 Brenner and Theodore, "Cities and the Geographies of 'Actually Existing Neoliberalism.'"

the structural inadequacies that encourage their use. Rather, it is to shift attention away from the modus operandi of illegal behaviour to *why* it happens.

Individuals use their legal authority to subvert the substance of law, with the effect of widening the gap between the state's legal and institutional structures. On a micro level, this case study demonstrated that officials in Indonesia exercise a great deal of discretion in making judgements about how to use the law in their work. The risk associated with such behaviour is that highly personalized regimes for performing public functions may develop, as is the case with how labour attachés in three countries did their work. More broadly, the practice lays bare power relations between the legislative, judicial and executive branches of the Indonesian state. The Ministry of Manpower's response to the legislature's attempts at mediation and the lengths to which the ministry went to subvert a Supreme Court judgement expose the extent to which the executive continues to dominate other branches of the state in Indonesia. Individual and systemic observations have important implications for efforts to refine Indonesia's far-reaching reform agenda, as they demonstrate the centrality of legal authority and discretion in determining how the state is constituted and imposed.

These findings reveal the complexities associated with implementing national government programmes through a diverse network of officials, agencies and tiers of government in a large and geographically dispersed country. As implementation of the overseas labour migration programme has demonstrated, institutional objectives and the private ambitions of those who determine them are intricately interwoven and place-specific. The book has also advanced the debate around the effects of discretion by refocusing attention on legal authority rather than illegality. This focus is useful because it scrutinizes the ability of government officials to make choices, which can and do bring different elements of the state to become mired in conflict over control of systems and their attending benefits in the pursuit of individual and institutional objectives.

Appendix: Organigrams

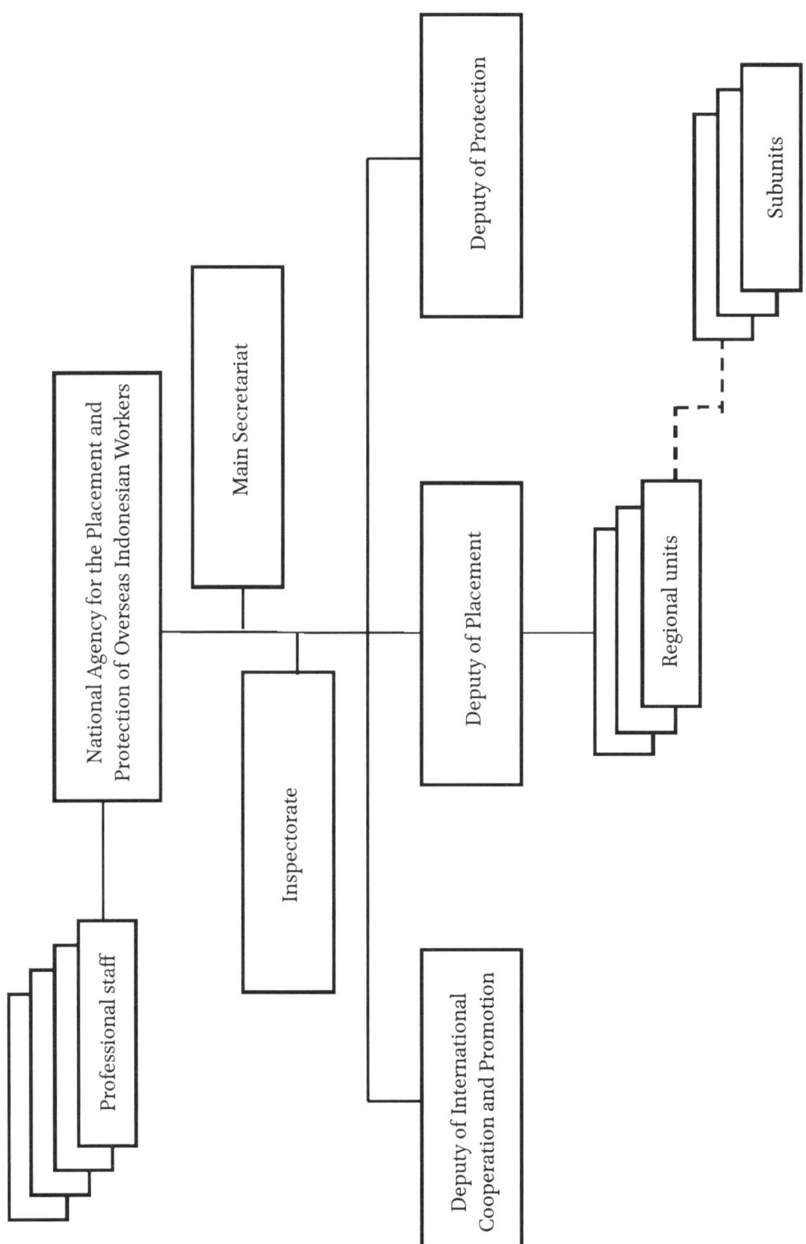

DIAGRAM 1 *National Agency for the Placement and Protection of Overseas Indonesian Workers*

 | DOI 10.1163/9789004325487_008

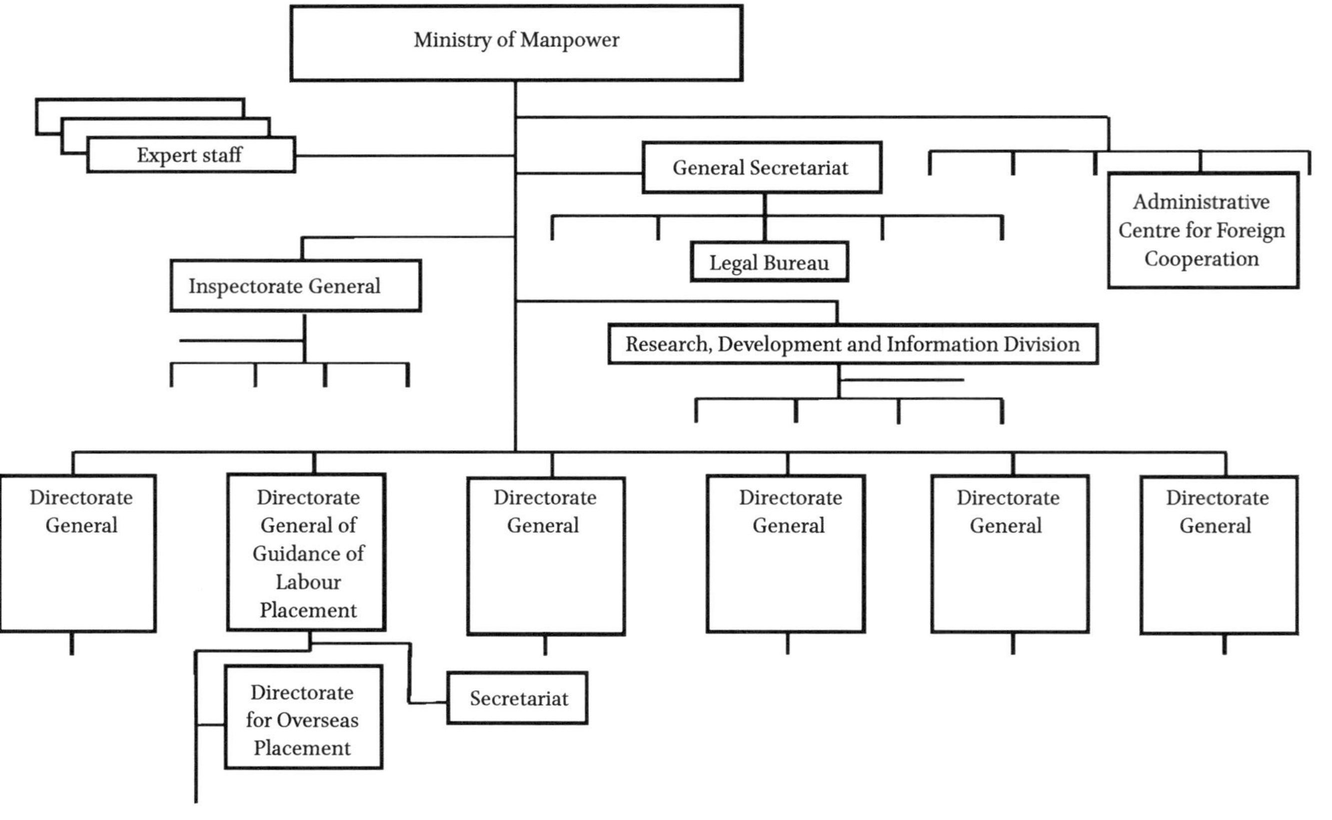

DIAGRAM 2 *Ministry of Manpower and Transmigration*

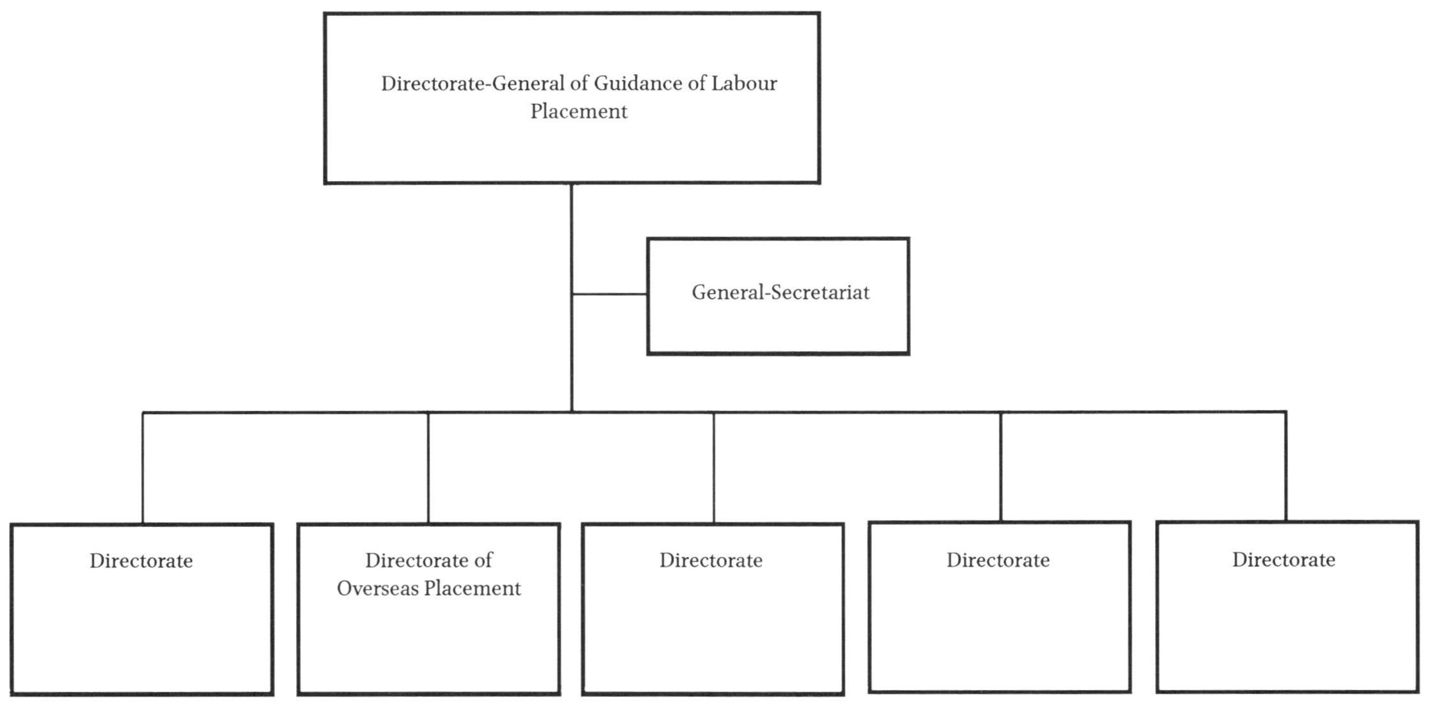

DIAGRAM 3 *Directorate-General of Guidance of Labour Placement*

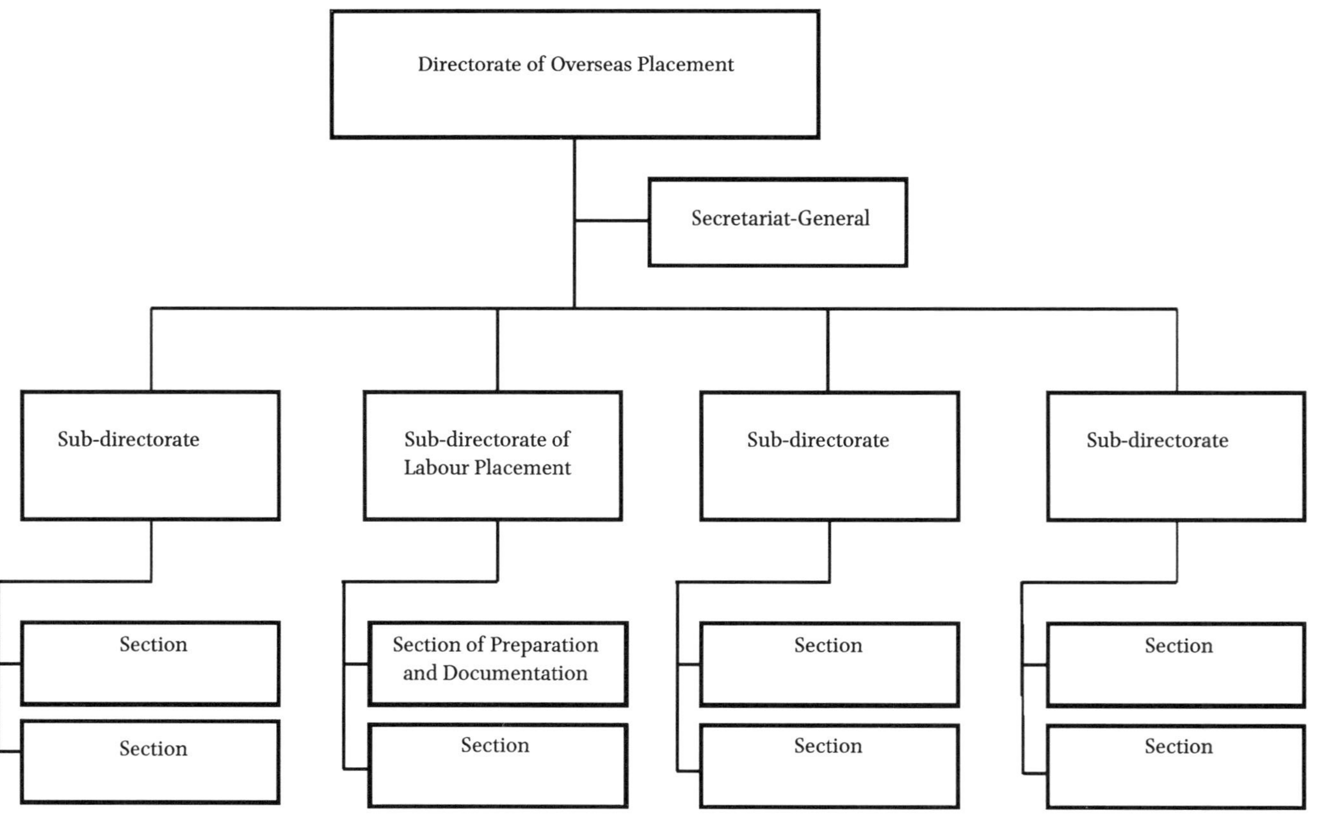

DIAGRAM 4 *Directorate of Overseas Placement*

References

"4.300 TKI Masuk Penampungan Baru." *Suaramerdeka.com*, September 16, 2002.

"12 Ormas Islam Mendesak Penghentian Pengiriman TKW." *Harian Terbit*, June 13, 2013.

"80% Masalah TKI Di Luar Negeri Berawal Dari Kampung Halaman." *Detik.com*, June 22, 2011.

"80 Persen Masalah BMI Terjadi Di Dalam Negeri," *VHR Media*, July 20, 2012.

Abrams, Philip. "Notes on the Difficulty of Studying the State (1977)." *Journal of Historical Sociology* 1, no. 1 (1988): 58–89.

Aditjondro, George. *Membongkar Gurita Cikeas: Di Balik Skandal Bank Century*. Jakarta: Galang Press, 2010.

Akzin, Benjamin. "Analysis of State and Law Structure." In *Law, State, and International Legal Order: Essays in Honor of Hans Kelsen*, edited by Salo Engel and Rudolf Métall, 1–20. Knoxville: University of Tennessee Press, 1964.

Al-Basry Establishment. "Letter of Authorization." Addressed to Departemen Tenaga Kerja dan Transmigrasi, April 2, 1979.

Amiati, Ati. *Memoir Bunda Seorang Aktivis*. Bandung: Mangle Panglipur, 2012.

Ananta, Aris, and Evi Arifin. "Should Southeast Asian Borders Be Opened?" In *International Migration in Southeast Asia*, edited by Aris Ananta and Evi Arifin, 1–27. Singapore: Institute of Southeast Asian Studies, 2004.

Anderson, Benedict. "Old State, New Society: Indonesia's New Order in Comparative Historical Perspective." *Journal of Asian Studies* 42, no. 3 (1983): 477–496.

"Anggota DPR Desak SBY Atasi Konflik BNP2TKI & Depnakertrans." *Myzone*, January 12, 2010.

"Arab Saudi Tunda 50 Ribu Visa Calon TKI," *Tempo*, August 7, 2007.

Asosiasi Jasa Penempatan Asia Pasifik. "Pengantar Rekrut SIP Agensi Al Ahliya (EST) Labour Suplay." Addressed to Direktur Jenderal Binapenta. 004/R-SIP/AJASPAC/XI/2008, November 5, 2008.

Asosiasi Perusahaan Jasa Tenaga Kerja Indonesia. "Anggaran Dasar: Asosiasi Perusahaan Penempatan Tenaga Kerja Indonesia Di Hong Kong," 1995.

———. "Biaya Penempatan TKI Ke Hong Kong." Addressed to Bapak Dirjen Binapenta Departemen Tenaga Kerja. 256/DPH/APJATI/V/99, May 18, 1999.

Aspinall, Edward. *Opposing Suharto: Compromise, Resistance and Regime Change in Indonesia*. Standford: Standford University Press, 2005.

Aspinall, Edward, and Greg Fealy, eds. *Local Power and Politics in Indonesia: Decentralisation and Democratisation*. Singapore: Institute of Southeast Asian Studies, 2003.

Aspinall, Edward, and Gerry van Klinken, eds. *The State and Illegality in Indonesia*. Leiden: KILTV, 2011.

Asuransi Jasindo. "Jasindo Bayar Klaim 4.985 TKI," June 13, 2007.

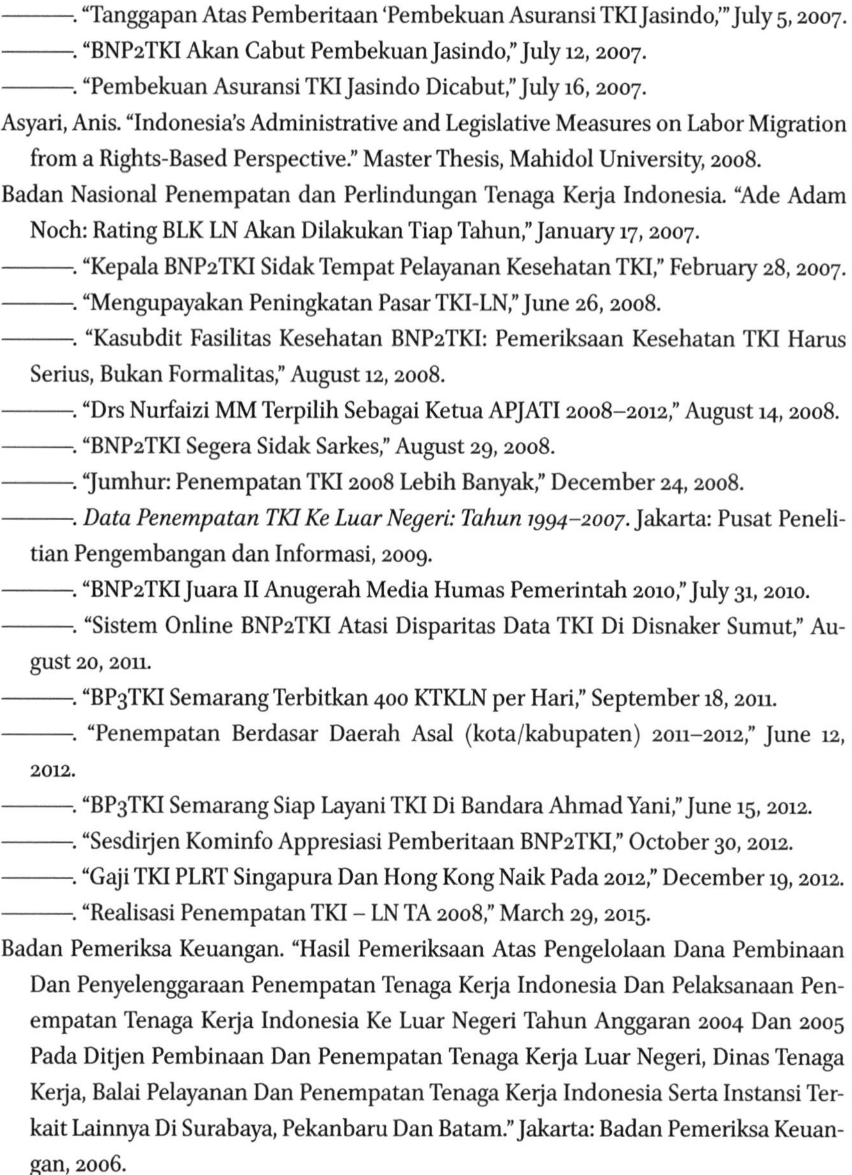

———. "Tanggapan Atas Pemberitaan 'Pembekuan Asuransi TKI Jasindo,'" July 5, 2007.

———. "BNP2TKI Akan Cabut Pembekuan Jasindo," July 12, 2007.

———. "Pembekuan Asuransi TKI Jasindo Dicabut," July 16, 2007.

Asyari, Anis. "Indonesia's Administrative and Legislative Measures on Labor Migration from a Rights-Based Perspective." Master Thesis, Mahidol University, 2008.

Badan Nasional Penempatan dan Perlindungan Tenaga Kerja Indonesia. "Ade Adam Noch: Rating BLK LN Akan Dilakukan Tiap Tahun," January 17, 2007.

———. "Kepala BNP2TKI Sidak Tempat Pelayanan Kesehatan TKI," February 28, 2007.

———. "Mengupayakan Peningkatan Pasar TKI-LN," June 26, 2008.

———. "Kasubdit Fasilitas Kesehatan BNP2TKI: Pemeriksaan Kesehatan TKI Harus Serius, Bukan Formalitas," August 12, 2008.

———. "Drs Nurfaizi MM Terpilih Sebagai Ketua APJATI 2008–2012," August 14, 2008.

———. "BNP2TKI Segera Sidak Sarkes," August 29, 2008.

———. "Jumhur: Penempatan TKI 2008 Lebih Banyak," December 24, 2008.

———. *Data Penempatan TKI Ke Luar Negeri: Tahun 1994–2007*. Jakarta: Pusat Penelitian Pengembangan dan Informasi, 2009.

———. "BNP2TKI Juara II Anugerah Media Humas Pemerintah 2010," July 31, 2010.

———. "Sistem Online BNP2TKI Atasi Disparitas Data TKI Di Disnaker Sumut," August 20, 2011.

———. "BP3TKI Semarang Terbitkan 400 KTKLN per Hari," September 18, 2011.

———. "Penempatan Berdasar Daerah Asal (kota/kabupaten) 2011–2012," June 12, 2012.

———. "BP3TKI Semarang Siap Layani TKI Di Bandara Ahmad Yani," June 15, 2012.

———. "Sesdirjen Kominfo Appresiasi Pemberitaan BNP2TKI," October 30, 2012.

———. "Gaji TKI PLRT Singapura Dan Hong Kong Naik Pada 2012," December 19, 2012.

———. "Realisasi Penempatan TKI – LN TA 2008," March 29, 2015.

Badan Pemeriksa Keuangan. "Hasil Pemeriksaan Atas Pengelolaan Dana Pembinaan Dan Penyelenggaraan Penempatan Tenaga Kerja Indonesia Dan Pelaksanaan Penempatan Tenaga Kerja Indonesia Ke Luar Negeri Tahun Anggaran 2004 Dan 2005 Pada Ditjen Pembinaan Dan Penempatan Tenaga Kerja Luar Negeri, Dinas Tenaga Kerja, Balai Pelayanan Dan Penempatan Tenaga Kerja Indonesia Serta Instansi Terkait Lainnya Di Surabaya, Pekanbaru Dan Batam." Jakarta: Badan Pemeriksa Keuangan, 2006.

Barker, Joshua, and Gerry van Klinken, eds. *State of Authority: State in Society in Indonesia*. New York: Southeast Asia Program Publications, 2009.

Bass, Bernard, and Ronald Riggio. *Transformational Leadership*. Mahwah: Lawrence Erlbaum Associates, 2006.

"Batas Usia Calon TKI Minimal 18 Dan 21 Tahun." *Portal CBN Cybernews*, September 4, 2004.

Batubara, Cosmas. *Cosmas Batubara, Sebuah Otobiografi Politik*. Jakarta: Penerbit Buku Kompas, 2007.

Becker, Gary, and George Stigler. "Law Enforcement, Malfeasance, and Compensation of Enforcers." *Journal of Legal Studies* 3 (1974): 1–18.

Bedner, Adriaan. *Administrative Courts in Indonesia: A Socio-Legal Study*. The Hague: Kluwer Law International, 2001.

"BNP2TKI Diminta Benahi Komite Korea." *Bursa.com*, July 4, 2007.

"BNP2TKI Tangani TKI Ke Korsel." *Suaramerdeka.com*, July 26, 2007.

"Bomer: Minggu Ini Ada Pergantian Eselon I Depnaker." *Antara*, May 23, 2000.

Booth, Anne. *The Oil Boom and after: Indonesian Economic Policy and Performance in the Soeharto Era*. Singapore: Oxford University Press, 1992.

Bourguignon, François, and Thierry Verdier. "Oligarchy, Democracy, Inequality and Growth." *Journal of Development Economics* 62 (2000): 285–313.

Brenner, Neil, and Nik Theodore. "Cities and the Geographies of 'Actually Existing Neoliberalism.'" *Antipode* 34, no. 3 (n.d.): 349–379.

Breton, Albert, and Ronald Wintrobe. "The Equilibrium of a Budget-Maximizing Bureau: A Note on Niskanen's Theory of Bureaucracy." *Journal of Political Economy* 83, no. 1 (1975): 195–208.

Brietzke, Paul. "Administrative Reform in Indonesia." In *Corruption in Asia: Rethinking the Governance Paradigm*, edited by Timothy Lindsey and Howard Dick, 109–126. Sydney: Federation Press, 2002.

Bünte, Marco. "Indonesia's Protracted Decentralization: Contested Reforms and Their Unintended Consequences." In *Democratization in Post-Suharto Indonesia*, edited by Marco Bünte and Andreas Ufen. Oxon and New York: Routledge, 2009.

Butt, Simon. *Corruption and Law in Indonesia*. New York: Routledge, 2010.

———. "Regional Autonomy and Legal Disorder: The Proliferation of Local Laws in Indonesia." *Sydney Law Review* 32, no. 2 (2010): 177–191.

Caraway, Teri. "Explaining the Dominance of Legacy Unions in New Democracies: Comparative Insights from Indonesia." *Comparative Political Studies* 41, no. 10 (2007): 1371–1397.

Christie, George. "Lawful Departures from Legal Rules: 'Jury Nullification' and Legitimated Disobedience." *California Law Review* 62 (1974): 1289–1310.

Constable, Nicole. *Maid to Order in Hong Kong: Stories of Migrant Workers*. 2nd ed. Ithaca and London: Cornell University Press, 2007.

———. *Born out of Place: Migrant Workers and the Politics of International Labor*. Hong Kong: Hong Kong University Press, 2014.

Corbin, Arthur. "Legal Analysis and Terminology." *Yale Law Journal* 29 (1919): 163–273.

Cremer, Georg. "Deployment of Indonesian Migrants in the Middle East: Present Situation and Prospects." *Bulletin of Indonesian Economic Studies* 24, no. 3 (1988): 73–86.

Cribb, Robert. "A System of Exemptions: Historicizing State Illegality in Indonesia." In *The State and Illegality in Indonesia*, edited by Edward Aspinall and Gerry van Klinken, 31–44. Leiden: KILTV, 2011.

"Dana Pungutan TKI Diusut Kejaksaan Agung." *Gatra*, February 28, 2001.

Darden, Keith. "Blackmail as a Tool of State Domination: Ukraine under Kuchma." *East European Constitutional Review* 10 (2001): 67–71.

———. "The Integrity of Corrupt States: Graft as an Informal State Institution." *Politics and Society* 36, no. 1 (2008): 35–60.

Departemen Pertahanan Keamanan. "Berbagai Usaha Pembinaan Dan Pengamanan Tenaga Kerja Indonesia Di Luar Negeri Khususnya Di Timur Tengah." In *Diskusi Panel: Peningkatan Usaha Pengiriman Tenaga Kerja Indonesia Ke Timur Tengah: Pengawasan Dan Perlindungan Tenaga Kerja Indonesia Di Timur Tengah*. Team Koordinasi Kegiatan Ekspor Timur Tengah: Departmen Perdagangan dan Koperasi, 1983.

Departemen Tenaga Kerja. *Perluasan Kesempatan Kerja Melalui Antar Kerja Antar Negara Ke Malaysia Timur*. Jakarta, 1987.

Departemen Tenaga Kerja Transmigrasi dan Koperasi. "Bulletin Tahunan: Statistik Tenaga Kerja Indonesia." Jakarta, 1972.

———. *Bulletin Tahunan: Statistik Tenaga Kerja Indonesia*, 1975.

———. *Bulletin Tahunan: Statistik Tenaga Kerja Indonesia*, 1977.

———. *Bulletin Tahunan: Statistik Tenaga Kerja Indonesia*, 1978.

———. *Bulletin Tahunan: Statistik Tenaga Kerja Indonesia*, 1983.

"Detail Biodata: Pejabat Menteri." perpusnas.go.id, Accessed July 1, 2013.

Dewan Perwakilan Rakyat. *Risalah Rapat Panitia Khusus Rancangan Undang-Undang Tentang Pemberantasan Tindak Pidana Perdagangan Orang: Rapat Dengar Pendapat Umum*. 1 February, 2006.

———. *Risalah Rapat Panitia Khusus Rancangan Undang-Undang Tentang Pemberantasan Tindak Pidana Perdagangan Orang: Rapat Dengar Pendapat Umum*. 9 February, 2006.

———. *Risalah Rapat Panitia Khusus Rancangan Undang-Undang Tentang Pemberantasan Tindak Pidana Perdagangan Orang: Rapat Dengar Pendapat Umum*. 8 March, 2006.

"Di Balik Pelengseran Wakil Bupati Kendal (2-Habis): Bagaimana Tanggung Jawab Panitia Pemilihan Dulu?" *Suaramerdeka.com*, July 20, 2002.

Dick, Howard, James Fox, and Jamie Mackie. *Balanced Development: East Java in the New Order*. New York: Oxford University Press, 1993.

Diederich, Mathias. "Indonesians in Saudi Arabia." In *Transnational Connections and the Arab Gulf*, edited by Madawi Al-Rasheed, 128–146. London and New York: Routledge, 2005.

"Dilarang Merekrut TKI Hingga Desember 2000." *Liputan6*, September 15, 2000.

Dinas Tenaga Kerja Transmigrasi dan Kependudukan. "Sejarah Lembaga Pelayanan Penempatan TKI Di Jatim." jatimprov.go.id, Accessed July 7, 2013.

Dinas Tenaga Kerja Transmigrasi dan Penduduk. "Mundur Dari APJATI, Deklarasikan IEMSA," April 20, 2011.

Direktur Jenderal Pembinaan dan Penempatan Tenaga Kerja. "Struktur Biaya Penempatan TKI Ke Hong Kong." Addressed to Direktur Bidang Kredit Bank Indonesia. B.603/BP/1999, May 21, 1999.

Direktur Jenderal Pembinaan dan Penggunaan Tenaga Kerja. "Garis-Garis Besar Antar Kerja Antar Negara." Departemen Tenaga Kerja dan Transmigrasi, 1982.

Direktur Penempatan Tenaga Kerja Luar Negeri. "Undangan." Addressed to list of invitees (attached). UND No. 136/PP-TKLN/III/2008, March 14, 2008.

"Dirjen Binapenta I Made Arka: Selama G to G Masih Ada, Dualisme Proses Pelayanan Pemberangkatan TKI." *Madina*, n.d.

Doig, Alan. "Good Government and Sustainable Anti-Corruption Strategies: A Role for Independent Anti-Corruption Agencies." *Public Administration and Development* 15 (1995): 151–165.

Dowling, John, and Jeffrey Pfeffer. "Organizational Legitimacy: Social Values and Organizational Behaviour." *Pacific Sociological Review* 18, no. 1 (1975): 122–136.

"Dualisme Kemenakertrans-BNP2TKI Berakhir." *Republika*, October 15, 2010.

"Dualisme Pengelolaan TKI Berakhir," *buruhmigran.co.id*, September 27, 2010.

Dwivedi, Onkar, and James Gow. *From Bureaucracy to Public Management: The Administrative Culture of the Government of Canada*. Petrerborough, Ontario: Broadview Press, 1999.

"Eks Pejabat Depnakertrans Divonis 3 Tahun Bui." *Detik.com*, January 5, 2010.

Embassy of Indonesia (Canada). "Company Profile: Eldy International, PT." indonesia.ottawa.org, Accessed June 26, 2013.

Emmerson, Donald. "Understanding the New Order: Bureaucratic Pluralism in Indonesia." *Asian Survey* 23, no. 11 (1983): 1220–1241.

———. "A Foreshadow Play." *A Survey of Asia* 31, no. 2 (1991): 179–187.

Epstein, David, and Sharyn O'Halloran. *A Transaction Cost Politics Approach to Policy Making under Separate Powers*. Cambridge: Cambridge University Press, 1999.

"Erman Suparno Siap Lepas Posisi Bendahara Umum PKB." *Detik.com*, December 6, 2005.

Falk, Sally. *Law as Process: An Anthropological Approach*. Münster-Hamburg and Oxford: LIT Verlag and James Currey, 2000.

Fayard, Anne-Laure, and John Weeks. "Photocopier and Water-Coolers: The Affordances of Informal Interaction." *Organization Studies* 28, no. 5 (2007): 605–634.

Feuer, Lewis. "End of Coolie Labor in New Caledonia." *Far Eastern Survey* 15, no. 17 (1946): 264–267.

Firman, Tommy. "In Search of a Governance Institution Model for Jakarta Metropolitan Area (JMA) under Indonesia's Decentralization Policy: Old Problems, New Challenges." *Public Administration and Development* 28 (2008): 280–290.

Ford, Michele. "After Nunukan: The Regulation of Indonesian Migration to Malaysia." In *Divided We Move: Mobility, Labour Migration and Border Controls in Asia*, edited by A. Kaur and I. Metcalfe, 228–247. New York: Palgrave Macmillan, 2006.

———. *Workers and Intellectuals: NGOs, Trade Unions and the Indonesian Labour Movement*. Singapore: NUS Press, 2009.

———. "Constructing Legality: The Management of Irregular Migration in Thailand and Malaysia." In *Labour History beyond Borders: Concepts and Explorations*, edited by Marcel van der Linden, 177–199. Leipzig: Akademische Verlagsanstalt, 2010.

Ford, Michele, and Lenore Lyons. "Travelling the Aspal Route: 'Grey' Labour Migration through an Indonesian Border Town." In *The State and Illegality in Indonesia*, edited by Edward Aspinall and Gerry van Klinken, 107–122. Leiden: KILTV, 2011.

Ford, Michele, and Thomas Pepinsky. "Beyond Oligarchy? Critical Exchanges on Political Power and Material Inequality in Indonesia." *Indonesia* 96, no. 2 (2013): 1–9.

Ford, Michele, Lenore Lyons, and Wayne Palmer. "Stopping the Hordes: A Critical Account of the Labor Government's Regional Approach to the Management of Asylum Seekers." *Local–global* 8 (2010): 28–35.

Fyre, Timothy. "Capture or Exchange? Business Lobbying in Russia." *Europe-Asia Studies* 54, no. 7 (2002): 1017–1036.

Garoupa, Nuno. "The Theory of Optimal Law Enforcement." *Journal of Economic Surveys* 11, no. 3 (1997): 267–295.

Gilardi, Fabrizio. "Policy Credibility and Delegation to Independent Regulatory Agencies: A Comparative Empirical Analysis." *Journal of European Public Policy* 9, no. 6 (2002): 873–893.

Gootenberg, Paul. "Talking like a State: Drugs, and the Language of Control." In *Illicit Flows and Criminal Things: States, Borders, and the Other Side of Globalization*, edited by Willem van Schendel and Itty Abraham, 101–127. Bloomington: Indiana University Press, 2005.

Government of Indonesia, and Government of Malaysia. "Memorandum of Understanding between the Government of the Republic of Indonesia and the Government of Malaysia on the Recruitment and Placement of Indonesian Migrant Workers," May 13, 2006.

Government of Indonesia, HOKINDO (Badan Otonom Hong Kong Indonesia), APPIH (Asosiasi PPTKI Hong Kong), and APJATI (Asosiasi Perusahaan Jasa Tenaga Kerja Indonesia). *Memorandum of Understanding: Struktur Biaya Penempatan TKI Ke Hong Kong*. 7 February, 2003.

Grant, Ronald M. "Indonesia 1978: A Third Term for President Suharto." *Asian Survey* 19, no. 2 (1979): 141–146.

Grzymala-Busse, Anna. "The Best Laid Plans: The Impact of Informal Rules on Formal Institutions in Transitional Regimes." *Studies in Comparative International Development* 45, no. 3 (2010): 311–333.

Hadiz, Vedi. *Localising Power in Post-Authoritarian Indonesia: A Southeast Asia Perspective*. Singapore: Institute of Southeast Asian Studies, 2011.

———. "Reformasi and Changing State and Labour Relations in Indonesia and Malaysia." In *Challenging Authoritarianism in Southeast Asia*, edited by Ariel Heryanto and Sumit Mandal, 2nd ed., 90–116. Oxon: Routledge, 2012.

Hadiz, Vedi, and Richard Robison. "The Political Economy of Oligarcy and the Reorganization of Power in Indonesia." *Indonesia* 96, no. 2 (2013): 35–57.

Hajnal, György. "The Spirit of Management Reforms." *Public Management Review* 7, no. 4 (2005): 495–513.

Hamilton-Hart, Natasha. "Anti-Corruption Strategies in Indonesia." *Bulletin of Indonesian Economic Studies* 37, no. 1 (2001): 65–82.

Hariani, Dyah, and Hesti Lestari. "Analisis Kualitas Pelayanan Di Balai Pelayanan Penempatan Dan Perlindungan Tenaga Kerja Indonesia (BP3TKI) Semarang Provinsi Jawa Tengah." *Journal of Public Policy and Management Review* 2, no. 2 (2013): 1–10.

Hart, Herbert. *The Concept of Law*. 3rd ed. Clarendon Law Series. Oxford: Oxford University Press, 2012.

Heather Sutherland. *The Making of a Bureaucratic Elite: The Colonial Transformation of the Javanese Priyayi*. Singapore: Heinemann, 1979.

Hein, Gordon. "Indonesia in 1981: Countdown to the General Elections." *Asian Survey* 22, no. 2 (1982): 200–211.

———. "Indonesia in 1989: A Question of Openness." *Asian Survey* 30, no. 2 (1990): 221–230.

Henderson, Lynne. "Legality and Empathy." *Michigan Law Review* 85 (1986): 1574–1653.

Hernawan, Ari, and Supriyadi. "Penerapan Sanksi Terhadap Pelanggaran PPTKIS Dalam Pra Penempatan TKI Di Luar Negeri." *Mimbar Hukum* 19, no. 3 (2007): 335–485.

Hill, Hal. "The Indonesian Economy: The Strange and Sudden Death of a Tiger." In *The Fall of Soeharto*, edited by Geoff Forrester and R May, 93–103. Bathurst: Crawford House, 1998.

———. *The Indonesian Economy*. 2nd ed. Cambridge: Cambridge University Press, 2000.

Hofstede, Geert, Gert Jan Hofstede, and Michael Minkov. *Cultures and Organizations: Software of the Mind*. 3rd ed. New York: McGraw-Hil, 2010.

Horowitz, Donald. *Constitutional Change and Democracy in Indonesia*. Cambridge and New York: Cambridge University Press, 2013.

Houben, Vincent, and J. Lindblad. *Coolie Labour in Colonial Indonesia: A Study of Labour Relations in the Outer Islands, C. 1900–1940*. Wiesbaden: Harrassowitz, 1999.

Hugo, Graeme. "Population Movement in Indonesia since 1971." *Tijdschrift Voor Economische En Sociale Geografie* 79, no. 4 (1988): 242–256.

———. "Indonesian Labour Migration to Malaysia: Trends and Policy Implications." *Asian Journal of Social Science* 21, no. 1 (1993): 36–70.

———. "Information, Exploitation and Empowerment: The Case of Indonesian Overseas Workers." *Asian and Pacific Migration Journal* 12, no. 4 (2003): 439–467.

Hugo, Graeme, and W. Bohning. "Providing Information to Outgoing Indonesian Migrant Workers." Report. International Labour Office, 2000.

hukumonline.com. "Pro-Kontra Citizen Law Suit: Belajar Dari Kasus Nunukan," May 14, 2003.

———. "RUU Perlindungan Tenaga Kerja Diharapkan Hapus Monopoli PJTKI," January 24, 2004.

———. "RUU Buruh Migran Versi Depnakertrans Dinilai Tidak Berorientasi Perlindungan," July 26, 2004.

———. "PPTKIS Siap Mengirim TKI Meski Tanpa BNP2TKI." February 7, 2009.

———. "Depnakertrans Jawab Permohonan Uji Materi Permenakertrans No. 22/2008," March 5, 2009.

———. "Mantan Dirjen Depnakertrans Divonis Tiga Tahun Penjara," January 5, 2010.

———. *Awas, Sesat Pikir Tentang Wajar Tanpa Pengecualian*. Jakarta, 2012.

Human Rights Watch. "Help Wanted: Abuses against Female Domestic Workers in Indonesia and Malaysia." Report. Human Rights Watch, 2004.

Idrus, Nurul. "Makkunrai Passimokolo': Bugis Migrant Women Workers in Malaysia." In *Women and Work in Indonesia*, edited by Michele Ford and Lyn Parker, 155–172. New York: Routledge, 2008.

"Ijin Operasional Jasindo Dibekukan BNP2TKI." *Pos Kota*, July 2, 2007.

"Indonesia-Malaysia Tandatangani MoU Perlindungan." *Tempo*, August 16, 2004.

Indonesian consulate (Hong Kong). "Renewal: Business Accreditation Certificate (BAC) to Operate an Indonesian Employment Agency." 44-B-XI/09-X, October 23, 2009.

"Indonesia-Pilipina Bekerjasama Dalam Penyaluran Tenaga Kerja Di Timur Tengah," September 1982.

"Indonesia Siapkan Evakuasi TKI Dari Timur Tengah." *Tempo*, February 12, 2003.

Indrawati, Agus. "Agus- Sorot-Depnaker," *asia.groups.yahoo.com*, November 6, 2009.

International Crisis Group. "Indonesia: Defying the State Asia Briefing No. 138." Jakarta/Brussels: International Crisis Group, 2012.

International Organization for Migration. "Labour Migration from Indonesia: An Overview of Indonesian Migration in Selected Destinations in Asia and the Middle East." Report. International Organization for Migration, 2010.

Jansen, Nils. *The Making of Legal Authority: Non-Legislative Codifications in Historical and Comparative Perspective*. Oxford: Oxford University Press, 2010.

John Jeffries Jr.. "Legality, Vagueness, and the Construction of Penal Statutes." *Virginia Law Review* 71 (1985): 189–245.

Jenkins, David. *Suharto and His Generals: Indonesian Military Politics, 1975–1983*. Jakarta and Kuala Lumpur: Equinox Publishing, 2010.

Jones, Sidney. *Making Money off Migrants*. Hong Kong: Asia 2000 and Centre for Asia Pacific Social Transformation Studies, University of Wollongong, 2000.

Jones-Correa, Michael, and Els de Graauw. "The Illegality Trap: The Politics of Immigration & the Lens of Illegality." *Daelus* 142, no. 3 (2013): 185–198.

"Jumhur: Asuransi TKI Berengsek Semua." *Detik.com*, January 9, 2008.

"Jumhur Ngaku Heran Menakertran Cabut Kewenangan BNP2TKI." *Pos Kota*, October 18, 2011.

Juridico, Elmor. "Overseas Employment and Recruitment Practices of Asian Labour-Sending Countries." International Labour Organization, 1989.

"Jusuf Kalla Akui Bocoran Wikileaks Benar." *Tempo*, March 11, 2011.

Kadish, Mortimer, and Sanford Kadish. *Discretion to Disobey: A Study of Lawful Departures from Legal Rules*. Stanford: Standord University Press, 1973.

Kassim, Azizah. "Filipino Refugees in Sabah: State Responses, Public Stereotypes and the Dilemma over Their Future." *Southeast Asian Studies* 47, no. 1 (2009): 52–88.

Katz, Joan. "The Games Bureaucrats Play: Hide and Seek under the Freedom of Information Act." *Texas Law Review* 48 (1969): 1261–1284.

Kaur, Amarjit. "Indonesian Migrant Workers in Malaysia: From Preferred Migrants to 'Last to Be Hired' Workers." *Review of Indonesian and Malaysian Affairs* 39, no. 2 (2005): 3–30.

"Kebijakan Penempatan Pekerja Indonesia Cuma Memosisikan TKI Sebagai Komoditas." *Kompas*, October 2, 2002.

Kelsen, Hans. *Pure Theory of Law*. Berkeley: University of California Press, 1967.

"Ke Mana Rp 1 Triliun Duit TKI." *Tempo*, February 7, 1998.

Kementerian Hukum dan HAM. Peran Pemerintah Daerah Di Wilayah Perbatasan Dalam Melindungi Warga Negara Indonesia Yang Dideportasi (Studi Di Propinsi Kalimantan Barat, Kepulauan Riau, Sumatera Utara, Dan Kalimantan Timur). Jakarta, 2011.

Kementerian Koordinator Kesejahteraan Rakyat. "Kinerja Tim Koordinasi Pemulangan Tenaga Kerja Indonesia Bermasalah Dan Keluarga Dari Malaysia (TK-PTKB) Tahun 2007." Jakarta: Kementerian Koordinator Kesejahteraan Rakyat, 2007.

———. "Kinerja Tim Koordinasi Pemulangan Tenaga Kerja Indonesia Bermasalah Dan Keluarga Dari Malaysia (TK-PTKB) Tahun 2008." Jakarta, 2008.

———. "Petunjuk Pelaksanaan Penanganan Dan Pemulangan Tenaga Kerja Indonesia Bermasalah Dan Keluarganya (TKI-B) Dari Malaysia." Jakarta: Kementerian Koordinator Kesejahteraan Rakyat, 2009.

"Kilas Balik Perjalanan Masduki Yusak." *Suaramerdeka.com*, July 18, 2002.

Killias, Olivia. "The Politics of Bondage in the Recruitment, Training and Placement of Indonesian Migrant Domestic Workers." *Sociologus* 2 (2009): 145–172.

———. "'Illegal' Migration as Resistance: Legality, Morality and Coercion in Indonesian Domestic Worker Migration to Malaysia." *Asian Journal of Social Science* 38, no. 6 (2010): 897–914.

Kipp, Rita. "Indonesia in 2003: Terror's Aftermath." *Asian Survey* 44, no. 1 (2004): 62–69.

Kloppenburg, Sanneke, and Peter Peters. "Confined Mobilities: Following Indonesian Migrant Workers on Their Way Home." *Tijdschrift Voor Economische En Sociale Geografie* 103, no. 5 (2012): 530–541.

"Koalisi Buruh Migran Menolak RUU PTKLN." *Liputan6*, September 2, 2004.

Komisi Yudisial. "Mantan Pejabat Depnakertrans Divonis 4 Tahun Penjara," April 30, 2008.

Koppelman, Andrew. "How 'Decentralization' Rationalizes Oligarchy: John McGinnis and the Rehnquist Court." *Constitutional Commentary* 20 (2003): 11–37.

Krisnawaty, Tati. "Reformasi Dibelenggu Birokrasi." Jakarta: Komnas Perempuan, 2006.

Kristiansen, Stein, and Muhid Ramli. "Buying an Income: The Market for Civil Service Positions in Indonesia." *Contemporary Southeast Asia* 28, no. 2 (2006): 207–233.

Kurus, Bilson. "Migrant Labor: The Sabah Experience." *Asian and Pacific Migration Journal* 7, nos. 2–3 (1998): 281–295.

Langbein, Laura. *Bureaucratic Discretion*. Vol. 2. Kluwer Academic Publishers, 2004.

Lindquist, Johan. "Labour Recruitment, Circuits of Capital and Gendered Mobility: Reconceptualizing the Indonesian Migration Industry." *Pacific Affairs* 83, no. 1 (2010): 115–132.

———. "The Elementary School Teacher, the Thug and His Grandmother: Informal Brokers and Transnational Migration from Indonesia." *Pacific Affairs* 85, no. 1 (2012): 69–89.

———. "Rescue, Return, in Place: Deportees, 'Victims,' and the Regulation of Indonesian Migration." In *Return: Nationalizing Transnational Mobility in Asia*, edited by Xiang Biao, Mika Toyota, and Brenda Yeoh. Durham and London: Durham University Press, 2013.

Lindquist, Johan, and Nicola Piper. "From HIV Prevention to Counter-Trafficking: Discursive Shifts and Institutional Continuities in South-East Asia." In *Human Trafficking*, edited by Maggy Lee, 138–158. Devon: Willian Publishing, 2007.

Liow, Jospeh. *The Politics of Indonesia-Malaysia Relations: One Kin Two Nations*. London: RoutledgeCurzon, 2005.

Lomnitz, Larissa Adler. "Informal Exchange Networks in Formal Systems: A Theoretical Model." *American Anthropologist* 90, no. 1 (1988): 42–55.

Lyons, Lenore, and Michele Ford. "The Chinese of Karimun: Citizenship and Belonging at Indonesia's Margins." In *Chinese Indonesians Reassessed: History, Religion and Belonging*, edited by Siew-Min Sai and Chang-Yau Hoon, 121–137. London: Taylor and Francis, 2013.

Machmudi, Yon. "Islamising Indonesia: The Rise of Jemaah Tarbiyah and the Prosperous Justice Party (PKS)," 2008.

MacIntyre, Andrew. "Indonesia in 1992: Coming to Terms with the Outside World." *Asian Survey* 33, no. 2 (1993): 204–210.

Mackie, Jamie. "Indonesia: Economic Growth and Depoliticization." In *Driven by Growth: Political Change in the Asia-Pacific Region*, edited by James Morley, 2nd ed., 123–141. London and New York: M.E. Sharpe, 1999.

———. "Indonesia's New 'National Unity' Cabinet." *Bulletin of Indonesian Economic Studies* 35, no. 3 (1999): 153–158.

Majelis Ulama Indonesia. "Fatwa: Pengiriman Tenaga Kerja Wanita (TKW) Ke Luar Negeri," July 29, 2000.

"Malaysia Acts to Stem Tide of Illegal Immigrants." *Straits Times*, January 29, 1987.

"Malaysia's Draft MoU One-Sided, Unrealistic." *Jakarta Post*, February 11, 2004.

Malley, Michael. "Indonesia in 2002: The Rising Cost of Inaction." *Asian Survey* 43, no. 1 (2003): 135–146.

"Mantan Menteri Soalkan Monopoli Asuransi TKI." *Viva.co.id*, October 29, 2010.

Masitah, Siti. "Urgensi Naskah Akademik Dalam Pembentukan Peraturan Daerah." *Jurnal Legislasi Indonesia* 10, no. 2 (2013): 109–122.

Massaro, Toni. "Empathy, Legal Storytelling, and the Rule of Law: New Worlds, Old Wounds?" *Michigan Law Review* 87, no. 8 (1989): 2099–2127.

Massey, Douglas. "Economic Development and International Migration in Comparative Perspective." *Population and Development Review* 14, no. 3 (1988): 383–413.

Matheson, Craig. "Rationality and Decision-Making in Australian Federal Government." *Australian Journal of Political Science* 33, no. 1 (1998): 57–72.

Matland, Richard. "Synthesizing the Implementation Literature: The Ambiguity-Conflict Model of Policy Implementation." *Journal of Public Administration Research and Theory* 5, no. 2 (1995): 145–174.

Maurer, Jean-Luc. *Les Javanais Du Caillou: Des Affres de L'exil Aux Aléas de L'intégration: Sociologie Historique de La Communauté Indonésienne de Nouvelle-Calédonie*. Paris: Association Archipel, 2006.

———. "The Thin Red Line between Indentured and Bonded Labour: Javanese Workers in New Caledonia in the Early 20th Century." *Asian Journal of Social Science* 38 (2010): 866–879.

McCarthy, John. "The Limits of Legality: State, Governance and Resource Control in Indonesia." In *The State and Illegality in Indonesia*, edited by Edward Aspinall and Gerry van Klinken. Leiden: KILTV, 2011.

McLeod, Ross. "Government-Business Relations in Indonesia." In *Reform and Recovery in East Asia: The Role of the State and Economic Enterprise*, edited by Peter Drysdale, 146–168. London: Routledge, 2000.

———. "Soeharto's Indonesia: A Better Class of Corruption." *Agenda* 7, no. 2 (2000): 99–112.

———. "Institutionalized Public Sector Corruption: A Legacy of the Soeharto Franchise." In *The State and Illegality in Indonesia*, edited by Edward Aspinall and Gerry van Klinken. Leiden: KILTV, 2011.

"Menlu: Moritorium Penempatan TKI," *Kompas*, June 17, 2009.

Menteri Tenaga Kerja dan Transmigrasi. "Pengiriman Tenaga Kerja Rumah Tangga Ke Arab." Addressed to Duta Besar Republik Indonesia di Jeddah. No. 414/M/XII/1982, December 29, 1982.

Metzger, Gillian. "Privatization as Delegation." *Columbia Law Review* 6, no. October (2003): 1367–1502.

Meyer, John, and Brian Rowan. "Institutionalized Organizations: Formal Structure as Myth and Ceremony." *American Journal of Sociology* 83, no. 2 (1977): 340–363.

Mietzner, Marcus. *Money, Power, and Ideology: Political Parties in Post-Authoritarian Indonesia*. Singapore: NUS Press, 2013.

———. "Party Financing in Post-Soeharto Indonesia: Between State Subsidies and Political Corruption." *Contemporary Southeast Asia: A Journal of International and Strategic Affairs* 29, no. 2 (2007): 238–263.

———. "The Ambivalence of Weak Legitimacy: Habibie's Interregnum Revisted." *Review of Indonesian and Malaysian Affairs* 42, no. 2 (2008): 1–33.

———. "Funding Pilkada: Illegal Campaign Financing In Indonesia's Local Elections." In *The State and Illegality in Indonesia*, edited by Edward Aspinall and Gerry van Klinken. Leiden: KILTV, 2011.

Migdal, Joel. *State in Society: Studying How States and Societies Transform and Constitute One Another*. Cambridge and New York: Cambridge University Press, 2001.

Minako Sakai, and Amelia Fauzia. "Islamic Orientations in Contemporary Indonesia: Islam on the Rise." *Asian Ethnicity* 15, no. 1 (2014): 41–61.

Ministry of Manpower. "Penjelasan Komite Pelaksanaan Penempatan TKI Ke Korea." B.300/SJ-HM/VI/2007, n.d.

Ministry of Manpower (Singapore). "Foreign Workforce in Numbers." mom.gov.sg, Accessed March 29, 2015.

———. "Labour Force." mom.gov.sg, Accessed March 29, 2015.

"Muhaimin Harus Bedakan Manajemen Parpol Dengan Pemerintahan." *Suara Pembaruan*, April 12, 2011.

"Muhaimin Target 'Lulus' Laporan Keuangan BPK: Pada 2009, Kemenakertrans Mendapat Label Wajar Dengan Pengecualian (WDP)." *Viva.co.id*, January 4, 2011.

Nana Oishi. *Women in Motion*. Standford: Standford University Press, 2005.

Nasution, Salman, Ahmad Ramadhan, Alexander Pramono, Siti Al, Jhony Pasaribu, and Cristine Wahyuni. "Blunder Jumhur Hidayat (Kepala BNP2TKI): Amburadulnya Pengelolaan TKI Dan Suburnya Praktik Percaloan Di BNP2TKI," *finance.groups.yahoo.com*, June 1, 2007.

n.d. "Latief Curi Uang TKI," *minihub.org*, July 24, 1998.

———. "History Perlawanan," *frontjakarta.blogspot.com.au*, Accessed July 27, 2012.

Niskanen, William. "Nonmarket Decision Making: The Peculiar Economics of Bureaucracy." *American Economic Review* 58, no. 2 (1968): 293–305.

Olowo, Bamidele. "Pride and Performance in African Public Services: Analysis of Institutional Breakdown and Rebuilding Efforts in Nigeria and Uganda." *International Review of Administrative Sciences* 67 (2001): 117–134.

Özden, Çaglar, and Eric Reinhardt. "The Perversity of Preferences: GSP and Developing Country Trade Policies, 1976–2000." *Journal of Development Economics* 78 (2005): 1–21.

Palmer, Wayne. "Learning to Lead (interview with Eni Lestari)." *Inside Indonesia*, 2010.

———. "Discretion and the Trafficking-like Practices of the Indonesian State." In *Labour Migration and Human Trafficking in Southeast Asia: Critical Perspectives*, edited by Michele Ford, Lenore Lyons, and Willem van Schendel, 149–166. London: Routledge, 2012.

———. "Public-Private Partnerships in the Administration and Control of Indonesian Migrant Labour in Hong Kong." *Political Geography* 34 (2013): 1–9.

Passoth, Jan-Hendrik, and Nicholas Rowland. "Actor-Network State: Integrating Actor-Network Theory and State Theory." *International Sociology* 25, no. 6 (2010): 818–841.

Pauker, Guy. "The Age of Reason?" *Asian Survey* 8, no. 2 (1968): 133–147.

———. "Indonesia in 1980: Regime Fatigue?" *Asian Survey* 21, no. 2 (1981): 232–244.

Paulson, Stanley. "Material and Formal Authorisation in Kelsen's Pure Theory." *Cambridge Law Journal* 39, no. 1 (1980): 172–193.

"Pemerintah Akan Buka Atase Tenaga Kerja Di Enam Negara." *Merdeka*, February 23, 2005.

"Penempatan TKI: PPTKIS Berharap BNP2TKI Terbuka Terhadap Masukan." *Suara Karya*, January 16, 2007.

"Penetapan Asuransi Dinilai Tak Transparan." *Bisnis Indonesia*, October 12, 2010.

Peng, Tey Nai. "Migration Issues in the Asia Pacific: Issues Paper from Malaysia." In *Asia Pacific Migration Research Network (APMRN): Migration Issues in the Asia Pacific Working Paper Series 1*, edited by Patrick Brownlee and Colleen Mitchell. Wollongong: APMRN Secretariat Centre for Multicultural Studies in cooperation with University of Wollongong Institute for Social Change & Critical Inquiry, 1997.

"Perlindungan TKI, Antara Asuransi Dan Jaminan Sosial." *Pelita*, n.d 2008.

Pierce, Steven. "Looking like a State: Colonialism and the Discourse of Corruption in Northern Nigeria." *Comparative Study of Society and History* 48, no. 4 (2006): 887–914.

"Polres Bandara Bingung Soal KTKLN." *Tangerang News*, January 11, 2010.

"Presiden Megawati Akan Menemui Keluarga Nirmala." *Liputan6*, May 26, 2004.

Presidential Executive Order (The Philippines) No. 797 on Reorganizing the Ministry of Labor and Employment, Creating the Philippine Overseas Employment Administration, and for Other Purposes, 1982.

Presidential Executive Order (The Philippines) No. 857 on Governing the Remittance to the Philippines of Foreign Exchange Earnings of Filipino Workers Abroad and for Other Purposes, 1982.

Presidential Executive Order (The Philippines) No. 1021 on Encouraging the Inward Remittances of Contract Workers Earnings through Official Channels, 1985.

Probokusumo, Pantyo. "Kondisi Dan Pelayanan Pekerja Migran Di Daerah Transit: Studi Kasus Di Kabupaten Nunukan Kalimantan Timur." *Junral PKS* IX, no. 31 (2010): 88–102.

Pye, Oliver, Ramlah Daud, Yuyun Harmono, and Tatat. "Precarious Lives: Transnational Biographies of Migrant Palm Workers." *Asia Pacific Viewpoint* 53, no. 3 (2012): 330–342.

Quinn, Robert, Herbert Hildebrandt, Priscilla Rogers, and Michael Thompson. "A Competing Value Framework for Analyzing Presentational Communication in Management Contexts." *Journal of Business Communication* 28, no. 3 (1991): 213–232.

Raharto, Aswatini, Daliyo, Fadjri Alihar, Graeme Hugo, Haning Romdati, Mita Noveria, Mujiyani, Suko Bandiyono, and Soewartoyo. "Kebutuhan Informasi Bagi Tenaga Kerja Migran Indonesia." Pusat Penelitian Kependudukan Lembaga Ilmu Pengetahuan, 2002.

Rajagukguk, Erman. "Teori Hukum Positif (Legal Positivism) 1: Kuliah 3 Firsafat Legal Positivism Menyangkut Ekonomi," January 25, 2011.

Ramcharran, Harri. "OPEC's Production under Fluctuating Oil Prices: Further Test of the Target Revenue Theory." *Energy Economics* 23 (2001): 667–681.

RDCMD-YTKI. *Prospek Pasar Kerja Di Arab Saudi Bagi Tenaga Kerja Indonesia.* RDCMD-YTKI in cooperation with Badan Perencanaan Pembangunan Nasional, 1986.

Reeve, David. *Golkar of Indonesia: An Alternative to the Party System.* Oxford, New York and Singapore: Oxford University Press, 1985.

"Rejection of Labour Placement in Saudi Arabia Regretted." *Indonesia Times*, July 19, 1982.

Rhodes, Rod. "Intergovernmental Relations in the United Kingdom." In *Centre-Periphery Relations in Western Europe*, edited by Yves Mény and Vincent Wright, 33–78. London: George Allen & Unwin, 1985.

———. "The Hollowing of the State: The Changing Nature of the Public Service in Britain." *Political Quarterly* 65, no. 2 (1994): 138–151.

Robinson, Kathryn. "Gender, Islam, and Nationality: Indonesian Domestic Servants in the Middle East." In *Home and Hegemony: Domestic Service and Identity Politics in South and Southeast Asia*, edited by Kathleen Adams and Sara Dickey, 249–282. Ann Arbor: University of Michigan Press, 2000.

Robison, Richard. *Indonesia, the Rise of Capital.* Sydney: Allen & Unwin, 1986.

Rodriguez, Robyn. *Migrants for Export: How the Philippine State Brokers Workers to the World*. Minneapolis: University of Minnesota Press, 2010.

Rose-Ackerman, Susan. *Corruption and Government: Causes, Consequences, and Reform*. New York: Cambridge University Press, 1999.

Rosenbloom, David. "Israel's Administrative Culture, Israeli Arabs, and Arab Subjects." *Syracuse Journal of International Law and Commerce* 13 (1986): 435–437.

Rubin, Barnett. *The Fragmentation of Afghanistan: State Formation and Collapse in the International System*. 2nd ed. New Haven: Yale University Press, 2002.

Ruth McVey. "The Beamtenstaat in Indonesia." In *Interpreting Indonesian Politics: Thirteen Contributions to the Debate*, 84–91. Ithaca, N.Y.: Cornell University Press, 1982.

Sadiq, Kamal. *Paper Citizens: How Illegal Immigrants Acquire Citizenship in Developing Countries*. Oxford: Oxford University Press, 2009.

Santosa, Mas Achmad, Iosi Khatarina, and Rifqi Siarief Assegaf. "Indonesia." In *Climate Change Liability: Transnational Law and Practice*, edited by QC Richard Lord, Silke Goldberg, Lavanya Rajamani, and Jutta Brunnée, 178–205. Cambridge: Cambridge University Press, 2012.

Schein, Edgar. *Organizational Psychology*. 3rd ed. Prentice Hall: Englewood Cliffs, 1988.

Schillemans, Thomas. "Accountability in the Shadow of Hierarchy: The Horizontal Accountability of Agencies." *Public Organization Review* 8 (2008): 175–194.

Schleifer, A., and R. Vishny. "Corruption." *Quarterly Journal of Economics* 108, no. 3 (1993): 599–611.

"Sekilas Mohammad Jumhur Hidayat." *Kompas*, November 1, 2011.

"Sending of Women Workers Abroad Allowed Now." *Indonesian Observer*, December 7, 1982.

Setiawati, Sri. "The Demographic and Socio-Economic Characteristics of Overseas Contract Workers (OCWs) from Indonesia." Masters Thesis, University of Adelaide, 1997.

Shapiro, Martin. "The Problems of Independent Agencies in the United States and the European Union." *Journal of European Public Policy* 4, no. 2 (1997): 276–291.

Shymala, Evelyn, and Chan Wai Meng. "Policies and Laws Regulating Migrant Workers in Malaysia: A Critical Appraisal." *Journal of Contemporary Asia* 44, no. 1 (2014): 19–35.

Silvey, Rachel. "Transnational Domestication: State Power and Indonesian Migrant Women in Saudi Arabia." *Political Geography* 23 (2004): 245–265.

———. "Unequal Borders: Indonesian Transnational Migrants at Immigration Control." *Geopolitics* 12, no. 2 (2007): 265–279.

———. "Gender, Difference, and Contestation: Economic Geography through the Lens of Transnational Migration." In *Economic Geography*, edited by Trevor Barnes, Jamie Peck, and Eric Sheppard, 421–430. Oxford: Blackwell Publishing, 2012.

Sim, Amy. "Organising Discontent: NGOs for Southeast Asian Migrant Workers in Hong Kong." *Asian Journal of Social Science* 31, no. 3 (2003): 478–510.

Slater Dan. "Indonesia's Accountability Trap: Party Cartels and Presidential Power after Democratic Transition." *Indonesia* 78, no. October (2004): 61–92.

SMERU. "Pelaksanaan Desentralisasi Dan Otonomi Daerah: Kasus Tiga Kabupaten Di Sulawesi Utara Dan Gorontalo." Report. Lembaga Penelitian SMERU, 2001. Lembaga Penelitian SMERU.

Spaan, Ernst. "Taikongs and Calos: The Role of Middlemen and Brokers in Javanese International Migration." *International Migration Review* 28, no. 1 (1994): 93–113.

Suchman, Mark. "Managing Legitimacy: Strategic and Institutional Approaches." *Academy of Management Review* 20, no. 3 (1995): 571–610.

Suparno, Erman. *Grand Strategy: Manajemen Pembangunan Negara Bangsa*. Jakarta: Empowering Society Institute, 2009.

———. *National Manpower Strategy: (Strategi Ketenagakerjaan Nasional)*. Jakarta: Kompas, 2009.

Suryadinata, Leo. "A Year of Upheaval and Uncertainty: The Fall of Soeharto and Rise of Habibie." *Southeast Asian Affairs*, 1999, 111–127.

———. "The Decline of the Hegemonic Party System in Indonesia: Golkar after the Fall of Soeharto." *Contemporary Southeast Asia: A Journal of International and Strategic Affairs* 29, no. 2 (2007): 333–358.

Tanguay-Renaud, François. "The Intelligibility of Extralegal State Action: A General Lesson for Debates on Public Emergencies and Legality." *Legal Theory* 16 (2010): 161–189.

Tan, Paige. "Anti-Party Reaction in Indonesia: Causes and Implications." *Contemporary Southeast Asia* 24, no. 3 (2002): 484–508.

Taylor, John. "Discretion versus Policy Rules in Practice." *Carnegie-Rochester Conference Series on Public Policy* 39 (1993): 195–214.

Team Koordinasi Kegiatan Ekspor Timur Tengah. "Gugus Kerja Pembinaan Tenaga Kerja Indonesia Di Timur Tengah." Jakarta: Departemen Perdagangan dan Koperasi, 1982.

———. *Hasil Diskusi Panel: Peningkatan Usaha Pengiriman Tenaga Kerja Indonesia Ke Timur Tengah*, 1983.

Tirtosudarmo, Riwanto. *Mencari Indonesia: Demografi-Politik Pasca-Soeharto*. Jakarta: LIPI Press, 2007.

"Tolak Pengiriman Tenaga Kerja Wanita Ke Luar Negeri." *Pelita*, December 8, 1982.

Toonen, Theo. "The Unitary State as a System of Co-Governance: The Case of The Netherlands." *Public Administration* 68 (1990): 281–296.

Trade Partnership. "The U.S. Generalized System of Preferences Program: An Update." Washington, D.C.: Prepared for the Coalition for GSP, 2011.

"Tragedi Nunukan: Enggan Pulang Kamupng, 17,600 Bertahan Di Nunukan." *Gatra*, September 9, 2002.

Troper, Michel. "Lars Vinx, Hans Kelsen's Pure Theory of Law: Legality and Legitimacy." *University of Toronto Law Journal* 58, no. 4 (2008): 521–527.

"Tugas BNP2TKI." *Realita*, September 27, 2010.

"Upah Minimum TKI Di Singapura Naik 20 Persen." *Antara*, June 4, 2007.

van Klinken, Gerry. "Decolonization and the Making of Middle Indonesia." *Urban Geography* 30, no. 8 (2009): 879–897.

Vinx, Lars. *Hans Kelsen's Pure Theory of Law: Legality and Legitimacy*. New York: Oxford University Press, 2007.

Vinzant, Janet, and Lane Crothers. *Street-Level Leadership: Discretion and Legitimacy in Front-Line Public Service*. Washington, D.C.: Georgetown University Press, 1998.

Vredenbregt, Jacob. "The Haddj: Some of Its Features and Functions in Indonesia." *Bijdragen Tot de Taal-, Land- En Volkenkunde* 118, no. 1 (1962): 91–152.

"Wakil Bupati Kendal Diberhentikan: Putusan Aklamasi Dewan." *Suaramerdeka.com*, July 18, 2002.

Wanandi, Yusuf. *Shades of Grey: A Political Memoir of Modern Indonesia, 1965–1998*. Jakarta and Singapore: Equinox, 2012.

Weber, Max. "Bureaucracy." In *Economy and Society*, edited by Guenther Roth and Claus Wittich. Berkeley: University of California Press, 1978.

Wijayanti, Asri. "Kendali Alokasi Sebagai Bentuk Perlindungan Hukum Bagi Tenaga Kerja Indonesia." *Jurnal Yustika* 7, no. 1 (2004): 63–82.

Winters, Jeffrey. "Oligarchy and Democracy in Indonesia." *Indonesia* 96, no. 2 (2013): 11–33.

Wirasmo. *Buku Panduan Tenaga Kerja Indonesia Di Arab Saudi*. Jakarta: Yayasan Dana Pendidikan Kesejahteraan Masyarakat, 1985.

Wittaker, Steve, David Frohlich, and Owen Daly-Jones. "Informal Workplace Communication: What Is It like and How Might We Support It?" In *Human Factors in Computing Systems*, 131–137, n.d.

Yusak, Masduki. "Mekanisme Pengiriman Tenaga Kerja Indonesia Ke Luar Negeri." Pusat Antar Kerja Antar Negara: Departemen Tenaga Kerja dan Transmigrasi, 1988.

Yusra, Abrar. *Tokoh Yang Berhati Rakyat: Biografi Harun Zain*. Jakarta: Yayasan Gebu Minang, 1997.

Indonesian Laws, Regulations, Policies and Legal Decisions

Agency Circular Memorandum (BNP2TKI) No. B.307/BNP2TKI/VI/2007 on Pemotongan Upah TKI Dan Penindakan Terhadap Agency Di Hong Kong, 2007.

Agency Circular Memorandum (BNP2TKI) No. 3/KA/VIII/2009 on Pelaksanaan Dan Perlindungan Tenaga Kerja Indonesia, 2009.

Agency Decree (BNP2TKI) No. 130/KA-BNP2TKI/V/2007 on Komite Pelaksanaan Penempatan Tenaga Kerja Indonesia Ke Korea Dalam Rangka Program G to G, 2007.

Agency Regulation (BNP2TKI) No. 31/KA/V/2008 on Prosedur Tetap Pelayanan Penerbitan Surat Izin Pengerahan Dan Persetujuan Penempatan Tenaga Kerja Indonesia Untuk Kepentingan Perusahaan Sendiri, 2008.

Chair Decree No. 6/SK/TT/VIII on Pembentukan Gugus Kerja Pembinaan Tenaga Kerja Indonesia, 1981.

Chair Decree (Trade) No. 1/SK/TT/I/83 on Penyelenggaran Diskusi Panel Mengenai Usaha-Usaha Pengembangan Pengiriman Tenaga Kerja Indonesia Ke Timur Tengah, 1983.

Director General Decree (Guidance and Placement of Labour) No. 15/BP/1995 on Petunjuk Teknis Pelaksanaan Penempatan Tenaga Kerja Ke Luar Negeri, 1995.

Director General Decree (Guidance of Labour Placement) No. 68/PPTK/III/2008 on Pembentukan Tim Pelaksana Pembekalan Penempatan Tenaga Kerja, 2008.

Director General Decree (Placement and Protection of Overseas Labour) No. 653/DP2TKLN on Biaya Penempatan Calon Tenaga Kerja Indonesia Informal Ke Hong Kong, 2004.

Director General Decree (Guidance of Labour Placement) No. 186/PPTK/VI/2008 on Komponen Dan Besarnya Biaya Penempatan Calon Tenaga Kerja Indonesia Penata Laksana Rumah Tangga, Perawat Bayi, Dan Perawat Orang Tua/jompo Untuk Negara Tujuan Hongkong, 2008.

Director General Memorandum Circular (Guidance of Placement of Labour) No. 14/PPTK-TKLN/X/2008 on Penerbitan Surat Ijin Pengerahan (SIP) Dan Surat Persetujuan Penempatan (SPP) Tenaga Kerja Indonesia Untuk Kepentingan Perusahaan Sendiri, 2008.

Director Memorandum Circular (Preparation and Departure) No. B. 539/PEN/VIII/2009 on Pelayanan Penempatan TKI, 2009.

Governmental Regulation No. 73/1999 on Tata Cara Penggunaan Penerimaan Negara Bukan Pajak Yang Bersumber Dari Kegiatan Tertentu, 1999.

Governmental Regulation No, 25/2000 on Kewenangan Pemerintah Dan Kewenangan Propinsi Sebagai Daerah Otonom, 2000.

Governmental Regulation No. 38/2008 on Pembagian Urusan Pemerintahan Antara Pemerintah, Pemerintahan Daerah Provinsi, Dan Pemerintahan Daerah Kabupaten/Kota, 2007.

Gubernatorial Regulation (East Java) No. 35/2000 on Dinas Tenaga Kerja, 2000.

Law No. 13 on Labour, 2003.

Law No. 14 on Important Points about Labour, 1969.

Law No. 21 on Eradication of the Crime of Trafficking in Persons, 2007.

Law No. 22 on Regional Governance, 1999.

Law No. 25 on Public Service, 2009.

Law No. 31 on Eradication of the Crime of Corruption, 1999.

Law No. 39 on Placement and Protection of Indonesian Workers Overseas, 2004.

Ministerial Decree (Trade) No. 242/KP/III/78 on Susunan Organisasi Dan Tata Kerja Team Koordinasi Kegiatan Ekspor Timur Tengah, 1978.

Ministerial Decree (Manpower) No. 408/MEN/1984 on Pengerahan Dan Pengiriman Tenaga Kerja Ke Malaysia, 1984.

Ministerial Decree (Manpower) No. 420/MEN/1985 on Persyaratan Dan Kewajiban Perusahaan Pengerahan Tenaga Kerja Indonesia Ke Luar Negeri, 1985.

Ministerial Decree (Manpower) No. 195/MEN/1991 on Petunjuk Pelaksanaan Antar Kerja Antar Negara, 1991.

Ministerial Decree (Manpower) No. 196/MEN/1991 on Petunjuk Teknis Pengerahan Tenaga Kerja Indonesia Ke Arab Saudi, 1991.

Ministerial Decree (Manpower) No. 141/MEN/1993 on Penunjukan PT. Oring Jabu Jaya Sebagai Pelaksana Jasa Pelayanan Angkutan Pumulangan TKI Ke Daerah Asal, 1993.

Ministerial Decree (Manpower) No. 44/MEN/1994 on Petunjuk Pelaksanaan Penempatan Tenaga Kerja Indonesia, 1994.

Ministerial Decree (Manpower) No. 137/MEN/1994 on Pelayanan Angkutan Pemulangan TKI Ke Daerah Asal, 1994.

Ministerial Decree (Manpower) No. 104A/MEN/2002 on Penempatan Tenaga Kerja Indonesia Ke Luar Negeri, 2002.

Ministerial Decree (Manpower) No. 14/MEN/I/2005 on Tim Pencegahan Pemberangkatan TKI Non-Prosedural Dan Pelayanan Pemulangan TKI, 2005.

Ministerial Regulation (Manpower) No. 200/MEN/IX/2008 on Penunjukan Pejabat Penerbitan Surat Izin Pengerahan, 2008.

Ministerial Decree (Manpower) No. 200/MEN/IX/2008 on Penunjukan Pejabat Penerbitan Surat Izin Pengerahan, 2008.

Ministerial Decree (Manpower) No. 201/MEN/IX/2008 on Penunjukan Pejabat Penerbitan Persetujuan Penempatan Tenaga Kerja Indonesia Di Luar Negeri Untuk Kepentingan Perusahaan Sendiri, 2008.

Ministerial Decree (Manpower) No. 156/MEN/V/2009 on Penunjukan Pejabat Penerbit Surat Izin Pengerahan, 2009.

Ministerial Regulation (Manpower) No. 38/1952 on Panjar Biaya Perjalanan Dan Pemindahan Tenaga Kerja, 1952.

Ministerial Regulation (Manpower) No. 4/1970 on Pengerahan Tenaga Kerja, 1970.

Ministerial Regulation (Manpower) No. 1/MEN/1983 on Perusahaan Pengerahan Tenaga Kerja Indonesia Ke Luar Negeri, 1983.

Ministerial Regulation (Manpower) No. 128/MEN/1983 on Penggunaan Kartu Identitas Tenaga Kerja Indonesia Yang Bekerja Di Luar Negeri, 1983.

Ministerial Regulation (Manpower) No. 01/MEN/1991 on Antar Kerja Antar Negara, 1991.

Ministerial Regulation (Manpower) No. 2/MEN/1994 on Penempatan Tenaga Kerja Di Dalam Dan Ke Luar Negeri, 1994.

Ministerial Regulation (Manpower) No. 7/MEN/IV/2005 on Standar Tempat Penampungan Calon Tenaga Kerja Indonesia, 2005.

Ministerial Regulation (Manpower) No. 5/MEN/III/2005 on Ketentuan Sanksi Administratif Dan Tata Cara Penjatuhan Sanksi Dalam Pelaksanaan Penempatan Dan Perlindungan Tenaga Kerja Indonesia Di Luar Negeri, 2005.

Ministerial Regulation (Manpower) No. 14/MEN/VII/2005 on Organisasi Dan Tata Kerja Departemen Tenaga Kerja Dan Transmigrasi, 2005.

Ministerial Regulation (Manpower) No. 6/MEN/III/2006 on Organisasi Dan Tata Kerja Unit Pelaksana Teknis Di Lingkungan Departemen Tenaga Kerja Dan Transmigrasi, 2006.

Ministerial Regulation (Manpower) No. 19/MEN/V/2006 on Pelaksanaan Penempatan Dan Perlindungan Tenaga Kerja Indonesia Di Luar Negeri, 2006.

Ministerial Regulation (Manpower) No. 23/MEN/V/2006 on Asuransi Tenaga Kerja Indonesia, 2006.

Ministerial Regulation No. 38/MEN/XII/2006 on Tata Cara Pemberian, Perpanjangan Dan Pencabutan Surat Izin Pelaksana Penempatan Tenaga Kerja Indonesia, 2006.

Ministerial Regulation (Manpower) No. 5/MEN/IV/2007 on Organisasi Dan Tata Kerja Departemen Tenaga Kerja Dan Transmigrasi, 2007.

Ministerial Regulation (Manpower) No. 18/MEN/IX/2007 on Pelaksanaan Penempatan Dan Perlindungan Tenaga Kerja Indonesia Di Luar Negeri, 2007.

Ministerial Regulation (Manpower) No. 20/MEN/X/2007 on Asuransi Tenaga Kerja Indonesia, 2007.

Ministerial Regulation (Manpower) No. 22/MEN/XII/2008 on Pelaksanaan Penempatan Dan Perlindungan Tenaga Kerja Indonesia Di Luar Negeri, 2008.

Ministerial Regulation (Manpower) No. 23/MEN/XII/2008 on Asuransi Tenaga Kerja Indonesia, 2008.

Ministerial Regulation (Manpower) No. 5/MEN/II/2009 on Pelaksanaan Penyiapan Calon TKI Untuk Bekerja Di Luar Negeri, 2009.

Ministerial Regulation (Manpower) No. 18/MEN/VIII/2009 on Bentuk, Persyaratan, Dan Tata Cara Memperoleh Kartu Tenaga Kerja Luar Negeri, 2009.

Ministerial Regulation (Manpower) No. 7/MEN/X/V/2010 on Asuransi Tenaga Kerja Indonesia, 2010.

Ministerial Regulation (Manpower) No. 14/MEN/X/2010 on Pelaksanaan Penempatan Dan Perlindungan Tenaga Kerja Indonesia Di Luar Negeri, 2010.

Presidential Decree No. 36/1977 on Pembentukan Team Koordinasi Kegiatan Ekspor Timur Tengah, 1977.

Presidential Decree No. 127/M/78 on Pengangkatan Ketua Team Koordinasi Kegiatan Ekspor Timur Tengah, 1978.

Presidential Decree No. 84/1982 on Kebijaksanaan Pemberian Surat Keterangan Fiskal Luar Negeri, 1982.

Presidential Decree No. 15/1984 on Susunan Organisasi Departemen, 1984.

Presidential Decree No. 104/1993 on Perubahan Atas Keputusan Presiden Nomor 15 Tahun 1984 Tentang Susunan Organisasi Departemen Sebagaimana Telah Duapuluh Kali Diubah, Terakhir Dengan Keputusan Presiden Nomor 83 Tahun 1993, 1993.

Presidential Decree No. 29/1999 on Badan Koordinasi Penempatan Tenaga Kerja Indonesia, 1999.

Presidential Decree No. 106/2004 on Tim Koordinasi Pemulangan Tenaga Kerja Indonesia Bermasalah Dan Keluarganya Dari Malaysia, 2004.

Presidential Instruction No. 6/2006 on Kebijakan Reformasi Sistem Penempatan Dan Perlindungan Tenaga Kerja Indonesia, 2006.

Presidential Regulation No. 81/2006 on Badan Nasional Penempatan Dan Perlindungan Tenaga Kerja Indonesia, 2006.

Presidential Regulation No. 72/2008 on Rincian Anggaran Belanja Pemerintah Pusat Tahun Anggaran 2009, 2008.

Presidential Regulation No. 43/2009 on Dana Alokasi Umum Daerah Provinsi, Kabupaten, Dan Kota Tahun 2010, 2009.

Presidential Regulation No. 64/2011 on Pemeriksaan Kesehatan Dan Psikologi Calon Tenaga Kerja Indonesia, 2011.

Supreme Court. “Legal Decision No. 5 P/HUM/2009,” March 19, 2009.

———. “Legal Decision No. 61 P/HUM/2010,” January 18, 2011.

Index